THE AMBIGUITY OF HENRY JAMES

University of Illinois Press

URBANA   CHICAGO   LONDON

THE
AMBIGUITY
OF
HENRY JAMES

Charles Thomas Samuels

for Nada

for Larry and Suzanne

CONTENTS

vii

A NOTE ON TEXTS

The following list indicates the edition cited for each of James's works. Where no edition is cited, the story is referred to but not quoted. The works are listed according to the chapter in which each is discussed. The date in parentheses is the date of original publication.

INTRODUCTION: *The Governess*
"The Turn of the Screw" (1898)   New York edition, 1908

CHAPTER ONE: *At the Bottom of the* Fount
The Sacred Fount (1901)   Hart-Davis, 1959
"The Patagonia" (1888)   *Complete Tales of Henry James*, ed. Leon Edel (Philadelphia, 1961–1964)
"The Aspern Papers" (1888)   New York edition, 1908

CHAPTER TWO: *The Mansion and the Child*
The American (1877)   Riverside edition, 1962
"A Passionate Pilgrim" (1871)
The Princess Casamassima (1886)   New York edition, 1908

CHAPTER THREE: *The Joys of Renunciation*
The Wings of the Dove (1902)   New York edition, 1909

It is so much easier to "dislike James" for his obscurities—without troubling very much to say what we mean—or to idolize him for his subtle ambiguities. Both positions are wholly safe, backed by troops in rank on rank, with traditions of honorable battle going back several decades. What is hard is to look squarely at the master and decide—without idolatry or iconoclasm—whether he has done, after all, as well as he might have.

—WAYNE BOOTH

James was not the dispassionate observer. He started with the moral obsession; before he had worked clear of it he was entoiled in the obsession of social tone. He has pages of clear depiction, even of satire, but the sentimentalist is always lurking just around the corner. This softens his edges.

—EZRA POUND

PREFACE

To his contemporaries, the excellence of Henry James—as of any living artist—was a matter for debate. But, in this case, the debate was particularly vigorous in response to James's uniqueness of manner and novelty of vision. During his lifetime he was lionized and vilified, commanded a large audience, and at last only a coterie.[1]

Now James is widely regarded with an admiration bordering on reverence. Zealous exegesis of his fiction is notoriously one of the main occupations of students of American literature. Yet among the forty-nine books in the representative check-list printed by *Modern Fiction Studies* fifty years after his death, thirty are interpretations of special topics, themes, or groups of novels, thirteen are biographical, and only six are evaluative. Of the latter, four were written before 1925 in the period immediately after James's death.[2] Another is F. W. Dupee's excellent survey of James's life and work. The one full-length recent critical study is an all-out attack by Maxwell Geismar, which, despite considerable failings, has the merit of proving that James's greatness can't be simply taken for granted.[3] The reasons for this were better established by Edmund Wilson in his famous essay on James's ambiguity.[4] Wilson contends that we frequently do not know how to judge the characters in a James story and that our perplexity is important because his fiction is judgmental. Unfortunately, this insight has not been pursued. Instead, critics have usually taken diametrical positions on each dubious character or questionable theme and have failed to ask whether James himself might be faulted for supplying contrary evidence. Some have admired James's ingenuity in posing insoluble puzzles; others have dissolved the puzzles in a wash of paradox.

But a multifaceted character or theme differs from one that invites and supports incompatible or contradictory responses. The former is a sign of control and profundity; the latter, a sign of confusion or deviousness. Such assumptions underlie my attempt to follow Edmund Wilson's lead and to differentiate between success and failure in James's art. To evaluate his fiction on grounds only of skill and form would be impertinent, because of the almost unexceptionably high level of his craftsmanship, and superficial, because, despite Geismar, James wasn't merely a sophisticated entertainer. If one seeks to establish the nature of his achievement, one must look at the heart of the matter: James's moral antinomies.

These have been well established by generations of critics. Running through James's fiction is a fundamental opposition between innocence and worldliness. James's innocent protagonists—usually American and frequently female—enter society (often by crossing the Atlantic) and find it opportunistic, selfish, venal. Dispossessed of their innocence, they nevertheless remain devoted to its underlying values, rejecting the world in order to save their souls. The society which they reject is elegant and cultivated, but James generally indicates that it is well lost.

This fundamental pattern is, however, qualified in several ways. First, James knew well enough that good and evil aren't absolutely discrete. He understood that innocence wasn't totally synonymous with virtue but might be quixotic, priggish, or even specious. Moreover, worldliness brought the benefits not only of elegance and charm but of a wisdom so important as to make innocence undesirable. Furthermore, James was as interested in epistemology as in ethics, so that he regarded all perceptions as subjective, nonuniversal. This realization produced his most important technical innovation (in narrative point of view), but it also interfered with his desire to establish general moral truths. How to assert the essential difference between good and evil without oversimplifying their opposition, how to establish the validity of moral judgments without ignoring personal bias: these are the two challenges that James had to meet in his fiction. His greatness as a writer is partly measured by the magnitude of these challenges, and his books are successful by the extent to which each meets them effectively.

In James's career, success and failure are not related to chronology. Sometimes earlier novels are better than later ones; a great achievement may be followed by an equally great failure. Explanation for this would require a book many times longer than the present volume, for the terms of comparative evaluation would then have to be combined with biographical investigation and a comprehensive theory of the psychology of creation. Therefore, I do not ask why James was or was not able to succeed in a given book except insofar as this question can be answered from the text itself.

Accordingly, the organization of this book is evaluative rather than chronological. I begin with the least successful novels (omitting a few that seem negligible—like *Watch and Ward*, *The Outcry*, and *The Other House*—and touching only on relevant stories);[5] I end with the most successful. Or in my terminology, I begin with James's confused novels, move through his ambiguous ones, and end with his examples of achieved complexity.

"Confusion" may mean "perplexity," "senseless order," or "mistaking something for something else." In James, it means all three, as I initially show in the paradigmatic case of "The Turn of the Screw." This controversial novella presents an extreme version of James's basic plot: innocence fighting worldly knowledge. But it leaves the reader in perplexity because the tale's structure allows us to think that James might have mistaken the governess's moral opportunism for righteousness and that worldliness isn't evil except in her overheated mind. In no other work is James so equivocal about good and evil, though several of his novels and stories are nearly as perplexing as "The Turn of the Screw." These are dealt with in Part One.

In "The Turn of the Screw" a notable absence of dramatized evil precludes the contrast necessary to prove that the governess is good. A similar absence haunts *The Sacred Fount,* in which James intimates that society is depraved and then fails to validate the presumed evidence. This failure suggests an ambivalence toward society that is dramatized not through its complex portrayal but in contradictory hints: society is vampiristic and the narrator is crazy to think so. The novels in Chapter Two (*The American* and *The Princess Casamassima*) are more assuredly antagonistic toward society, against which they set natural men— the symbolically named Newman and Hyacinth. But in each of these books, James subverts his melodramatic pattern at a surprisingly late stage of the plot and begins to suggest that society isn't as bad as we had been led to find it. As a result, the hero, who had seemed good because he opposed society, suddenly falters and either leaves the fray (Newman) or immolates himself (Hyacinth) rather than harm what we had thought his deserved enemy. All three novels effectively work against themselves. *The Sacred Fount* is a moral mystery which excites us about finding the culprit but then won't point him out. *The American* and *The Princess Casamassima* are moral melodramas in which the heroes and villains begin to change sides or to act in ways that deny their original formulation.

My final instances of Jamesian confusion display the obverse flaw. Whereas the previous novels suggest unresolved ambivalence toward society, these are disconcertingly ambivalent toward innocence. Both *The Wings of the Dove* and *The Spoils of Poynton* feature heroines, amply celebrated by plotting and authorial intrusion, whose virtuous renunciations of the world seem suspiciously self-serving. Plot and rhetoric tell us that Milly Theale dies in judgment of Kate Croy's duplicity, but a disconcerting amount of evidence in the book suggests that she dies of disappointment at losing her man. James calls Fleda Vetch a "free spirit" and wants us to believe that she gave up Owen Gereth to her ideal of freedom; but we can also believe from evidence in the text that he is a sacrifice to her fear. Yet, instead of maintaining a double perspective on each heroine, James solicits one response while, with seeming inadvertence, allowing another.

The next group of novels I label "ambiguities," expecting my reader to recall that the term is itself ambiguous, meaning both "confused" and, in the Empsonian sense, "complex." As I try to show, *The Bostonians* and *The Portrait of a Lady* are novels with elements of confused—because contradictory—doubleness, but also with doubleness designedly apparent in plotting and characterization.

For example, Isabel Archer's disastrous marriage is partly caused by her own errors and partly by a trick played on her. Because James wants us to be sympathetic to her, he sometimes confuses her responsibility with her victimization and thus perplexes us about the exact process of her downfall. To this degree, the novel is faulty. However, from the start, James acknowledges that Isabel is both arrogant and pure (as he does not in the case of Milly Theale) so that she is complex whereas Milly is contradictory. The theme of *The Portrait of a Lady* (innocence is both its own recommendation and scourge) is, in consequence, clear and rich, whereas the theme of *The Wings of the Dove* is unconvincing.

In his confused novels, James makes us expect clear advocacy or derogation and then either fails to validate or actually blurs his own distinctions. The ambiguous books reflect such errors but don't succumb to them. The complex novels avoid them entirely. In these novels, James does not try for single-minded opposition between virtue and vice, but rather builds a dialectic between them into narrative structure, characterization, and rhetoric. This bespeaks an ironic, skeptical perspective that never makes simple judgments and thus escapes contradiction. Intimating that society is literally vampiristic seems a case of protesting too much, so that we ought not to be surprised when James doesn't make the protest work. In contrast, *The Europeans, Washington Square, The Awkward Age, What Maisie Knew,* and *The Ambassadors* dramatize an indictment of society that is all the more convincing for being both realistic and qualified. On the other hand, these books present innocence in a more authentic guise, not through renunciations that turn out to be self-serving but through energetic assertions of values and ideals. In his masterpieces, *What Maisie Knew* and *The Ambassadors*, the innocent protagonists don't establish their moral supremacy by renouncing the world but instead express their high vision of its possibility by working for what they believe.

In short, when James tries to assert too complete a distinction between innocence and worldliness or virtue and vice, his intelligence pulls against the attempt, producing disorderly structure, dubious characterization, equivocal themes. His best works are those in which all that can be said for the world and against innocence is built so firmly into his design that his fundamental dislike of the one and loyalty to the other are both clear and tenable.

In one novel, *The Golden Bowl,* James tries to go beyond moral distinctions entirely, emphasizing not the relative merits of his antagonists but the prospects for combining innocence with worldliness. Maggie Verver grows up, passes through disillusionment, does not renounce—and then goes a step further: she tries to become a true princess, a worldling of worldlings. But her story is dogged by old sentimentalities that can be traced back to novels like *The Wings of the Dove.* For this reason, *The Golden Bowl* provides the perfect vantage point for summarizing the distinctions I have tried to make.

Why have I thought these distinctions worth making? First, as I have said, James criticism is too exclusively interpretive. Most of it assumes James's greatness and thus neglects the new reader eager to sift good from bad or the experienced reader who is still troubled by parts of the corpus. This neglect of evaluation has also kept us from establishing the sort of canon that exists for James's forebears, like Hawthorne and Melville, or even for the most notable of his successors: Faulkner.

More important, in seeking to explain the basis of my judgments, I perforce deal with problems that must be considered even by the reader wanting exegesis. While judging their excellence, I have also tried to illuminate James's novels, just as I have tried to illuminate the essence of his total achievement. So far as I can tell, an author's flaws are as characteristic as his virtues; the latter are, in a profound sense, his victories over the former. Though my readers won't be impressed with this fact for four chapters, I think James is America's greatest novelist, and I always intended that my book should help demonstrate why that is so by first acknowledging why it might not have been.

I have received help from numerous people in my endeavors. My seminar students at Williams participated in my first flounderings on the subject. Robert J. Allen, Jonas A. Barish, and

Frederick C. Crews read and made helpful comments on early chapters in the manuscript. Peter Berek read and improved the whole of the text, as did Lawrence and Suzanne Graver, who also offered more emotional sustenance than I could possibly acknowledge. As always, my fiercest reader, both in her standards and her loyalty, was my wife.

I wish to thank the American Council of Learned Societies for a fellowship that enabled me to complete this book and Williams College for its continued support in the form of summer humanities grants and an assistant professor's leave. Thanks are also due *The American Scholar* for permission to reprint some of the material from "Giovanni and the Governess" and to *Novel,* in which part of the first chapter made its initial appearance. I am also grateful for the hospitality offered by institutions in which several of these chapters were delivered as lectures: Marlboro College, the University of Minnesota, the University of California at Davis, and the University of Southern California.

The Governess

Since Edmund Wilson began his study of Jamesian ambiguity with "The Turn of the Screw," few literary works have generated a dispute so seemingly interminable.[6] To some readers, the governess is a heroine fighting to shield innocence from the force of evil, while to others she is a neurotic violating innocence because of her own delusions. Unfortunately, the tale offers evidence for both readings, and we can't see how exemplary are its problems until we recall this fact.

The futility of trying to show that the governess imagined the ghosts is indicated by Wilson's attempt to explain two details that embarrass his position. If she is hallucinating, how can the governess accurately describe Peter Quint to Mrs. Grose, and since the casement was closed, who produced the cold wind that chilled her and blew out Miles's candle during their interview? In meeting the first point, Wilson is forced to adopt John Silver's theory that the governess heard about Quint during a trip to town;[7] in meeting the second, he must maintain that she is too far gone to know if the wind is blowing. However, the first argument is based on a fact not reported in the text, whereas the second begs us not to consider facts but to reject them. Once we agree to such a procedure, there is no telling where to stop.

In addition, critics who argue against Wilson correctly assert that every one of the story's details suits its gothic classification. Moreover, Quint and Miss Jessel were evidently bad enough in life to be symbolized by something unnatural. Before we accuse the poor governess of neurotic hysteria then, we should ask ourselves how we might feel in charge of a haunted house with only an illiterate sentimentalist and two children for company, when the former sees nothing and the latter might see a great deal but won't admit any of it. Probably, we would feel frightened and helpless, would wonder if we were losing our grip, and would do everything possible to prove the contrary.

All this fits the governess's tone well enough to make her account plausible; even Wilson admits, in the first version of his essay, that "The Turn of the Screw" can be read with or without believing in the phantoms. Nevertheless, he conjectures that James planned it this way in order to fool the audience, which anticipated a mere thriller, so as to present them with a case study. Judging from James's other work, however, this intention is highly unlikely, as Wilson went on to admit in the second version of his essay, after having examined James's comments on the tale.

These comments indicate that the ghosts are meant to be the prime movers and that the governess is merely a device to record their evil and the children's victimization. Thus, in a letter to H. G. Wells in 1898, James explained why he had not characterized his narrator: ". . . I had, about my young woman, to take a very sharp line. The grotesque business I had to make her picture and the childish psychology I had to make her trace and

present, were, for me at least, a very difficult job, in which absolute lucidity and logic, a singleness of effect, were imperative.
Therefore I had to rule out subjective complications of her own—
play of tone etc.; and keep her impersonal save for the most obvious and indispensable little note of neatness, firmness and courage—without which she wouldn't have her data. But the thing is
essentially a potboiler and a *jeu d'esprit*."[8] In 1900, when he confided to his notebook a plan for *The Sense of the Past*, he was
still belittling "The Turn of the Screw," and his 1908 preface to
the story boasts that it cannot "be baited by earnest criticism."[9]

But, as Wilson and Leon Edel have both noted, several other
comments in the New York preface indicate that the author dimly
realized that his story was not the simple thriller that this suggests. For James admits, "We have surely as much of [the governess's] own nature as we can swallow in watching it reflect her
anxieties and inductions," and though he delights in "the general
proposition of our young woman's keeping crystalline her record
of so many intense anomalies and obscurities," he calls "her explanation of them, a different matter."[10]

James's comments do draw attention to a question about the
tale, but not one concerning the ghosts. Instead, he expresses
concern about the governess. What James felt proud of was her
lucidity of description, for that is what he relied on to make his
tale credible; what worried him were those complicated explanations, necessarily reflecting her personality, which could divert
attention from the tale's horrific events. If we take a close look at
the governess, however, we begin to suspect that James had a
deeper reason for being concerned. For even if the ghosts are
real, the governess is not the neat figure he had intended.

Rather, from her very entrance, she seems concerned with out-
ward events primarily as they bear on herself. A little country
girl on her first job, the governess is avid for indications of
heightened stature. Greeted by the servants, "as if I had been the

mistress or a distinguished visitor," she wonders why, although Mrs. Grose is glad to see her, she is "positively on her guard against showing it too much." In retrospect, we are perhaps meant to take this as evidence of her tremendous sensitivity, because Mrs. Grose does have ample reason to long for relief. But when we read the passage, we wonder at the governess's vanity, a suspicion confirmed when she speaks happily of the "large impressive room, one of the best in the house, the great state bed, as I almost felt it, the figured full draperies, the long glasses in which, for the first time, I could see myself from head to foot. . . ."

Her account of meeting the master at Harley Street shows that her vanity can be defensive. "You *will* be carried away by the little gentleman!" Mrs. Grose beams, talking of Miles. And the governess replies: " 'Well, that, I think, is what I came for—to be carried away. I'm afraid, however,' I remember feeling the impulse to add, 'I'm rather easily carried away. I was carried away in London!' I can still see Mrs. Grose's broad face as she took this in. 'In Harley Street?' 'In Harley Street.' 'Well, Miss, you're not the first—and you won't be the last.' 'Oh I've no pretensions,' I could laugh, 'to being the only one.' " She may be unaware of the sexual nuance in "carried away," but she is clearly conscious of not wishing to appear presumptuous; "I could laugh" acknowledges a temporary triumph of humility. By the end of the first chapter however, pride reasserts itself along with her childish imagination, and she has the "view of a castle of romance inhabited by a rosy sprite . . . a building . . . in which I had the fancy of our being almost as lost as a handful of passengers in a great drifting ship. Well, I was strangely at the helm!" Thus is born a sense of power. About to occupy a place formerly denied by fortune, the little parson's daughter accepts it with a confident tremor of delight.

The governess is a good little bourgeoise, hell-bent to establish her place in the eye of God; and James underlines her combination of social and intellectual pretentiousness with touches of grotesque humor. That the young woman is the only one who can see the ghosts makes her pitiable; but as a result she must try to persuade Mrs. Grose of what she sees, and this makes her comic. Since the old lady is both too loving and too ignorant to enter into the governess's subtle visions, her companion is forced constantly to cue her in. "Of what other things have you got hold?" the dazzled housekeeper once asks.

"Why of the very things that have delighted, fascinated and yet, at bottom, as I now so strangely see, mystified and troubled me. Their more than earthly beauty, their absolutely unnatural goodness. It's a game," I went on; "it's a policy and a fraud!"

"On the part of little darlings—?"

"As yet mere lovely babies? Yes, mad as that seems!" The very act of bringing it out really helped me to trace it—follow it all up and piece it all together. "They haven't been good—they've only been absent. It has been easy to live with them because they're simply leading a life of their own. They're not mine—they're not ours. They're his and they're hers!"

"Quint's and that woman's?"

"Quint's and that woman's. They want to get to them."

Oh how, at this, poor Mrs. Grose appeared to study them! "But for what?"

"For the love of all the evil that, in those dreadful days, the pair put into them. And to ply them with that evil still, to keep up the work of demons, is what brings the others back."

"Laws!" said my friend under her breath. The exclamation was homely, but it revealed a real acceptance of my further proof. . . .

The governess is always having to "press" Mrs. Grose, to supply the right word, to help the old woman make things out. When Mrs. Grose falters at the prodigies of supposition required of her, the governess consoles, "You do know, you dear thing . . . only you haven't my dreadful boldness of mind, and you keep back, out of timidity and modesty and delicacy. . . ." The illiterate Mrs. Grose cannot derive evidence of Miles's corruption from the headmaster's letter, and she cannot see the ghosts. When, at last, she comes in triumph with a contribution to the governess's burgeoning theory of childish vice, it turns out simply to be the news that Flora had called the governess names.

Yet through her ability to bully a frightened, ignorant old servant into a vision of "depths, depths," the governess derives absolute confirmation of her position. She confirms her virtue merely through a walk around the house: ". . . I could take a turn into the grounds and enjoy, almost with a sense of property that amused and flattered me, the beauty and dignity of the place. It was a pleasure at these moments to feel myself tranquil and justified; doubtless perhaps also to reflect that by my discretion, my quiet good sense and general high propriety, I was giving pleasure—if he ever thought of it!—to the person to whose pressure I had yielded. What I was doing was what he had earnestly hoped and directly asked of me, and that I *could*, after all, do it proved even a greater joy than I had expected."

Because of her innate virtue, the low-class governess feels worthy to possess Bly; eventually, she begins to criticize the person who actually does: "He was not a trouble-loving gentleman," she decides, "nor so very particular perhaps about some of the company he himself kept." However, though she is quick to declare her superiority, she is always on the lookout for a chance to show it. This the ghosts provide. Come as if in answer to her prayers, they embody a proving ground for her soul.

But what they let her prove is the danger of moral absolutes. Like evil, good is an abstraction, false to the shaded substance of humanity. When once the governess gets hold of the idea that the apparently good Miles and Flora might also be tainted with evil, she determines to wash them clean. In addition, if, unschooled and unaided, as a woman and a social inferior, she can purify the

great house which her employer has left so reprehensibly unguarded, how much will her own virtue shine forth. "I dare say,"
she concludes while strolling through Bly before her first vision
of Quint, "I fancied myself . . . a remarkable young woman and
took comfort in the faith that this would more publicly appear."

Instead, what ultimately appears from the governess's ruthless
pursuit of indivisible goodness is the ambivalence of her own
nature. For her, allurements are simultaneously snares. "I learnt
something," she says, speaking of the first days at Bly, "that had
not been one of the teachings of my small smothered life; learnt
to be amused, and even amusing, and not to think for the mor-
row. It was the first time . . . that I had known space and air
and freedom, all the music of summer and all the mystery of
nature. And then there was consideration—and consideration
was sweet. Oh it was a trap—not designed but deep—to my imagination, to my delicacy, perhaps to my vanity; to whatever in me
was most excitable. . . . I was off my guard."

Threatened though she feels, she awaits Miles's return from
school with "a curiosity that . . . was to deepen almost to pain,"
while James underlines her prudish excess of virtue. Worrying
over the headmaster's note, the governess asks Mrs. Grose to declare that she has never known Miles to be bad. "Oh," Mrs. Grose
protests, "never known him—I don't pretend *that!*"

> I was upset again. "Then you *have* known him—?"
> "Yes indeed, Miss, thank God!"
> On reflexion I accepted this. "You mean that a boy who never
> is—?"
> "Is no boy for *me!*"
> I held her tighter. "You like them with the spirit to be naughty?"
> Then, keeping pace with her answer, "So do I!" I eagerly brought
> out. "But not to the degree to contaminate—"
> "To contaminate?"—my big word left her at a loss.
> I explained it. "To corrupt."

She stared, taking my meaning in; but it produced in her an odd laugh. "Are you afraid he'll corrupt *you?*" She put the question with such a fine bold humour that with a laugh, a little silly doubtless, to match her own, I gave way for the time to the apprehension of ridicule.

But the next day . . . I cropped up in another place.

Forgetting the absurdity in her fear of a ten-year-old child, the governess prepares, as she awaits her charge, for a great moral test. When he arrives, his beauty and apparent freedom from evil or suffering become themselves proof of his contamination. She imagines herself in Eden, "in charge of a pair of little grandees [who must be] fenced about and ordered and arranged [by] a really royal extension of the garden and the park." Yet she simultaneously feels this romantic setting to be a "hush in which something gathers or crouches . . . like the spring of a beast." The beast must spring; to the governess "all futures are rough!" Beautiful and favored as they are, the children must be menaced —and she must save them.

Her sense of propriety (the obverse of her careerism) connives with her sense of depravity (the obverse of her romanticism). When she sees Quint for a second time, he seems like one she "had been looking at . . . for years and had known . . . always." Casting about for an analogy that can convey the horror of so eternal a threat, she can only compare him to an actor. For the governess, evil is a confused mélange of vice and bad manners. "There was but one sane inference," she thinks after the first visitation, "some one had taken a liberty rather monstrous"; but the monstrousness is only Quint's appearing at Bly without having been announced. In a similar manner, she is horrified that he wears no hat. When Mrs. Grose tells her that he also used to wear the master's clothes and consorted with Miles despite his menial status, the governess's mind converts such breaches of etiquette into bottomless, demonic evils. Her taut sensibility meets that of her stolid companion only in their mutual horror that Quint was of a lower station than Miss Jessel. The offense against caste rather than the licentiousness is what they dwell upon; sometimes it seems as if one produces the other. Thus, true or not, the conclusions to which the governess leaps reflect her prejudices, confirm her needs and deficiencies.

The governess demonstrates an affinity for the ghosts, though they threaten the children, whereas she begins to hate those consigned to her protection. For the ghosts provide an opportunity to be heroic, but the children, by perversely denying the ghosts' existence, threaten to remove the opportunity. As a result, the governess begins to pursue the spectres almost with a sense of comradeship. She thinks of leaving the ghosts and the children, but she never thinks of leaving with the children or of calling for outside help, for that would mean opting out of the contest. When she sees Miss Jessel with Flora beside the lake, her terror is mixed with a dreadful joy: "She was there, so I was justified; she was there, so I was neither cruel nor mad. She was there for poor scared Mrs. Grose, but she was there most for Flora; and no moment of my monstrous time was perhaps so extraordinary as that in which I consciously threw out to her—with the sense that, pale and ravenous demon as she was, she would catch and understand it—an inarticulate message of gratitude." When Mrs. Grose comes to the governess with her poor scrap of evidence concerning Flora's depravity, the governess shouts, "Oh thank God!" Mrs. Grose springs up with a groan: " 'Thank God'!" "It so justifies me!" the governess replies.

Perfectly matched adversaries, the ghosts seek to give the children the power of evil, while the governess wishes to claim them for good. But she is no less exploitive than the ghosts, though ultimately more deadly. Her story declares a terrible irony: when virtue seeks public recognition of its power, it begins to take on the avidity of vice. The phrase that denotes an increase in horror when used in the prologue is used in quite another connection by the governess in her narrative: "I could only get on at all [she consoles herself] by taking 'nature' into my confidence and my account, by treating my monstrous ordeal as a push in a direction unusual, of course, and unpleasant, but demanding after all, for a fair front, only another turn of the screw of ordinary human virtue." The governess's virtue is what turns the screws.

That James wished to focus on a surprising equation between the heroine and her adversaries seems a very persuasive way of reading "The Turn of the Screw" (and I have merely outlined the evidence). Yet James always insisted, even when he admitted falling short of the mark, that his intended focus was the spectres. We should remember, however, that the spectres are designedly left to the reader's imagination, while the governess is provided, by means of the prologue, with a complicated personal history. In short, James seems consciously to have intended a common heroine suffering and routing evil and to have made this reading possible. But as he wrote the tale, doubts concerning her welled up from some part of his imagination, so that he also made it possible to find her a highly individualized moralist who is, ironically, a snob and a prude, conceited and self-justifying, and murderously ruthless in the expression of her ideals. What one wants to determine then is what might have made James admire her, since it is what she represents that makes his ambivalence exemplary.

Moralist that his works declare him, James might have admired the governess for her dependence on virtue and her sense of its prerogatives. Thus, to highlight her natural aristocracy, he contrasts it with the actual aristocracy that is manifestly inferior. For this reason, the Harley Street master is described as a ladies' man unconcerned with duty, and Peter Quint, his valet, is shadowed by the imputation of mysterious rites in an unguarded house full of women. As a result, Bly was quite unsuitable for children, and the governess, to her honor, was attempting to reform things.

Enraged by these efforts, the licentious servants, who had already suffered the wages of sin, sought to reverse this process by means literally diabolical. In order to prove that the governess *was* outstanding, and thus worthy of the stature to which she aspired, James also made her so prodigiously intelligent that no one else could see how matters stood.

It is this latter quality, however, that permits us to see the governess rather differently. Even if the ghosts exist, since no one corroborates her reading of their intentions, we are free to suspect that her reading is distorted by self-interest. In that case, the governess, in order to provide an opportunity for her own advancement, has merely assumed that Quint and Miss Jessel have come back for the children. Moreover, this assumption is itself an expression of moral pretension and class envy. The important question, then, is not the existence of the ghosts but the governess's interpretation.

Why then did James leave this interpretation in doubt? Even if he had wanted the open ending for effect, he still could have prevented aspersions on his heroine by having Mrs. Grose or even a minor character find one single item to back her up. Instead, he makes Mrs. Grose both a reluctant and an incompetent witness and excludes from the action anyone who could have taken her place. But it is this very isolation which constitutes the governess's sharpest note of heroism. Though we may deplore her explanations and her actions, we must grant her some credit for having the courage of her convictions. The more so, if, as James shows everywhere in his work, reality so nearly confounds one's motive for belief.

To summarize: the governess represents Jamesian values of innocence, moral commitment, and faith in one's perception. But James also shows, however inadvertently, that these "values" might, ironically, be only prudishness, moral opportunism, and intellectual presumption. In "The Turn of the Screw," since he did not decide whether the governess validates or exposes them, he could not make a good case for the values she represents. Moreover, though on this score the evidence is less full, "The Turn of the Screw" suggests that James also had difficulty presenting what he deplored. In trying to place my criticism of the governess on firm grounds, I have rejected Wilson's antiapparitionist reading. But one must finally remember, as I have said, that James deliberately refused to demonstrate what made the ghosts wicked. When you add to this the manifestly greater vividness of what is wrong with the heroine, it becomes possible to conclude that James was as unable to castigate evil as he was to affirm virtue. For if the governess may be no better than the spectres, the spectres may be no worse than she.

Good and bad are equally dubious in "The Turn of the Screw," though the former is emphasized and the latter merely hinted at. Despite recent criticism, both pro- and antiapparitionist, James was close to the truth when he derided the story as a potboiler.[11] Although "The Turn of the Screw" imitates James's major concerns, it has nothing definite to say about them. Through its fantasy James merely plays with the two obsessive questions in his work: how sound are morality and innocence? how bad are the upper classes? By looking at more serious efforts, we can learn his methods of evading or confronting these issues, and by so doing we can form a standard for judging his work.

Part One

CONFUSIONS

CHAPTER ONE

At the Bottom
of the Fount

Written not long after "The Turn of the Screw," *The Sacred Fount* also displays an inexperienced hero who thinks he has discovered something diabolical; but in the novel James gives a fuller account of the enemy than he did in the tale. Nevertheless, as Edmund Wilson contends, *The Sacred Fount* is "not merely mystifying but maddening though if one got to the bottom of it, a good deal of light would be thrown on the author."[12]

The narrator's relentless attempt, in Rebecca West's derisive words, "to discover whether there exists between certain of his fellow-guests a relationship not more interesting among these vacuous people than it is among sparrows,"[13] might seem to guarantee a negative response. However, James conveys so powerful a sense of Newmarch's corruption that the narrator's moral zealousness becomes heroic by default. Moreover, his obsessive in-

quiries are either initiated or corroborated by the other characters, who are all less compassionate in their gossip. Almost
immediately after he grasps his general law (Grace is getting
younger at Briss's expense, therefore Gilbert Long must be
getting wittier at the expense of some woman), he becomes
conscience-stricken on learning that the woman is May Server.
His dizzying circumlocutions and tortured evasions are in part
an effort to protect May from Grace Brissenden, who is simultaneously his confederate and his quarry. When Grace learns
that his inferences threaten to expose her egoistic wasting of
Briss, she puts him to rout not with her logic (always specious
and perhaps even mendacious) but by means of her tone. His
moral intelligence seems to have been checked (as James puts
it in *The American*) by Grace's "habit of unquestioned authority
and the absoluteness of a social theory favorable to [her]self."

Notebook entries and a letter to Mrs. Humphrey Ward show
that James intended the novel to be read in this fashion.[14] However, since, as in "The Turn of the Screw," the climax neither
confirms nor denies the narrator's supposition, and since the
action raises so many doubts about the purity of his motives, it is
not surprising that many critics have found the narrator no easier
to admire than the governess. But this difficulty doesn't simply
recall the most problematic of James's stories. It recurs in several
others ("The Liar," "A Light Man," "Louisa Pallant," to name
a few).

"The Patagonia" (1888) is a particularly relevant example
since, like *The Sacred Fount*, it was originally designed as a tale
of upper-class egotism. Aboard a ship taking Grace Mavis to a
hateful *mariage de convenance*, the narrator suspects that her
shipmate, Jasper Nettlepoint, is trifling with the girl; and when
Grace jumps overboard shortly before the Patagonia is to dock,
his suspicions seem confirmed. Yet James never really establishes
the accuracy of this interpretation (though there is ample ev-

idence, Jasper's name is about as incontrovertible as it ever gets), and he introduces a glimmer of doubt about the narrator's part in the tragedy which blurs things further (". . . I had a singular, a perverse and rather an embarrassed sense of having . . . interfered with her situation to her loss"). Since the narrator also speaks of himself as imaginative and cold and indulges, with Jasper's mother, in discussions about the morality of his observer's role, the resemblance between "The Patagonia" and *The Sacred Fount* is inescapable.[15] Why didn't James clearly weigh the moral responsibility of narrator and subject in "The Patagonia," "The Turn of the Screw," or *The Sacred Fount*? Why did he create a spokesman only to disenfranchise him? These are the questions that take us to the bottom of the *Fount*.

Although James's original conception is reflected in *The Sacred Fount*, as it is in "The Turn of the Screw," most salient textual details indicate that the narrator is faulty. Though the finale doesn't prove him wrong, it also doesn't prove the contrary; throughout, the narrator acts very like the governess. Here, too, self-interested behavior begins on the first page, where he responds to Gilbert Long and Grace in blatant reflection of their manners toward him. And since their manners toward him only improve when he presses his inquiries at Newmarch, we are led to suspect that he investigates them in order to gain approbation. "*I* alone was magnificently and absurdly aware," he crows, taking conscious pleasure in a gift he shares with the governess; "everyone else was benightedly out of it." But whereas the governess is uniquely perceptive because her adversaries manifest themselves only to her, the narrator's preeminence is self-invented. When he has not actually created what he alone knows, he refuses to share his knowledge with those who make it possible. Worse, his obscure speeches form a kind of private orgy in which his mind, innocent of experience, imaginatively invents experience in order to make it titillating. Accusing him of seeing "horrors," Mrs.

Brissenden wryly suggests that it would be better if he performed a few. Instead, the narrator seems to be battening on vice under the respectable cover of censure. When he goes to meet May Server in the garden, he feels suitably "as if I were trapping a bird or stalking a fawn." But her beauty does not excite him; talking, not stalking, he "groan[s] . . . as if for very ecstasy." The nearest he comes to the hanky-panky that may be afoot at Newmarch is "the last intellectual intimacy" in which he is "steeped" with Grace Brissenden.

No less than his motives, his methods fail to inspire confidence. When his analogies break down, he creates new ones. Absence of proof is proof; nothing is so revealing to him as a turned back, and his most intense conversations occur in total silence. Though he doubts, his doubts are short-lived. Though he is aware how threatening and sterile is his prying into the lives of his fellow guests, he decides, usually during his most guilt-stricken moments, that he can do nothing but push on. From ample evidence within the text, the narrator is a puerile, slightly perverse, logically dubious, and egoistic old maid. As Grace Brissenden tells him, he seems crazy.

Yet one must remember that her equivocations, shifts, and avowed fibs lend credence to the narrator's contention that she merely wishes to throw sand in his eyes. Moreover, though James throws plenty of pies at him, there are plenty of passages in which, face cleaned and remade, the narrator appears before us in a hush of eloquence to declare the supreme importance of his play: "I was just conscious, vaguely, of being on the track of a law, a law that would fit, that would strike me as governing the delicate phenomena—delicate though so marked—that my imagination found itself playing with. A part of the amusement they yielded came, I daresay, from my exaggerating them—grouping them into a larger mystery (and thereby a larger 'law') than the facts, as observed, yet warranted; but that is the common fault of minds for which the vision of life is an obsession."

This passage so characteristic of the book seems also characteristic of James's frequent self-definition. Therefore, *The Sacred Fount* has widely been thought to reveal something fundamental about the mind of its creator. But what does it reveal? If the narrator is a hero, it reveals that James could conceive of himself as a social critic ultimately rendered ineffective by society's arrogance. If the narrator is a fool, it reveals James's awareness, however unself-conscious, that his secondhand investigative method contained inherent weaknesses. If the former, *The Sacred Fount* is a moral exemplum based on social realities. If the latter, it is a satire in which an ingenious display of reason mocks itself. Either it is about morality or it is about thinking. Contradictorily, it is about both.

Whichever impulse we decide was James's guide, the other can be shown to operate against it. A moment's reflection will tell us that both impulses are always present in James's work. *The Portrait of a Lady*, for example, is about the evil of Osmond which victimizes the goodness of Isabel Archer; but she is also betrayed by her own interpretive errors, since (as the great description of Osmond's Florentine villa attests) human beings see only what they want to see. *The Ambassadors* follows Strether's moral maturation, but this process is itself inseparable from the comedy of his misperceptions. What we see in *The Sacred Fount* is that these subjects, ethics and epistemology, need not enrich one another. For *The Sacred Fount* is two novels—a moral allegory of ultimate evil and an epistemological comedy of ultimate imperception—joined imperfectly in a theory which evaporates before our eyes. The last pages of *The Sacred Fount*, like the last pages of "The Turn of the Screw," do not tell us whether the narrator was on the scent of evil or on the scent of nothing at all. The point we have now to see is that James himself doesn't try to know.

In his preface to "The Turn of the Screw," James argued that by not specifying the ghostly evil of Bly he had seduced his readers' imaginations and thus produced something more terrible than mere unaided narrative could accomplish. As a result, however, that terror story about evil has no certain evil in it. Because the governess's interpretation is never corroborated, the governess, so intensely realized, seems finally more threatening than the ghosts. This effect is evidently opposed to James's stated intention. A similar effect damages *The Sacred Fount*. Self-defeated fool or vanquished critic, the narrator of *The Sacred Fount* appeals to our understanding through the theory that he is seeking to prove. If it is silly or unverifiable, he is a fool; if it is important, though unproven, he is a heroic victim. The question of verification, as I have shown, is not answered. As in "The Turn of the Screw" and "The Patagonia," the ending concludes nothing. What I now propose to show is that the narrator's theory was faulty and confused from the outset.

The theory of the sacred fount is most easily and plausibly understood as a metaphor. The idea that intimate human relations always posit a partner who gives and one who takes is neither original nor farfetched; the sacred fount formulation merely exaggerates this contention for the purpose of dramatic clarity and vigor. So understood, the narrator's attempt to test the theory by observing the Brissendens, May Server, and Gilbert Long is an affecting image of the intellect at its benighted work. The sacred fount theory, then, can be regarded as a metaphor for the dangers of egoistic love or sexuality. Indeed such matters are at various points in the book explicitly discussed, and the fount image itself unavoidably suggests sex. Yet James goes to considerable lengths to separate the fount theory from all questions of a specifically sexual nature and thus effectively denies that it is metaphoric.

Adultery or illicit sexuality is not what the narrator is seeking to prove. The other characters are represented as being aware of sexual liaisons at Newmarch, but the narrator regards these as matters of a comparatively vulgar concern. This strange distinction is made clearest in a long conversation which he has with Lady John in chapter 9. Coming upon her and Briss, he finds that her greeting has the effect of dismissing her previous partner. Conventionally, they now set to work gossiping about him and about May Server. Throughout their talk he is delighted at the errors and grossness of vision which she manifests (in this scene his pride asserts itself most repulsively). For when they spy Gilbert Long and Grace talking alone on a "small sofa," Lady John immediately assumes that the lovers of the guests they have been discussing are themselves involved in an affair. To Lady John's Newmarch mentality, this is the real relationship between Grace and Long and between Briss and May Server. Yet the narrator believes that sex is not the adhesive. To him, Gilbert and Grace are conspiring together against his detective work, and the "idiotised" May Server is seeking commiseration from the octogenarian Briss. "She read all things, Lady John, heaven knows, in the light of the universal possibility of a 'relation'; but most of the relations that she had up her sleeve could thrust themselves into my theory only to find themselves, the next minute, eliminated." The narrator isn't using the sacred fount as a metaphor for sex; he really means that May is sacrificing her wit and that Briss is sacrificing his youth.

If the sacred fount is literal, James has intruded a fanciful element in an otherwise realistic, indeed, socially oriented novel. We can credit the significance of the narrator's behavior, for all its relentless excess, if what he is searching for, however he states it, is some actual fact of human intercourse. What happens when we perceive the fact to be in every sense fantastic? There is no need to argue against this incompatibility on generic grounds. Works like *What Maisie Knew* demonstrate that James can go very far in straining our sense of the plausible without violating the deepest facts of human life. But the sacred fount theory in the book undergoes a blurring that makes it finally quite unconvincing. It is not a plot metaphor but a rather absurd literalism; ultimately, it withers into an empty figure of speech.

The narrator first formulates his theory in response to a failure to recognize Grace Brissenden at the Paddington train. He learns from Gilbert that she is about forty-two or forty-three, though she now looks younger and prettier than she did five years ago at her wedding. In their subsequent discussion they consider many of the ways in which her alteration might be described. Gilbert believes not that she has grown younger but that she has kept her looks. The narrator objects that not aging is the same as growing younger and speaks, incorrectly, of Grace's "fifty years." A few moments later, when the narrator tells Grace that she looks quite twenty-five, she inadvertently gives a plausible explanation for the apparent change. Jokingly giving her age as ninety-three, she tells him that she does not dress appropriately for a twenty-five-year-old. "No," the narrator replies, "you dress, I make out, ninety-three. If you *would* only dress twenty-five you'd look fifteen." In short, Grace's rejuvenation is a cosmetic trick: by dressing in a manner suitable to a much older woman, her beauty and youth by contrast appear the more striking.

This is not only flimsy evidence for the narrator's subsequent harassment of Grace, it raises the deepest question about the actual relevance of his theory. It would be tedious to trace all the details in the book which suggest that his theory is not only vanquished but nonexistent, but one further example may establish the point. In the narrator's last conversation with Ford

Obert, Obert says that Briss, who momentarily enters, looks a hundred years old. The narrator tops him, saying that Briss looks two hundred or a thousand. This can only be taken as hyperbole. But if we take it as such, what is to prevent us from taking the narrator's entire theory as a monstrously overblown figure of speech which cannot be verified, not because the vampires vanquish him, or because he is a fool, or because the mind can never fathom experience, but because, strictly speaking, there isn't any theory at all?

As a result, *The Sacred Fount* contains no convincing portrayal of evil. Using it as an example, one can partly differentiate between James's successes and failures by distinguishing *Sacred Fount*-like villainies from those which are convincing. Nothing could be of greater significance for a writer whose main interest was the definition of good. Whenever James refuses to clarify the nature of evil, he cannot, as a consequence, validate the power of its opposite. In works like "The Turn of the Screw" and *The Sacred Fount* the protagonist's dubiousness is founded on the vagueness of his adversary.

However, this is not, as one might argue, simply a function of form: James's failure in *The Sacred Fount* goes deeper than his use of a first-person narrator who, as he recognized, risks a "terrible *fluidity* of self-revelation."[16] We can see this by comparing the novel to a similarly narrated story that *does* clearly engage evil.

As usual, Edmund Wilson was the first to point out the family resemblance between *The Sacred Fount* and "The Aspern Papers," and he was quite right in maintaining that the novella is innocent of such confusion as makes *The Sacred Fount* "maddening." The narrator in "The Aspern Papers" is not trying to prove anything, but in all other respects he resembles the narrator of *The Sacred Fount*. He is on the track of scandal, he is avowedly monomaniacal, this monomania makes him sexually unresponsive if not sterile, and he is routed in his quest by persons more in touch with life's libidinal sources. On the other hand, as Wilson saw, we are never in doubt that James wishes us to condemn him. Whatever faults he possesses, the plot shows that he is worse than he realizes. He is a fool, as we see from his absurd sentimentalizing of Juliana's past; he is a voyeur, as we see from his pursuit not of living sex but of musty records of ancient misdeeds; he is morally as well as sexually insensitive, as we see from his appalling attempts both to escape the love of Miss Tina and to ignore the full hideousness in his exploitation of her.

The epistemological theme crops up only once in "The Aspern Papers," when the narrator gets his cherished opportunity to meet Juliana. "Do you think it's right to rake up the past?" she asks, and the narrator replies:

> "I don't feel that I know what you mean by raking it up. How can we get at it unless we dig a little? The present has such a rough way of treading it down."
>
> "Oh I like the past, but I don't like critics," [the old woman declared, with her fine tranquillity].
>
> "Neither do I, but I like their discoveries."
>
> "Aren't they mostly lies?"
>
> "The lies are what they sometimes discover," I said, smiling at the quiet impertinence of this. "They often lay bare the truth."
>
> "The truth is God's, it isn't man's: we had better leave it alone. Who can judge of it?—who can say?"

This exchange has small effect on our understanding of a story that emphasizes the antiquarian lust of the glandless narrator. But it does recall a remark which James makes in the New York edition preface to "The Aspern Papers." Remembering that the idea for his tale came when he heard that Jane Clairmont, Byron's mistress, was still alive in Florence, James reveals that he had been undecided about whether or not he ought to visit her. Attached as he was to the period in which she flourished, he feared that her reality might compromise his romantic image of the Byronic age. Fortunately she soon died, settling the question for him.

As we see, James himself entertained both the narrator's romantic nostalgia and Juliana's shrewd belief that a love for the past is not incompatible with judicious ignorance. But there is no necessary contradiction between these attitudes, as Juliana's remarks tell us. Apparently, James identified the more ludicrous implications of his nostalgia with the narrator and united his positive reverence for the past to Juliana. This effective purging of his own sentimentality by affixing it to a villain is made possible by the commitment which enables Juliana to love the past more appealingly—her commitment to individual privacy and dignity. Thus Juliana is willing to sell Jeffrey Aspern's picture, but only to someone who appreciates its worth. She rightly perceives that the narrator's interest in Aspern is antithetical to the very genius which the narrator covets.

James was as implicated in "The Aspern Papers" as he was in *The Sacred Fount*. Why then could he see one reflection of himself so clearly and the other in a manner so deeply confused? Wilson tends to believe that James balked whenever he confronted sex. By comparing "The Aspern Papers" and *The Sacred Fount* we can see that sex was not his main problem.

In "The Aspern Papers" the heroine has a "past." But Juliana's illicit love affair does not, in James's eyes, keep her from being a fit representative of as exalted a conception of the past as is present anywhere in his work. Indeed, it is because Juliana had a lover that we admire her. Aspern was one indication of the devotion to love, the giving quality of her nature, that redeems her from charges of vulgarity, mendacity, and vice. We almost begin to think that love has kept her alive so much longer than man's normal term. Her very willingness to deal with the narrator illustrates the power of her love: she covets the opportunity he provides to insure Miss Tina's future. When she sees him rummaging through her furniture, desecrating her very god, she starts to die in Tina's arms.

Juliana's sexuality is related to values which James deeply believed—the sanctity of the individual, the inviolable mystery of individual memories and collective history—and she is James's heroine. In contrast, the narrator—with his lack of human feeling, his antiquarian folly—is clearly a villain. Whether or not the papers really exist makes no difference to the moral and psychological actuality of the tale's principal characters. James was so certain that moral issues were his focus in "The Aspern Papers" that questions of truth became irrelevant.[17]

Questions of truth are unanswerable in *The Sacred Fount* because James was uncertain about its moral issues. He was uncertain about its moral issues because he was ambivalent about the morality of its antagonists. In "The Aspern Papers" the narrator's antagonists represent fundamental Jamesian values. In *The Sacred Fount* the narrator's antagonists represent society, and society is a subject toward which James had a disturbingly ambivalent response. There is a beautiful passage in *The Sacred Fount* that formulates the narrator's relationship to society and thereby suggests James's problem:

> I remember feeling seriously warned, while dinner lasted, not to yield further to my idle habit of reading into mere human things an interest so much deeper than mere human things were in general prepared to supply. This especial hour, at Newmarch, had always a splendour that asked little of interpretation, that even carried itself with an amiable arrogance, as indifferent to what the imagination could do for it. I think the imagination, in those halls of art and fortune, was almost inevitably accounted a poor matter; the whole place and its participants abounded so in pleasantness and picture, in all the felicities, for every sense, taken for granted there by the very basis of life, that even the sense most

finely poetic, aspiring to extract the moral, could scarce have helped feeling itself treated to something of the snub that affects—when it does affect—the uninvited reporter in whose face a door is closed.

The narrator fears that he might be overreading the data presented by Newmarch, that his aspiration toward moral clarity might lead him away from the truth. But this fear is based not so much on his consciousness that imagination has its limits as on his suspicion that society's sheer vigor and sensuous display make imagination irrelevant and can end by shutting it out. Imagination may lead one astray, but may it not also lead one into solitude and rejection? If we take this worry as a projection, however unconscious, of James's own sense of the fate of imagination, we can see why he found it so difficult to tell us whether the narrator was right and Newmarch was a den of vice.

Since, like his narrator, James was an observer and a moral historian, his awareness that man's mind was dreadfully distant from the objects which it sought to know would have made exclusion from society an unmitigated disaster. If society scorned his imagination or closed the door in his face, how could he ever come even to that modicum of knowledge which his epistemological sophistication declared the optimum? Yet if he told the truth about society, would it not act, like Grace Brissenden, to protect itself? Wouldn't rejection, as the narrator effectively maintains, be, in fact, the highest tribute society could pay to his perceptual soundness? The desire to be right could only produce a slamming door which would keep him from his material and thereby perhaps keep him from ever being right again. He had to find a way for telling the truth so oblique as to maintain his position in the enemy camp.

I do not mean by this to imply vulgar timidity or pandering on James's part; the need to muffle his censure might have been a response to some internalized form of the dilemma I have described. He could justify his commitment to the world through his devotion to knowledge, but his devotion to morality would not find this argument very soothing in view of the patent immorality which the world exhibits. In his hunger for virtue and truth in a world that radically denies their connection, James was like his first surrogate heroine, Isabel Archer, for whom "the love of knowledge co-existed in [the] mind with the finest capacity for ignorance." He wished to know society, but he wished to ignore anything that would suggest the futility of idealism. He wished to plumb the depths of vice but not so far as to deny the primacy of virtue.

The Sacred Fount both reveals these difficulties and desperately tries to solve them. James's intellectual need for society colliding with his moral antipathy toward it finds an evasive release in fantasy. By making evil not ordinary sexual exploitation but a literal vampirism, James sidesteps his dilemma. He creates an ambience of vice for which the vampirism is a symbol and into which it emotionally fits. In this way, he can bear witness to society's wickedness and satisfy himself that his investigations have not been basely dispassionate or voyeuristic. At the same time, since vampirism is patently impossible, he need not face an evil which is invincible because common or one which would make the world morally untouchable for so universally fostering it. The sacred fount theory is designed, with considerable unconscious guile, to envelop the harsh outlines of evil in the evanescent mists of fancy. In addition, by throwing doubts over the narrator's correctness (though the notebooks and the letter to Mrs. Ward indicate that these doubts were never meant to be decisive), James almost denies that Newmarch is evil.

Indeed, he went too far. In "The Aspern Papers," the very clarity with which he sees the narrator's evil shows that James was disowning his creature, declaring himself on the right side. But in *The Sacred Fount* there is no right side. James is the narrator, but he is also Newmarch. He has a commitment to the observer, but he also has a commitment to the world. He cannot define a worldly evil that would compromise his interest in society, nor can he denounce society without renouncing it. Yet *The Sacred Fount*, the only James novel with a writer-hero, is also the first major James novel that does not involve renunciation. The narrator is sent away from Newmarch; he does not really choose to leave it.

The novel's insoluble ambiguity is partly due, as I have said, to a logical contradiction between James's need for moral judgments and his knowledge that judgments are ultimately private. But it is also a defense against the threat to his idealism which was involved in any admission of just how irredeemably wicked was the world he had devoted his life to understanding. By not facing the evil at Newmarch, James allows us to find the narrator a greater horror than any he suspects. It is a fitting irony that James's need to protect society and thereby protect his idealistic hope for it should eventually cast doubts on both. Lacking a clear portrayal of vice, he can give no clearly contrasting virtue. Newmarch and the narrator are both so indistinct that we cannot confirm the moral value of either. But we can see James's evasion. That is what is at the bottom of the *Fount*.

CHAPTER TWO

The Mansion and the Child

Henry James castigates evil in order to celebrate good. Therefore, since he was both a moralist and an incisive social critic, he faced a dilemma. Because his critical intelligence told him that society was bad, while his moral idealism insisted that it be redeemable, he evidently felt a temptation either to muffle his censure of worldliness or to qualify his need for virtue. In his greatest books, he does both things simultaneously, achieving a balance that earns credibility without compromising his essential preference. In weaker books, he merely equivocates.

In "The Turn of the Screw" and *The Sacred Fount* he equivocates about evil, thus ironically vitiating his portrayal of good. The novel helps us see why: its fantasy indicates James's need to bear witness against English society without losing his own sense of access to it. But having things both ways destroys the novel's structure, turning it into an insoluble contradiction that fascinates students of James but maddens the common reader. Both a more realistic and a more charming book, *The American* shares flaws with its successor, while it also further clarifies the nature of James's commitment to worldliness. Society was not precious to James only because it provided him with his chosen material (the field, as the Newmarch narrator puts it, where one finds "laws" that govern life). Society *per se* appealed to James, for qualities of pleasantness, cultivation, and style. As we recall, those very qualities make the narrator feel inferior and finally show him the door.

Being shown the door is the central crisis of *The American*, whose hero seeks and is denied admittance to French society. But in this novel as in the similar *Princess Casamassima*, the rejected hero vanquishes his adversaries as his counterpart in *The Sacred Fount* does not. The victories of Newman and Hyacinth, however, are rather odd. Instead of protesting his exclusion by a morally inferior force, Newman suffers his rebuff in silence, and Hyacinth immolates himself. Behind each act stands that same ambivalence toward society which expressed itself through fantasy in the later novel but which was first hidden behind a specious naturalism.

Still, the surface panorama is unquestionably cunning—so cunning in *The American*'s case that one wants to yield to its charm, its vigor, its adroit comedy of manners. Even the most devoted admirer of the later fiction must sometimes regret that James lost this opening note: "On a brilliant day in May, in the year 1868, a gentleman was reclining at his ease on the great circular divan which at that period occupied the centre of the Salon Carré, in the Museum of the Louvre. This commodious ottoman has since been removed, to the extreme regret of all weak-kneed lovers of the fine arts; but the gentleman in question had taken serene possession of its softest spot, and, with his head thrown back and his legs outstretched, was staring at Murillo's beautiful moon-borne Madonna in profound enjoyment of his posture."

How often, even in James, does one find so perfectly easy a combination of the witty and the expository? How delightful to combine workmanlike swiftness of characterization with a joke so pithy as Newman's delectation not of the Murillo but of his seat! When M. Nioche is presently introduced, we are at once informed and tickled about his past: "Adversity had not only ruined him, it had frightened him, and he was evidently going through his remnant of life on tiptoe, for fear of waking up the hostile fates." The plot is as entertaining as the characters: Newman's confrontation with the Bellegardes comes as close as a refined reader could wish to the thrills of a last-reel duel in a western movie. And all this in behalf of James's great theme: the discovery by a child of the great, wide, ugly world. *The American* brings Newman from his first view of Paris as paradise ("the scene [of] a kind of primordial, pastoral simplicity") to his anguished vision of "a region of convents and prisons, of streets bordered by long dead walls. . . . This seemed the goal of his journey; it was what he had come for."

Because it is the first deeply Jamesian book in situation and moral concern and because it does not sacrifice wit to seriousness, one feels reluctant to expose its deeper pretensions. Yet James himself acknowledged his self-deception when writing about the novel for the New York edition. In an unusually candid self-arraignment, he admits that the book, planned as moral realism, became blatant romance. Had he tried to be faithful to the actualities of the case, the Bellegardes would have swooped down upon Newman, under cover of darkness to be sure, and secured his millions for their ancient but impoverished *ménage*. James now realizes that his interest in Newman's magnanimity required that the Bellegardes provide a supreme test, even though to oblige they had to violate verisimilitude: "I had been plotting arch-romance without knowing it,"[18] he handsomely concedes. James also alludes to another serious flaw in *The American*: the obscure

motivation of Claire de Cintré. "The delicate clue to her character is never definitely placed in the reader's hand: I must have
liked verily to think it *was* delicate and to flatter myself it was to
be felt with finger-tips rather than heavily tugged at."[19] Together
with his confession concerning the Bellegardes, this amounts to
James's gentle acknowledgment that Newman is the novel's one
plausible character.

Also implausible is the plot. Although *The American* is presumably a love story, Newman hardly displays the proper interest
in his beloved: "He claimed, at least, none of the exemptions and
emoluments of the romantic passion. . . . What he felt was an
intense all-consuming tenderness. . . . [Mme de Cintré] seemed
to him so felicitous a product of nature and circumstance, that
his invention, musing on future combinations, was constantly
catching its breath with the fear of stumbling into some brutal
compression or mutilation of her beautiful personal harmony."
Newman's feeling, James tells us, "had the quality of a young
mother's eagerness to protect the sleep of her first-born child."
When Newman makes love, he assures Claire that she will be "as
safe . . . as in your father's arms." Though Claire seems pallid
to the reader, to Newman she is too hot to handle—except in
swaddling.

Since he is so timid in reaching for her, we can only find disproportionate the violence with which she rejects him. At any
rate, the motive on which she stands at their obligatory farewell
is no more than a gothic mystification: "Why do such dreadful
things happen to us—why is my brother Valentin killed, like a
beast, in the midst of his youth and his gaiety and his brightness
and all that we loved him for? Why are there things I can't ask
about—that I am afraid to know? Why are there places I can't
look at, sounds I can't hear?" To these plaintive questions, the
answer is "why indeed"; Valentin's death in a duel fought over
Noémie Nioche is an affair irrelevant to Claire's romance: none

of Claire's expostulations explains what is keeping her back or why. James makes one more attempt to suggest her motives when Mrs. Bread exhales, "She was like a fair peach . . . with just one little speck. . . . You pushed her into the sunshine, sir, and it almost disappeared. Then they pulled her back into the shade and in a moment it began to spread." This odd metaphor is comprehensible only on the grounds that Claire knew of her father's murder; but there is not the slightest evidence of such knowledge, and the murder itself is, as we shall see, uncertain. One critic, John A. Clair, even supposes that Mrs. Bread refers here to Claire's possible illegitimacy, and Newman is never sure himself why his betrothed enters a convent.[20]

But Newman scarcely cares, for he is quick to see the benefit which her mysterious gesture provides: "She has moved off, like her brother Valentin," he tells Mrs. Bread, "to give me room to work. It's as if it were done on purpose." Here, with the melodrama at its gaudiest, Newman starts to show true zest. The book's last scenes are what he has been waiting for: "[Newman] was nursing his thunderbolt; he loved it; he was unwilling to part with it. He seemed to be holding it aloft in the rumbling, vaguely-flashing air, directly over the heads of his victims, and he fancied he could see their pale upturned faces." We are indeed following a theatrical story of the sort that makes for best sellers, though the wish fulfilled in *The American* is rather more special. What greater delight for the provincial abashed before the glories of civilization than to have secret proof that civilization is a calculated ruse—and then to keep the proof to himself so as to be both superior and not vulgarly public about it!

Not love but the fraudulence of civilization is the subject of James's *American*. He had already written stories about impressionable compatriots exploited by a venal Europe that could never match their dream of it. In "A Passionate Pilgrim" (1871), for example, the hero journeys to England in a spirit of reverence only to find his English relative accusing him of greed. Determined to hold on to the family mansion he believes the American covets, the Englishman behaves very treacherously, until his villainy is cut short by a horse. However, before the house can fall to him, the American places himself above the battle by dying, but not before he provides an impoverished British worker with the means toward a new life in the States.

This early tale, with its disillusionment about Europe and its operatic proof of American magnanimity, is a crude but characteristic prefigurement of the novel. Despite its suavity and wit, *The American* even exceeds the story's display of European wickedness and enhances the American's grandeur by making his renunciation not an accident of nature but a calculated act.

Most vivid in the novel's pages is an exposure of European bogusness that establishes, through contrast, the humanity of the artless native. Chapter 10, where Newman meets the Bellegardes, achieves this contrast triumphantly. Newman attempts to ingratiate himself, but the Bellegardes confound him with haughtiness. Yet behind their frigid manner is a mean avidity. "Will you let [my courtship pass]?" Newman asks the Marquise. "You don't know what you ask," she replies; "I am a very proud and meddlesome old woman." "Well, I am very rich." And the answer shoots back: "How rich?"

Nor are the Bellegardes unusual examples of their *monde*. When Valentin shows Newman around Paris, he takes him to the home of a young woman whose obvious flirtations court disaster, yet he warns Newman of the futility in attempts to save her. At the ball which the Bellegardes give in Newman's honor, the most august guest is one Mme de la Rochefidèle, who had an "aged cadaverous face, with a falling of the lower jaw which prevented her from bringing her lips together, and reduced her conversation to a series of impressive but inarticulate gutturals."

The climax comes when Newman visits the leader of this society, Mme d'Outreville, in order to expose for her censure the Bellegardes' sin. But he realizes after all that he has nothing to tell her: "Wherein would it profit him to tell her that the Bellegardes were traitors and that the old lady, into the bargain, was a murderess? . . . What in the world had he been thinking of when he fancied the duchess could help him, and that it would conduce to his comfort to make her think ill of the Bellegardes? What did her opinion of the Bellegardes matter to him? It was only a shade more important than the opinion the Bellegardes entertained of her." Freedom from a provincial's nagging sense of inferiority is the boon that makes *The American* so light in tone for all its baleful plotting and which enables Newman to accept so readily the loss of Claire. The phantom Mme de Cintré and the incredibly vicious Bellegardes provide Newman with the outcast's dearest if not his only pleasure: the sense of being "a good fellow wronged." "He saw himself trustful, generous, liberal, patient, easy, pocketing frequent irritation and furnishing unlimited modesty. To have eaten humble pie, to have been snubbed and patronised and satirised, and have consented to take it as one of the conditions of the bargain—to have done this, and done it all for nothing. . . ." But not really for nothing. Children mistreated by their elders, young men from the provinces shown the door, and provincials snubbed by the establishment can all console themselves with martyrdom and self-aggrandizing fantasy.

Though James likes his moral provincial so much that he sacrifices credibility in order to enhance him, a contradictory attitude toward Newman is also evident. As a result, Newman possesses flaws that nearly justify the Bellegardes' refusal to swallow him. Not only is he acquisitive in the manner of an American businessman, he is guilty of the Jamesian sin of treating people as things. Throughout his courtship, he behaves as if he were purchasing a mate, with the same Philistine ignorance of all but quantitative matters that he shows when purchasing paintings wholesale from Noémie Nioche. His proposal, for example, might have been suitable for a girl's father—it is a veritable audit of his accounts—but it is hardly designed to win the girl. In the light of these ugly signs of crass indifference to emotion, the reader is free to interpret Newman's response to losing Claire as all too predictably loveless.

Though it is not developed (as one can see by going no further than *The Portrait of a Lady*), there are also hints of a "fortunate fall" motif that qualifies the novel's crisis. Newman's "most vivid conception of a supernatural element in the world's affairs," James tells us, was of the devil, "and he was accordingly seized with an intense personal enmity to this impertinent force." The Bellegardes at least teach him that resistance to his will is very pertinent, that he cannot trample on the loyalties of others, and that he cannot buy everything he wants. In one sense, they give him a salutary lesson in human relations.

J. A. Ward, in his book on James's notion of evil, has read the novel as if Newman were a rather rough sort whom the Bellegardes manage to polish.[21] Even Leon Edel and Richard Poirier, who are sure that Newman was intended as a fabulous hero, take pains to delineate his objectionable side. Poirier conjectures that the novel would have been more coherent had this side been developed; the Bellegardes would then have had a justifiable motive for turning Newman off, and the plot would not have remained so patently irrational.[22]

In any case, the irrationality of the plot points to James's anxiety that we sympathize with his hero, for by adding lack of motive to the Bellegardes' broken promise, their crime against Newman is made more intolerable. Ironically, James's ploy also has the contrary effect. Because the Bellegardes don't have any clear reason for turning Newman off, we are invited to search his character for the cause; and, as I have shown, the search bears fruit. Though not so damaging as in "The Turn of the Screw," this ambiguity recalls the earlier work. Seeking to enhance the governess by adding uniqueness of perception to her other virtues, James also creates a skepticism toward her that would not otherwise have occurred.

But in Newman's case, his charm overwhelms our suspicions. Though ambiguity in *The American* is not so serious as in the novella, it is aggravated by some plotting that recalls *The Sacred Fount*. The Bellegardes recall the Newmarch guests in two ways. Both are involved in terrible crimes, and neither is surely involved in them. Because the writing is so much clearer in the earlier novel, the evil of the Bellegardes seems more unequivocally established than the vampirism at Newmarch. But the matter is less simple than it seems.

In the essay I have mentioned, John Clair reinterprets the novel in a way that clarifies its mysteries: ". . . Mrs. Bread, the true mother of Claire de Cintré, was a blackmailer claiming both Newman and the Marquise de Bellegarde as victims . . . and . . . Claire's refusal to accept Newman in marriage came as a direct result of her having been informed by the Bellegardes of her true parents. . . ."[23] On the face of it, this reading is implausible, since it amounts to claiming that James, in the manner of Nabokov, wrote a novel concealing the real novel which is to be inferred from verbal hints buried in the false text. Yet it is true that James denies absolute evidence of the Marquise's guilt, while he presents several hints that Catherine Bread is an interested informer.

To the end the Bellegardes maintain that Mrs. Bread is both false and vindictive. Though it might seem mere pluck, Newman admires the conviction with which they play this last card. Moreover, James permits Mrs. Bread herself to lend credence to their contention out of her own mouth:

> "One day I had a red ribbon in my cap, and my lady flew out at me and ordered me to take it off. She accused me of putting it on to

make the marquis look at me. I don't know that I was impertinent, but I spoke up like an honest girl and didn't count my words. A red ribbon indeed! As if it was my ribbons the marquis looked at! My lady knew afterwards that I was perfectly respectable, but she never said a word to show that she believed it. But the marquis did! . . . I took off my red ribbon and put it away in a drawer, where I have kept it to this day. It's faded, now, it's very pale pink; but there it lies. My grudge has faded, too; the red has all gone out of it; but it lies here yet." And Mrs. Bread stroked her black satin bodice.

There is reason to credit the Bellegardes' self-defense; and if we do even for a minute, we must go beyond Newman's grudging admiration for their nerve to an active sympathy for the brutality they suffer at his hands. As they say, they have already borne both Mrs. Bread's malice and the loss of two children. If we can conceive of them as heroic figures in their final grief and pride, what is to prevent us from admiring the heroic principle they display in rejecting Newman? When they spurn him, they admit they would have preferred his money but could not compromise by taking the vulgarity to which it was joined. Since Newman is surely vulgar and since their evil is far from sure, it is possible to read the novel in a way that exactly reverses the conventional, James's avowed interpretation.

No doubt such a reading would be in error, and since most of the evidence goes the other way, we do not confront in *The American* the problems maddeningly characteristic of "The Turn of the Screw" and *The Sacred Fount*. To wholly admire the later works, one must either cleave to a single reading, ignoring contrary evidence in the text, or celebrate James for anticipating the current belief that stories ought to be about the incommunicability of experience and the duplicity of language. Since *The American* cannot be regarded as a precursor of the *nouvelle roman*, however, the likeliest defense against its ambiguities is that they make its character seem more life-like. Indeed, I shall myself argue in a similar fashion during the second and third parts of this book; but there is an important distinction to be made. That Strether is not all-virtuous, Mme de Vionnet not all-wicked, suits the complex structure and theme of *The Ambassadors*, a tragicomedy about James's deepest ethical and epistemological concerns. On the other hand, *The American* is a simple melodrama, most of whose facts don't prepare us to look askance at Newman or to doubt the villainy of the Bellegardes. Consequently, what are fundamental ironies in *The Ambassadors* are peripheral equivocations in *The American*. The moral relativism toward which the whole of *The Ambassadors* moves is in *The American* a disfunctional smudging of an otherwise bright and hard-edged design. In particular, James's refusal to certify the wickedness of the Bellegardes is wholly regrettable, recalling the ambivalence toward society that damages *The Sacred Fount*.

Because *The Princess Casamassima* concerns revolution, it afforded James an opportunity to resolve this ambivalence. Instead, it shows more blatantly even than *The American* that James loved society's stylishness so much he could paradoxically ignore defects of which he himself was a profound critic. The ambivalence that drains *The Sacred Fount* of clarity drains *The Princess Casamassima* of drama. As Yvor Winters claimed, the book's revolutionaries "have little more force or dignity than a small boy under a sheet at Hallowe'en."[24] Having chosen to write about people who shared his negative attitudes toward society, James was prevented by the depth of his positive attitudes from imagining them powerfully. Like *The American*, *The Princess Casamassima* initially raises the question of plausibility, though James had more candidly recognized this problem about the earlier book. In the New York preface to *The Princess*, he rather tries to rationalize the lapse. Though alive to "probably ironic reflexions on the full license for sketchiness and vagueness and dimness . . . [in his] picture," James asserts that such was his intention: ". . . the value I wished most to render and the effect I wished most to produce were precisely those of our not knowing, of society's not knowing, but only guessing and suspecting and trying to ignore, what 'goes on' irreconcilably, subversively, beneath the vast smug surface."[25] Remembering James's prefatory explanation for the absence of described evil at Bly and his notebook confession, while composing *The Princess*, that he had "never yet become engaged in a novel in which, after I had begun to write and send off my MS., the details had remained so vague,"[26] we may suspect that society was not the only observer uncertain of what was going on.

At any rate, *The Princess Casamassima* is no more about politics than *The American* is about love. Before the book is really under way, James pricks the anarchists' pretensions with such force that they remain bloodless phantoms unable to provide more than the merest semblance of rebellion. This, for example, is James's initial description of Eustache Poupin, Hyacinth's guide to the anarchist underworld: "M. Poupin was an aggressive socialist . . . and a constructive democrat . . . and a theorist and an optimist and a collectivist and a perfectionist and a visionary; he believed the day was to come when all the nations of the earth would abolish their frontiers and armies and customhouses, and embrace on both cheeks and cover the globe with boulevards, radiating from Paris, where the human family would sit in groups at little tables, according to affinities, drinking coffee (not tea, *par exemple!*) and listening to the music of the spheres." "Whatever his occupation or his topic," Poupin's eyes have "the same declamatory, reclamatory, proclamatory, the same universally inaugurative expression." When he speaks about the impending revolution, his "wife" makes "a very cheerful clatter with a big spoon in a saucepan." The only chapter that shows an anarchist conclave resembles nothing so much as the debate of the devils in *Paradise Lost*.

Of the three principal characters attached to the anarchists, Christina and Paul Muniment are probably lacking in sincere political convictions and Hyacinth is ultimately repelled by the very idea of politics. The only true revolutionary in the book, Hoffendahl, never appears.

At times, James tries to center the novel in Hyacinth's internal struggles between his anarchist and aristocratic leanings, schematized, in a manner unusually banal for James, as a re-enactment of the murderous conflict between his aristocratic father and his working-class mother. But these attempts are uniformly unconvincing.

> There was no peace for him between the two currents that flowed in his nature [James tells us shortly before the catastrophe]. . . . They continued to toss him from one side to the other; they arrayed him in intolerable defiances and revenges against himself. He had a high ambition: he wanted neither more nor less than to get hold of the truth and wear it in his heart. He believed with the candour of youth that it is brilliant and clear-cut, like a royal diamond; but to whatever quarter he turned in the effort to find it he seemed to know that behind him, bent on him in reproach, was a tragic wounded face.

There is little trace of such suffering in Hyacinth, but James mentions "these dim broodings not because they belong in an especial degree to the history of our young man during the winter of the Princess's residence in Madeira Crescent, but because they were a constant element in his moral life and need to be remembered in any view of him at a given time." If the plaintive retrospection of this avowal were not sufficient to establish James's negligence, the almost unique inelegance of the sentence structure would give the flaw away.

Since the conspirators, as George Woodcock has argued, are

consistently viewed with either "contempt or fear,"[27] and since none of the principal characters is really to be understood as taking form within a context of internal or external controversy, the ostensible subject of *The Princess Casamassima*, like the ostensible subject of *The American*, is a red herring. The real subject follows the outline of the earlier book. Like Christopher Newman, Hyacinth Robinson is a social inferior, placed in a category that prevents him from entering the world of fabulous elegance toward which he yearns, who proves his innate superiority to that world by renouncing an act of violence that threatens its existence.

In Hyacinth's case, James is so zealous at keeping the hero's innate superiority before us that he makes incredible the internal division upon which the plot is meant to turn. Hyacinth's guardian, Miss Pynsent, "had from his earliest age made him feel that there was a grandeur in his past," and everything he does or says in the book bears witness to the efficacy of her child-rearing. In his first appearance, when he is ten years old, we recognize his "aristocratic manner," and his walks, while a young man, through low-class London are impelled by a sense of the picturesque that no denizen could possess. Moreover, James informs us that "the nature of his mind . . . was perpetually, almost morbidly conscious that the circle in which he lived was an infinitesimally small shallow eddy in the roaring vortex of London," and that Hyacinth was sustained by "the hope of being carried to some brighter, happier vision—the vision of societies where, in splendid rooms, with smiles and soft voices, distinguished men, with women who were both proud and gentle, talked of art, literature and history." In the light of these early revelations, we can only smile at his later animadversions about the iniquities of the social system.

The very act which tragically crowns his putative conflict has no connection to politics. Long before Hyacinth is given orders to kill the Duke, he confesses that his sympathies are with the aristocracy. His motive for obedience, then, can only be a quixotic if not aristocratic code of honor. Suggestively, when Hyacinth's friend, Mr. Vetch, comes to the Princess begging that she persuade the youth to reveal his task, he says that Hyacinth hasn't confided in him because "it would be like a man giving notice when he's going to fight a duel."

Hyacinth's acceptance of his homicidal order has nothing to do with revolution and everything to do with self-expression: " 'Isn't it enough now to give my life to the beastly cause,' the young man broke out, 'without giving my sympathy?' 'The beastly cause?' the Princess murmured, opening her deep eyes. 'Of course it's really just as holy as ever; only the people I find myself pitying now are the rich, the happy.' . . . 'You're very remarkable. Yes, you're splendid.' To which he made an answer: 'Well, it's what I want to be!' " This wish is fulfilled. By accepting Hoffendahl's orders, he proves himself more splendid than the slightly ridiculous conspirators. Then, by shooting himself rather than the Duke, he augments his original splendor with the protection of an unheeding aristocracy. As in Newman's case, his final thrill is the austere lack of publicity with which the self-abasement is performed.

Hyacinth Robinson is one of the many projections in James's fiction of a child-like and therefore pure outsider who establishes the grandeur underlying his apparent unfitness for adult life by exposing the world's evil in an exemplary act of self-sacrifice. "He's a thin-skinned, morbid, mooning, introspective little beggar," Mr. Vetch says, "with a good deal of imagination and not much perseverance, who'll expect a good deal more of life than he'll find in it. That's why he won't be happy." It is the heart of this description that unhappiness be the proof of distinction. The bullet in Hyacinth's chest, like the empty hands of Christopher Newman, is the authentic Jamesian badge of honor.

Unfortunately, Hyacinth is not what James wanted him to be. Newman has his famous charm; Hyacinth, at most, has mere pathos. Moreover, James was not able to give Hyacinth some of his own intelligence, probably because he lacked the ability to dramatize internal debate. *The Bostonians,* James's more successful venture into revolution, succeeds in part because James can externalize dialectic in the opposing characters of Basil Ransom and Olive Chancellor. One searches in vain throughout his fiction for the kind of inner ideological turmoil that alone could have made Hyacinth's ordeal convincing. In the words of F. W. Dupee: "Unlike Isabel and Newman, whose superior gallantry is vivid, positive, and intelligible, Hyacinth seems a case merely of unrequited sensibility, of the man who is too good for this world. No doubt James's mind was in this instance *too* inviolable to ideas; he could have done with a few. Surely Hyacinth travels far to learn what he could have read any day in the *Times*: that radicals are envious."[28]

Of more immediate consequence to the plot, Hyacinth travels far to learn that Paul and the Princess are frauds. "It was very difficult, with Hyacinth, to make reservations or mysteries," James boasts; "he wanted to know everything about everything." When told everything however, he makes a mystery where none exists. Mme Grandoni warns him that Christina is a *"capricciosa,"* and Rose Muniment confesses herself unable to vouch for her brother's convictions, yet Hyacinth persists in worshiping the dubious pair and resists knowledge when he discovers what we have known all along.

When all this has been said, however, *The Princess* does present a more mature conception of evil than the earlier novel. *The American*'s great triumph is the chapter which brings Newman to the Bellegarde house. The great triumph of *The Princess Casamassima* comes when Paul pays his first visit to Madeira Crescent. This scene belongs with the marvelous confrontations in James: Merle confessing to Isabel, Maisie challenging Claude at the railway station, Strether and Marie de Vionnet saying farewell. In it, two shallow egotists take full measure of one another. "Whatever you are you'll succeed," Christina tells him. "Hyacinth won't, but you will."

> "It depends upon what you call success! . . . You've got a lovely home."
> "Lovely? My dear sir, it's hideous. That's what I like it for." . . .
> "Well, I like it, but perhaps I don't know the reason. I thought you had given up everything—pitched your goods out of window for a grand scramble."
> "It's what I *have* done. You should have seen me before."
> "I should have liked that . . . I like to see solid wealth."
> "Ah you're as bad as Hyacinth. I'm the only consistent one! . . ."
> "You've a great deal left, for a person who has given everything away."

At their last meeting, when Paul reduces Christina to her first anguish in the novel, she buries her face in a pedantically deprived sofa while Paul remarks casually that she shall certainly return to her husband.

Muniment and the Princess are promising depictions of moral vacancy, but they are not well developed. Though she lends her name to the novel, Christina never takes the center of the stage, and Paul is discussed far more than exhibited. Moreover, though James has rendered important ironies in this ascetic revolutionary and the bored aristocrat playing at politics, their characters are fairly simple and remain so.

Nonetheless, particularly in Christina's case, James provides the same final rehabilitation of a bad character that one sees in *The American* and perhaps in *The Sacred Fount*. On the testimony of her friends, her actions, and her ludicrous rhetoric, there is no reason for thinking Christina sincere. Yet in her last meeting with Hyacinth, James devotes to her passages of such approbation that she is turned into Hyacinth's revolutionary muse. The hero perceives in her tone "something so inspiring in the great union of her beauty, her sincerity and her energy that the image of a heroism not less great flashed up again before him in all the splendour it had lost—the idea of a tremendous risk and an unregarded sacrifice. Such a woman as that, at such an hour, one who could shine like silver and ring like crystal, made every scruple a poor prudence and every compunction a cowardice." So brilliant is her example of revolutionary fervor that, in this moment before his ultimate renunciation, Hyacinth can find nothing more worthy of esteem: " 'There's no one in the world and has never been any one in the world like you.' 'Oh thank you!' said the Princess impatiently. And she turned from him as with a beat of great white wings that raised her straight out of the bad air of the personal. It took her up too high, it put an end to their talk; expressing an indifference to what it might interest him to think of her to-day, and even a contempt for it, which brought tears to his eyes. His tears, however, were concealed by the fact that he bent his head low over the hand he had taken to kiss; after which he left the room without looking at her." Hyacinth's behavior either reminds us that he has been consistently overgenerous in his vision of the Princess, or, since he is the novel's hero, it cautions us against being critical of her ourselves. If the former, this seems an odd time to remind us of Hyacinth's naiveté; more likely, James is presenting here his own feeling for Christina. But the physical difficulty of Hyacinth's parting gesture nicely measures the illogic of James's *machina* for his *dea*; Christina is, after all, being cruelly indifferent to the obvious suffering of someone she is purported to admire. We can accept Hyacinth's failure to recoil against her untimely *hauteur*, but what are we to make of James's failure to indicate that Hyacinth is being too devotional?

Van Wyck Brooks's notion of James's career has been justly

condemned for its tendentious simplicity, but passages such as Hyacinth's farewell to the Princess Casamassima vouch for his portion of truth: "Henry James had travelled over land and sea, known men and cities, watched and labored, he had become withal the most formidable of artists; and still the dreams of his prime lurked at the bottom of his heart. The great world had remained for him what the world of fairies is for other souls: it was the unquestionable, the sublime, the world beyond good and evil. To enter it was to cross the threshold of Utopia."[29]

The ambiguity concerning Christina is surely not so serious or striking as that concerning the Bellegardes. But one cannot escape the conclusion, while reading *The Princess Casamassima*, that James had a respect for culture, as maintained and enhanced by a privileged class, which was both prior to and infinitely deeper than his concern for man's attempts to alter the daily condition. That is why Christina can be great in the midst of her revolutionary games. After all, they are unimportant and probably transitory, whereas her stylish grandeur will survive. Hyacinth confesses that his life taught him to admire

the great achievements of which man has been capable in spite of [social iniquities]—the splendid accumulations of the happier few, to which doubtless the miserable many have also in their degree contributed. . . . The monuments and treasures of art, the great palaces and properties, the conquests of learning and taste, the general fabric of civilisation as we know it, based if you will upon all the despotisms, the cruelties, the exclusions, the monopolies, and the rapacities of the past, but thanks to which, all the same, the world is less of a "bloody sell" and life more of a lark—our friend Hoffendahl seems to me to hold them too cheap and to wish to substitute for them something in which I can't somehow believe as I do in things with which the yearnings and the tears of generations have been mixed.

Since James also seems to support Mr. Vetch's contention that all change is a "new combination of the same elements," *The Princess Casamassima* is the most fundamentally misleading of his major novels. Written out of what seems instinctive aestheticism and a total uninterest in political reform, the book's subject is a large-scale irrelevance. Since James cannot impartially dramatize the debate between culture and politics, since his devotion is assumed and not tested through action, since his politicians are fools without programs and his aristocrats are grand in the midst of their folly, the book is devoid of movement. As a result, though less successfully than in *The American,* James is forced to rely on melodrama.

However, in neither book does he give us the simple melodramatic pleasure that is initially promised. Though he obviously designed his plots to demonstrate the hero's magnanimity, Newman's nobility is qualified by egotism and gullibility, Hyacinth's by what seems very like witlessness. On the other hand, though the Bellegardes are exaggeratedly wicked and the anarchists exaggeratedly false, each is partly rehabilitated because of their style. Nevertheless both novels are too intense and vigorous to be placed with James's examples of mere professionalism (*Confidence, The Other House, The Outcry*). Instead, they stand, though insecurely, beside those works that make James one of the great stylists and moralists in the history of the novel.

All James's great novels celebrate those "who expect too much of life"; but the superior works oppose more credible evils than we find in *The American* or *The Princess Casamassima,* and they are less sentimental toward gestures by means of which the hero affirms himself. In these books James only makes his heroes flawed because he too much admires their opponents. Each novel signals a conflict between James's taste for civilized society and his love for an innocence society does not foster. In *The American* society is so melodramatically criminal that James has little trouble preferring his hero, but he does have trouble. In *The Princess*

Casamassima James attempts to assuage the conflict by making the hero great in the act of affirming society. In that sense, *The Princess* is the most unreal of his books; never again would he imagine a story in which civilization is so sacrificially embraced.

CHAPTER THREE

The Joys of Renunciation

Each of the previous novels is flawed because James's commitment to the protagonist is compromised by admiration for the enemy. *The Wings of the Dove* and *The Spoils of Poynton* are damaged for nearly the obverse reason: in these books evil is persuasive, but virtue—inadvertently—is not. However, since both novels come at the height of James's career and since both are concerned with the central theme of renunciation, neither seems so vulnerable as *The American* or *The Princess Casamassima*. In particular, *The Wings of the Dove* is obviously brilliant, its portrait of corruption supreme. How could a novel fail with Kate Croy?

Kate, the book's chief embodiment of evil, is one of James's major creations. Our first glimpse of her "face positively pale with . . . irritation" in "a vulgar little room" on a "vulgar little street" establishes a reality that never falters. Though powerful in her own right, Kate has been twisted into the shape of evil by other hands. In a world whose only values are material, she belongs to a family that cannot gratify the acquisitive taste it fosters. Moreover, Kate is ashamed of what she is like: "She saw . . . how material things spoke to her. She saw, and she blushed to see, that if in contrast with some of its old aspects life now affected her as a dress successfully 'done up,' this was exactly by reason of the trimmings and lace, was a matter of ribbons and silk and velvet. She had a dire accessibility to pleasure from such sources." Thus, she tries to elude the machinations of her greedy aunt, "Brittania of the Market Place," and at the same time save herself from the greasy poverty of her sister, Mrs. Condrip. With ambition as naively vaunting as classic hybris, she tells her lover, Merton Densher, early in the book: "I shall sacrifice nobody and nothing, and that's just my situation, that I want and that I shall try for everything. That . . . is how I see myself (and how I see you quite as much)." Kate wants more from life than she can get. She thinks she can possess through duplicity and still not lose her soul, but she is wrong; and James traces her error as movingly as the errors of those fastidious moralizers who stand closer to his heart.

With Kate, the author neither blinks at nor misjudges sexual issues that are troublesome in more typically Jamesian characters. Kate's greatest sin is her use of Milly Theale, but to use Milly she must use her own passion for Merton Densher. At our first view of the lovers, Kate is counseling restraint so that they may ultimately possess each other and money. Throughout the book, what is most shocking about her, most indicative of increasing dehumanization, is this way she has of separating herself from her own feeling and of "dol[ing] it out," as Densher says, like a housewife dispensing sugar from her cupboard—or, as one might better say, like a trainer giving inducements to a prize horse. Having misappropriated passion, Kate will suffer its degradation when she is taken by Densher not in healthy lust but in his need to restore the self-direction she had deprived him of. Finally, she will lose his love, not only, as she shallowly thinks, because he has fallen in love with Milly but because she had for too long made his love her instrument. At the end, he is ready to marry her if she will take him for himself. In the end, however, Kate cannot respond to that self, for she has turned it into the means not of passion but of cash.

Kate Croy represents the destructive power of egoism on a selflessness that must exist even in erotic love. Yet she is a tragic and not a melodramatic villainess, because the motive for her villainy is so sympathetic and she acts throughout in the belief that her machinations are expedient, but no worse. In this, she epitomizes a way of life, a kind of polite league of predators that has trained her to be a member of the society in which "it would never occur [to the inner circle] that they were eating you up. They did that without tasting."

Maud, the main lioness in that London zoo, is dreadful at bottom, but her surface is suavely considerate. Like Kate, she is convinced that her exploitation of Milly is acceptable because Milly herself will gain from it. The evil of her set is a banal evil, supported by a ghastly instrumentalism: the greatest good to the greatest number means that a dying girl requires a smaller share. When Milly's attendant, Susan Shepherd Stringham, sits anxiously amidst the inner circle, she looks "very much as some spectator in an old-time circus might have watched the oddity of a Christian maiden, in the arena, mildly, caressingly, martyred. It was the nosing and fumbling not of lions and tigers but of domestic animals let loose as for the joke." The very gentleness of their desecration of Milly is what makes the Lowder set one of James's most profound depictions of "the high brutality of good intentions." When one recalls this polite ruthlessness, the striking biblical imagery which is meant to highlight its significance, and the great scenes in which the animals pace and pounce, it seems obvious that *The Wings of the Dove* deserves a high place in James's *oeuvre*.

Evil in this book is a convincing, because familiar, reality. When we begin to examine its opposite, however, we come to an emptiness whose prototypes we noted in the ghosts, the vampires, the Bellegardes, and the anarchists. The central emptiness in *The Wings of the Dove* is the dove herself. In the novels I have already discussed, James did not adequately face evil because he did not face an evil real enough to vanquish good. For a deeper sentimentality in James's devotion to virtue, Milly Theale is his definitive symbol. Going beyond all reasonable limits of ethical advocacy, his love for her produces expostulations like this: "[Milly] worked—and seemingly quite without design—upon the sympathy, the curiosity, the fancy of her associates, and we shall really ourselves scarce otherwise come closer to her than by feeling their impression and sharing, if need be, their confusion." That James would so compromise his creed of authorial reticence suggests the fervor of his admiration, which attains a volume exceeding even the governess's hosannas: "When Milly smiled it was a public event—when she didn't it was a chapter of history." This claim is made in the impressionable mind of Mrs. Stringham, but James never attempts to qualify its spirit. On the contrary, *his* mind associates Milly with Jesus Christ.

This connection is made when Milly and Susan are journeying through the Alps before they reach Lancaster Gate. Susan gets a glimpse of her companion "looking down on the kingdoms of the earth," and wonders "was she choosing among them or did she want them all?" If one reads *The Wings of the Dove* allegorically, this allusion may seem inspirational, but if we recall that Milly isn't God but rather a fabulously rich girl avid for life, the implication is sinister. James, however, ignores the irony, and later falls into contradiction. He means Milly to be Christ-like in her mercy and selflessness (when she dies, she releases her fortune to the man who had betrayed her), but he also means her to be a brave girl seizing life even at the moment that it is slipping away. Each of these qualities—selfless mercy and appetite for life—is admirable, but in quite incompatible ways. One is directed toward others; the other is self-serving. Though Milly's function in the plot emphasizes the former, her character displays principally the latter.

She is, for one thing, frequently presented in the role of collector. On her first visit to Sir Luke, her physician, James compares his concern for her to "a great . . . crystal-clean . . . empty cup," which becomes a "relation" that she bears off as a "special trophy." However, trophies presented to Milly aren't persuasive testimonials since, with the exception of Sir Luke, all the givers have interested motives. As a result, these testimonials ultimately detract from her stature when Milly is shown receiving compliments with striking complacency. When Kate calls her a dove, Milly feels herself "ever so delicately, so considerately, embraced" and concludes that Kate's appellation is entirely warranted. When she returns from Sir Luke's operatic admiration to Susie's solicitude, she accepts the combination this way: "If devotion, in a word, was what it would come up for the interested pair to organise, she was herself ready to consume it as the dressed and served dish. He had talked to her of 'appetite,' her account of which, she felt, must have been vague. But for devotion, she could now see, this appetite would be of the best. Gross, greedy, ravenous—these were doubtless the proper names for her: she was at all events resigned in advance to the machinations of sympathy." There is potential irony here, but James never acknowledges Milly's air of chilling condescension. Instead, he protects his heroine in a manner tellingly compared by Marius Bewley to Hawthorne's presentation of Hilda in *The Marble Faun*: "Milly's 'Princess' equates with Hilda's 'Saint,' and both girls have a treasure of gilt-edged metaphors deposited in their names enabling them to draw lavishly on dividends that neither one of them has done much to earn."[30]

Since good characters are notoriously difficult to make convincing in fiction, admirers may safely grant the unfortunate notes of avidity and self-righteousness that Milly sometimes strikes. Her situation and her action, they can say, earn our respect nevertheless. However, should we take this line, we are again faced with a contradiction based on James's desire that Milly win our sympathy in all ways at once. Because she is victimized by something recognizably wicked, we are quite prepared to pity her. Yet James is not satisfied that Milly win the sympathy reserved for victims; he wishes also to make her ordeal heroic because willed. Therefore, Milly connives in her own betrayal in much the same manner as James's major protagonist, Lambert Strether. She is given ample reason to suspect Kate Croy, but, like Strether, she ignores available evidence. However, Strether's ignorance celebrates the putative virtue of Chad and Mme de Vionnet whereas Milly's ignorance is self-interested. Because of her zeal for life, she wants Merton Densher; and if getting Merton Densher means pulling the wool over her own eyes, she is perfectly willing to do so. James tries to have it both ways, to make her a victim who is self-sacrificed, but her sacrifice looks suspiciously like a gambit lost.

When Milly first enters the world of Lancaster Gate, she is certain that Kate is lying about her affairs: "It now came over her as in a clear cold wave that there was a possible account of their relations in which the quantity her new friend told her might have figured as small, as smallest, beside the quantity she hadn't." In subsequent chapters, James clearly shows how the others deceived Milly to quiet her suspicions of Kate, but they do not have to work at it. After her visit to Mrs. Condrip, for example, Susie asks if Milly had been told that Kate is not in love with Densher: " 'You mean she thinks her sister distinctly doesn't care for him?'

. . . 'If she did care Mrs. Condrip would have told me.' . . .
'But did you ask her?' 'Ah, no!' 'Oh!' said Susan Shepherd."
"Merton Densher was in love," Milly decides, "and Kate couldn't
help it—could only be sorry and kind: wouldn't that, without
wild flurries, cover everything? Milly at all events tried it as a
cover, tried it hard, for the time; pulled it over her, in the front,
the larger room, drew it up to her chin with energy. If it didn't,
so treated, do everything for her, it did so much that she could
herself supply the rest."

I am not suggesting that Milly is any less pathetic for conniving
in her own destruction; I am suggesting that she does connive.
Since she loves Densher, we can forgive her credulity as a callow
sign of her affection; but, in that case, Milly is pathetic, not god-
like. However, James wants us to think Milly divinely unselfish,
so at the end of Book Four she decides to leave London before
Densher's return in order to avoid a confrontation that would
reveal their prior friendship and might cause Kate to suspect
Densher of infidelity. By leaving London for such a reason, she is
affirming to herself a liaison with Densher that never existed. In
addition to being callow, the action contains a supersubtle but
readily identified sexual interest that is hardly Christ-like.

Densher's willingness to lend himself, however passively, to
Kate's design surely makes him responsible for Milly's death.
But for reasons we shall presently take up, James wanted to keep
Densher's participation from being ostentatious. As a result, the
journalist gives the girl little visible reason to believe that he is
in love with her, thus placing additional responsibility for Milly's
death on her own shoulders. Throughout the book she displays
not only a hunger for love but an odd ability to spot it before it
occurs. When we recall her desire for Densher, her credulity,
and her vanity, we have cause to think her death not a Christ-like
renunciation but the sentimental death in Venice of a young girl
who couldn't get her man. One doesn't want to make too much

of it, but we ought to remind ourselves that Milly's final generosity, whatever else it may produce, wrests Densher from her rival.

Such aspersions would be untenable if we accept Quentin Anderson's famous interpretation of *The Wings of the Dove* as a Swedenborgian allegory. But aside from the fact that James always denied interest in his father's ideas and was never in his career technically an allegorist, Anderson's reading involves an inaccurate version of the novel's plot. According to Anderson, "the action of the novel consists in the movement of the redeeming love to the point at which Milly is exposed to the 'lusts of personal aggrandizement.' Endowed with money as Christ had been endowed with the title to rule over the kingdom, she rejects every lure that the world can offer and determines that the best mode of expressing her love for mankind and her forgiveness for its selfishness and greed is to die for it."[31] Even if we prefer Anderson's emphasis on Milly's forgiveness to mine on her avidity, we cannot assert that she "determines to express her love" by dying, for that ignores Mark's climactic revelation of Densher's betrayal, whose fatal effect on Milly alone makes "forgiveness" a meaningful option.

Nevertheless, Anderson's reading is pertinent. The novel's system of biblical allusions cannot have been accidental; James clearly wished the reader to think Milly divine. Unfortunately, he does not show us that she is, either in action or in martyrdom (the latter of which is kept offstage). With Merton Densher, who, as it were, plays apostle to Milly's Christ, James's failure to dramatize is even more striking.

Densher begins as a blank to be filled in by experience. Less worldly than Kate, he is solely devoted to love; and if he is at times embarrassingly eager, his lust has the merit of being uncalculated. In the scheming London jungle, however, lust seeks bigger game. When Densher returns to London after his American trip, his naiveté is both winning and significant. He is delighted that Kate and Milly are friends, since he believes that Milly will camouflage their intercourse: "The charming girl adored [Kate] . . . and would protect, would lend a hand, to their interviews. These might take place, in other words, on her premises, which would remove them still better from the streets." Not having counted on Kate's deviousness, he innocently approaches Milly, thus properly situating himself for Kate's plan. When finally he sees what Kate wants, he exacts payment for it: "He had absolutely to *see* her . . . incapable of refuge, stand . . . for him in all the light of the day and of his admirable merciless meaning." Therefore, when Kate gives herself, she does so to gratify not his passion but his desire to see her subjugated. Though Densher has by this time unwittingly lost Kate, he carries through her plan with Milly, learning from Milly's ordeal the depths of his villainy and loving the dead girl for having declined to make him publicly repent. Symbolically, on Christmas Eve, contrite and disillusioned, Densher goes to church. On Christmas Day, "the season of gifts," Milly gives him a new life of ascetic withdrawal from the world that had inspired and then dirtied his healthy lust for it.

Densher's conversion seems proof of Milly's magnificence, just as Milly's magnificence seems the cause of his conversion. But the relationship between these two main facts in *The Wings of the Dove* is not so smoothly symbiotic. Though Densher's conversion is the surest sign we get of Milly's worth, bringing the two people together necessitates the prior existence of a sexual appetite in Milly that keeps her from being the complete antithesis of Kate Croy—reducing her instead to a rival whose illness is at least partly counterbalanced by her fabulous means. Moreover, Densher's conversion is itself implausible and no less unarguable a sign of Milly's greatness than her own behavior.

Bluntly stated, James wanted Densher to be morally imperceptive, since in proportion as his initial morality is lacking the morality he obtains from Milly is miraculous. But since he is so imperceptive and since James does not dramatize his conversion any more than Milly's martyrdom, the miracle is unconvincing.

"Imperceptive" is hardly the word though. In the early stages of Densher's reaction to Kate's plan, he is almost a moral moron.[32] Thinking that he should refuse Kate's request, he decides to go ahead with it because

> he liked too much every one concerned. . . . He liked Kate, good-ness knew, and he also clearly enough liked Mrs. Lowder. He liked in particular Milly herself; and hadn't it come up for him the evening before that he quite liked even Susan Shepherd? He had never known himself so generally merciful. It was a footing, at all events, whatever accounted for it, on which he would surely be rather a muff not to manage by one turn or another to escape dis-obliging. Should he find he couldn't work it there would still be time enough. The idea of working it crystallised before him in such guise as not only to promise much interest—fairly, in case of suc-cess, much enthusiasm; but positively to impart to failure an ap-pearance of barbarity.

(The irony here is coruscating, but that is precisely my point: James will ask us to believe that a man this sophistical can ul-timately emerge spotless.) "Wouldn't it be virtually as indelicate to challenge [Milly] as to leave her deluded?" Densher later thinks; "and this quite apart from the exposure, so to speak, of Kate, as to whom it would constitute a kind of betrayal. Kate's de-sign was something so extraordinarily special to Kate that he felt himself shrink from the complications involved in judging it. Not to give away the woman one loved, but to back her up in her mistakes—once they had gone a certain length—that was per-haps the chief among the inevitabilities of the abjection of love." In the thick of the intrigue, separated both from Kate's person and the sophistries which it inspires, Densher is still able to make light of his degradation: "as he hadn't really 'begun' anything," he assures himself, "had only submitted, consented, but too generously indulged and condoned the beginnings of others, he had no call to treat himself with superstitious rigor." On another occasion, he decides he cannot leave Venice because it would be ungenerous to decline Milly's generosity. Still later, a few pages before his offstage conversion, he assuages his conscience with the preposterous contention that he had not really understood that Milly was dying.

Densher's stupidities and sophistries constitute a compelling portrayal of decorous evil. Like the characteristics of Kate and Aunt Maud, they comprise one of James's most convincing depictions of a brutality that thrives on ignorance. It is only when James tries to relate this evil to good, tries to prove that good can redeem evil, that the very richness of the depiction becomes an error.

Not only is Milly's goodness meager; being meager, it cannot fill up so cavernous a moral vacuum as Densher. James seems almost to admit as much in his attempt to deny that Densher was evil and thus to make the conversion plausible. Surely this is one reason that James has Lord Mark deliver the deathblow. Densher himself takes this fact as somehow diminishing his own sin, and James never corrects his brutal casuistry. Moreover, James forces the one utterly disinterested member of Milly's entourage, Sir Luke, to nearly exonerate the indirect cause of her effectual murder. In one of his last interviews with Kate, Densher is able to tell her that Luke "understood." "But understood what?" Kate asks. "That I had meant awfully well," Densher replies.

This interview is one of the novel's finest scenes, underlining the suavity of wickedness by transpiring while the lovers serve each other tea, and Kate, recalling an earlier image, doles out Densher's sugar. But it triumphs in depicting evil; as a testimonial to Densher's goodness, it is ingeniously evasive. James apparently wants us to think Densher less depraved because he does not share Kate's willingness to lie to Milly right up to the end:"You might have lied to her from pity, and she have seen you and felt you lie, and yet—since it was all for tenderness—she would have thanked you and blessed you and clung to you but the more." But his comparative innocence is only impressive if we forget his easy sins of omission. Only his symbolic gesture of entering church and his rather tardy comprehension of Kate declare Densher a new man. We do not see a change but only a long-delayed and undramatized recognition of what he has been.

The novel's plot is as implausible as its heroine, for Milly's virtue and Densher's conversion are equally frail defenses against the solid Lowder world. Yet how can James have written a book so brilliant in conception and so flimsy in detail between a novel that is his masterpiece and one that, however flawed, breaks new ground? Of the last three books, *The Wings of the Dove* is neither a culmination nor a departure but a regression. Its sentimentalities had been evident in James's work from the beginning.

His second work of short fiction, "The Story of a Year" (1865), initiates the group of relevant renunciation fantasies. Its hero, John Ford, goes to fight in the Civil War hoping that his fiancée will prove faithful. However, when she fulfills his mother's prophecy by yielding to her first suitor, Ford recognizes that he half expected this himself. However, when he returns home a wounded man, he makes no protest. Rather, he does the magnanimous Jamesian thing: he dies. To be sure, the girl immediately renounces the rival, but James wryly suggests that her scruples will eventually be overcome.

Three years later James published another story with a Civil War background that develops the sacrificial hero of the earlier tale. In "A Most Extraordinary Case" the sick lover not only gives up the girl, he leaves her his fortune, and the man she marries is his physician. Both tales interestingly prefigure *The Wings*

of the Dove by lionizing a sick swain who renounces his suit
with increasingly notable generosity. In a story published in
1878, "Longstaff's Marriage," the sick saint becomes a woman,
and the relationship between disease and sexuality, so shrouded
in the novel, emerges clearly.

Too bizarre to have intrinsic merit, "Longstaff's Marriage" is
important as a model for things to come. It tells of young, virginal
Diana Belfield, beset by suitors and admired by a dying man
named Longstaff. On his deathbed, Longstaff proposes that Diana
marry him so that he can give her his fortune if not himself.
Understandably, the prudent girl fears that the latter might
linger behind with the former and so declines. Her scorn mirac-
ulously cures the sick man, and for several years neither hears
from the other. In the interim, Diana is magically stricken with
love for him, while James makes clear that erotic longing is al-
lied to illness: "The beautiful statue had grown human and taken
on some of the imperfections of humanity." Now mortal and
thus love-sick, Diana sends for Longstaff to match his dying request of her. But second thoughts afflict Diana, and she mag-
nanimously dies, releasing him from a pledge that, ironically,
he would gladly have carried out. The point of the story, however, is that dying for him is a more significant proof of love
than living would have been.

Of the entire group, the most blatant prefigurement of the
novel, as noted by other critics, is the 1884 tale "Georgina's Reasons." This story concerns a young woman, strongly resembling
Kate Croy, who is ardently in love with an impecunious sailor,
unacceptable to her parents. Like Kate, she wishes to enjoy the
young man without forfeiting any worldly opportunities, but the
means she employs are less plausible. She insists that Benyon
marry her surreptitiously, and after a brief though fruitful intercourse she renounces him and gives their baby for adoption to a
Neapolitan peasant. Years later, Benyon becomes an intimate of

the Theory family (its sisters are named Kate and Milly) and decides to marry Kate. Fearful of being a bigamist, however, he hesitates. By chance, he discovers that no such scruple entered Georgina's mind. Face to face with the woman who had ruined his life and child, he can exact vengeance by exposing her. Since this is a Jamesian story, he does not stoop to retribution, choosing instead to affirm his morality by not marrying the woman he now loves.

Putting these stories together, we have in essential form every plot element in the novel: the greedy woman who sins against her lover, the dying lover who cedes a fortune to a rival after having experienced and been sickened by desire, the scrupulous young person who disdains vengeance when presented with the opportunity. All that is lacking is the aura of asceticism and death worship which gives the novel its poignancy or, to anyone not voluntarily devout, its strange power to repel. This is provided by one of James's most famous tales, "The Altar of the Dead" (1895).

Like the novel, this important story contains within it an ethical issue that may redeem its atmosphere for some readers. In the course of his death worship, Stransom is taught by Mary Antrim to forgive the man who had wronged him, but the process by which she brings him to accept Acton Hague and the seriousness of his gesture are far less striking than the atmosphere of the tale. The atmosphere of "The Altar of the Dead," as overpowering as the incense that fills Stransom's private chapel, as lurid as the candles that blaze there, is an atmosphere of total lifelessness.

The stories with affinities to *The Wings of the Dove* cluster about a life denial that is neither satiric nor tragic but morbidly sentimental. These magnanimous invalids who woo lovers with death exemplify what is most unpleasant in James's work. At his best, James comprehends the dangers of worldliness in a manner that places him among the great moralists of world literature. At his worst, in order to affirm the antidote of virtue, James ignores the self-righteousness and morbidity of those who help him to imaginatively redeem the world.

Throughout his career, James would admire characters who renounce life insofar as he detested the life they renounced. With such characters, we must always ask two questions: is the life they confront authentically detestable and do they renounce it with authentic magnanimity? In books like *The American* and *The Princess Casamassima*, James fails the first test. But failures of the second test are more frequent, and because James is so devoted to virtue, more significant. When James presents a character who is really good or a good character whose flaws he objectively discerns, James can display a hopefulness commanded by few writers so essentially pessimistic. This is perhaps why Jacobites often treat James as if he were revealing divine mysteries. For there is something divine in Lambert Strether and Maisie, just as there is something divine in Prince Myshkin and Faulkner's Dilsey. But in characters like Milly Theale there is mostly sickness and sexual incapacity. The underside of James's genius is that these life-denying qualities had for him an immense appeal.

Innocent and doomed, Milly has already attained the failure (which is success for James) that Newman and Hyacinth labor to achieve. Thus she cannot be dramatic even in the way they are. Into the vacuum produced by her immobility, James rushes with encomia that progressively reveal their divergence from the rendered facts of her case. In *The Spoils of Poynton*, James chooses a single character who does develop so that this book is more dynamic than *The Wings of the Dove*. Moreover, since it is the first fruit of James's theatrical experiment and since it begins in a mood of buoyant satire, this tight, humorous novel is the most considerable of James's flawed hymns to renunciation.

The first third of *The Spoils of Poynton* contains some of James's best social comedy. The idea of the book (more completely traced in the notebooks than any novel discussed there) was an important social anomaly: "the situation in which, in England, there has *always* seemed to me to be a story—the situation of the mother *deposed*, by the ugly English custom, turned out of the big house on the son's marriage and relegated."[33] As we see from James's statement, this idea also contained ample opportunity for sentimental melodrama, but he avoids this trap by making mother and son a pair evenly matched in virtue and silliness.

Mrs. Gereth, ostensibly the wronged party, is a prodigy of taste, which "ruling passion had in a manner despoiled her of her humanity." Presented through comic exaggeration (she is "kept awake for hours by the wall-paper in her room"), the pathos of her situation is mitigated by her inherently ludicrous character. Though handsome and sweet-tempered, Owen Gereth is also a tremendous dolt who must have been a constant torment to his mother: "He was sometimes closeted for an hour in a room of his own that was the one monstrosity of Poynton: all tobacco-pots and bootjacks, his mother had said—such an array of arms of aggression and castigation that he himself had confessed to eighteen rifles and forty whips." Mother and son have always stared at one another across an abyss with those superb accumulations of Poynton on her side and the whips and bootjacks on his. In part, the alienation is sexual. When Owen underlines this fact, in normal fashion, by wishing to marry, their abyss becomes a battlefield. The mock-heroic imagery which fills the novel is the perfect reflection of that inevitable family strife which the plot recounts.

Yet in their battle, Owen is no fit opponent. As James adroitly shows, such wars belong to women. Throughout the book Owen is a sort of adjutant to his fiancée, since Mona Brigstock is better equipped to map strategy: "She belonged to the type in which speech is an unaided emission of sound, in which the secret of being is impenetrably and incorruptibly kept. Her expression would probably have been beautiful if she had had one, but whatever she communicated she communicated, in a manner best known to herself, without signs." Before her stolid advance, Mrs. Gereth's voluble connoisseurship is a force full of alarms and firings but doomed to a fluttery retreat: "If I should wish to take anything, [Mrs. Gereth moans] she would simply say, with that motionless mask, 'It goes with the house.' And day after day, in the face of every argument, of every consideration of generosity, she would repeat, without winking, in that voice like the squeeze of a doll's stomach, 'It goes with the house—it goes with the house.' "

Their battle is "love" for "love"; since Owen's feeling for Mona is no more than a coltish eroticism, Mrs. Gereth feels she may take up her position in a thunderous maternal mystique. What if she and Owen have had little in common,

> One's mother, gracious goodness, if one were the kind of fine young man one ought to be, the only kind Mrs. Gereth cared for, was a subject for poetry, for idolatry. Hadn't she often told Fleda of her friend Madame de Jaume, the wittiest of women, but a small black crooked person, each of whose three boys, when absent, wrote to her every day of their lives? She had the house in Paris, she had the house in Poitou, she had more than in the lifetime of her husband— to whom, in spite of her appearance, she had afforded repeated cause for jealousy—because she was to have till the end of her days the supreme word about everything. It was easy to see how Mrs. Gereth would have given again and again her complexion, her figure, and even perhaps the spotless virtue she had still more successfully retained, to have been the consecrated Madame de Jaume.

At one moment in the conflict, when Fleda reports that she acknowledged Mrs. Gereth's hardness to her son, the mother replies: " 'Quite right, my dear: I'm a rank bigot. . . . I've never denied it. I'd kidnap—to save them, to convert them—the children of heretics. When I know I'm right, I go to the stake. Oh he may burn me alive!' she cried with a happy face. 'Did he abuse me?' she then demanded." And when the smoke clears, the delighted reader perceives that Mrs. Gereth and Mona are indeed sisters in arms. Mrs. Gereth confesses that she wore the pants in her family, just as Mona is busy wresting them from Owen, and we now see why Mr. Gereth might have failed to will Poynton to his wife.

The conflict in the novel is so funny and perceptive that *The Spoils of Poynton* might have been a supreme example of those excellent comedies which include *The Europeans* and *The Bostonians*. But in his notebook James admitted finding the tale ugly and in need of purification.[34] Fleda Vetch, the novel's heroine, was originally designed as a "reflector," yet with a bit of gilding she would do very nicely as a shield for James against the ugliness of his fable. Unintentionally however, Fleda is another of those Jamesian shields off which virtue bounces with a dubious glitter.

The novel's New York preface falsifies the genesis so fully detailed in the notebooks. Having received the germ of the story, James tells us, "I instantly became aware, with my 'sense for the subject,' of the prick of innoculation; the *whole* of the virus, as I have called it, being infused by that single touch."[35] In fact, the development of *The Spoils of Poynton* was so gradual that James was still changing his conception while the book was being serialized (a matter to which we shall return). The famous celebration of a "free spirit" that ultimately conditioned the behavior of Fleda Vetch was a late development.

The other characters in his comedy were less important to James than they are likely to seem to us. "The fools are interesting by contrast, by the salience they acquire, and by a hundred other of their advantages; and the free spirit, always much tormented, and by no means always triumphant, is heroic, ironic, pathetic or whatever, and, as exemplified in the record of Fleda Vetch, for instance, 'successful,' only through having remained free."[36] In other words, the comic characters are valuable only to set Fleda off, and Fleda is valuable because she maintains her virtue by renouncing their worldliness. Moreover, she bears the unmistakable sign of James's regard: she is a failure.

With Fleda, James cannot be accused of ignoring his heroine's shortcomings ("Fleda . . . was only intelligent, not distinctively able"),[37] but ever since Yvor Winters called her a "moral hysteric," most critics have found her more unable than James recognized.[38] In his important article, Patrick Quinn made a strong case that Fleda Vetch is "a study in the psychology of ethical absolutism." "There is a sharp, baffling disparity between her characterization as it exists in the scenes and incidents of the novel, and her characterization as it existed in the mind of the novelist," Quinn acknowledges; but he goes on to say, "*The Spoils of Poynton* is a greater achievement than its author realized."[39]

Before one accepts Quinn's sweeping transvaluation, the book should be reviewed. For there is much to say in Fleda's behalf. She is distinguished from Mrs. Gereth by virtue of her respect for feelings that aren't aesthetic. Thus she can appreciate the affectionate furnishings of Ricks, which Mrs. Gereth despises on purely artistic grounds (see chapter 5). Then too, her initial feeling for Owen is disinterested. Although some commentators have found it ironic that a girl so morally nice spends much of her time lying, that irony operates against Mrs. Gereth—not the heroine. Mrs. Gereth, after all, had thrown Fleda at Owen with quite as much selfish vulgarity as the girl judges, and Fleda lies to her patroness only because she is caught in a conflict of loyalties.

Responsible critics of Fleda Vetch concentrate instead on her fine-spun refusals of Owen's love. Yet here too, she has compelling motives. First, she is deeply aware that everyone from Mrs. Gereth to her family wants her to make the match not for the welfare of herself and Owen but for material reasons. Because of her poverty and dependence on Owen's mother she is unwilling to yield to a desire for Poynton which would be shameless if it took advantage of Mrs. Gereth's interested offer of help. To his credit, James is much more aware of Fleda's avidity than of Milly Theale's, and Fleda wins our admiration, in part because, aware herself, she attempts to resist it. More importantly, she admires in Owen a generosity, a freedom from greed, a fair-mindedness, which would all be compromised if he either sought Poynton for himself or denied Mona's claim to seek it through him. If winning Owen requires that she violate the very virtues that made him attractive to her, we can easily understand her reluctance.

Even if we insist that such scruples are blocked by the development of the plot (Owen has kept faith with Mona, but Mona reveals that her interest isn't in him, and he, in turn, finds himself preferring Fleda), still the girl has cause for hesitation. She has reason to fear that Owen's transfer of affection is adventitious, a mere consequence of his trouble with Mona. Under the circumstances, it is perfectly acceptable that Fleda insist on Owen's officially breaking his engagement with Mona as a sign that his love for her is sincere. One can go further. Since both Mona and Mrs. Gereth are women who use their femininity to win earthly goods through men, it is more than admirable that Fleda leaves the whole matter to Owen. Her love for him is both validated and shown to be superior by her insistence that he follow his own course.

That Fleda is willing to sacrifice her chance for marriage, in the face of all practical and emotional compulsions, to her ideal that Owen be free to work his own will fully justifies the high value James places on her. A reader who fails to respond to this authentic note of heroism fails to respond to the moral center of James's universe. Good, in James, is no more than this act of Fleda's: the ability to restrain egoism in our relations with others so that they may fulfill their own souls, just as evil is the exploitation of others for personal ends.

Nevertheless, Quinn's objections are cogent. Though Fleda Vetch is more convincingly heroic than Milly Theale, James's habit of claiming too much excites a scrutiny that ultimately works to the heroine's disadvantage. Insofar as Fleda is able to discipline her desire, we can grant her high marks for deportment. But there are hints throughout *The Spoils of Poynton* that Fleda's desire is deficient if not perverse and that her failure is an inverted erotic fulfillment. Before Owen declares himself, she takes special delight in not showing her feelings. This reticence is comprehensible in a Victorian setting, but we should remember that four years before the publication of the novel, James was able to tell, without the slightest tinge of irony, a story concerning a young girl who dies of remorse for having confessed her love before her suitor did ("The Visits"). Once Owen's passion is revealed, Fleda responds with a "sense of desolation." Her despair might come from a fear that their love is doomed to frustration, but she herself has made that fate likely. The novel's central scene, in which Owen finally breaks down, almost works within the context of Fleda's motivation as I have previously described it, but James pushes things over the line.

As I have said, Fleda has valid reasons. When Owen speaks slightingly of Mona, Fleda judiciously inquires, "Can you take such pleasure in her being 'finished'—a poor girl you've once loved?" And when Owen tries to get around this by declaring that he never loved Mona, Fleda still more ardently pursues, "Then how am I to know you 'really' love—anybody else?" Still, we join Owen in his "dread . . . of some darksome process in her mind" because of the ferocity, unrelated to ethics, with which she "seemed to whirl [his passion] out of the room." Fleda "would only be impeccable even though she should have to be sententious," and Owen recognizes that her behavior is absurd. To her expostulation, "You'll be happy if you're perfect," he inwardly responds, "No one was happy just because no one could be what she so easily prescribed."

Suspicions about Fleda's lack of sexual feeling are perhaps partly due to the novel's serialization. Unfortunately, James hit upon the notion that Owen would fall for Fleda after much of the book had been written. ("I had intended to make Fleda 'fall in love' with Owen. . . . But I had not intended to represent a feeling of this kind on Owen's part.")[40] Matters would have been worse had Owen's declaration not occurred, but it comes rather late. Because James seems not to have originally envisaged this turn in the plot, the first part of the book raises all sorts of doubt concerning Fleda's objectivity. When Fleda meets Owen accidentally in London, for example, in the absence of any evidence that he loves her, the reader can only find her hesitancies peculiarly prim ("She had read in novels about gentlemen who on the eve of marriage, winding up the past, had surrendered themselves for the occasion to the influence of a former tie") and perversely proud ("She must have counted very little if she didn't count too much for a romp in a restaurant"). Since she is not a former tie, since a restaurant is safe even for a well-brought-up Victorian virgin, and since Owen's behavior seems hardly more than civil, the reader can only wonder why Fleda is "as frightened as some thoughtless girl who finds herself the object of an overture from a married man." Halfway through the book, Owen is still "declaring himself" in total silence, so there is no wonder that Fleda's conclusions have inspired the sort of radical debunking we

have become accustomed to when a literal-minded reader notices textual discrepancies ignored by convinced Jacobites.[41]
Owen does finally speak his passion, but by that time the damage to Fleda's credibility has already been done.

To add to her sexual frigidity and overzealous suggestibility
is that self-delectation with which James always provides the
more sentimentally perceived of his heroines. In the midst of
her behavior, Fleda is likely to "see her [future] only as some
high and delicate deed." In addition, almost like the governess,
she seems actively to seek complications, the better to reveal
her grandeur. The only fault with Poynton in her mind is that
it contains no ghosts. And her climactic speech to Mrs. Gereth,
for all its incisiveness, has a double edge: "You simplify far
too much. You always did and you always will. The tangle of
life is much more intricate than you've ever, I think, felt it to
be. You slash into it . . . with a great pair of shears; you nip at
it as if you were one of the Fates!" To which Mrs. Gereth
replies: "I do simplify, doubtless, if to simplify is to fail to
comprehend the inanity of a passion that bewilders a young
blockhead with bugaboo barriers, with hideous and monstrous
sacrifices. I can only repeat that you're beyond me. Your perversity's a thing to howl over." This judgment has found ample
critical expression.

The effect of Fleda's behavior unfortunately supports the
practical condemnation of Mrs. Gereth. But Fleda is essentially
right. For this reason, *The Spoils of Poynton* comes closer than
any novel we have thus far considered to finding adequate expression for James's moral views. Certainly, James incorpor-
ates in the text a greater awareness of Fleda's outrageous qualities than he manages in the case of any protagonist previously
discussed. Before Fleda's moral somersaults get too complicated, he warns us against an expectedly gross response: "It
would not perhaps if revealed be generally understood, inas-

much as the effect of the special pressure she proposed to exercise would be, should success attend it, to keep him tied to an affection that had died a sudden and violent death. Even in the ardour of her meditation Fleda remained in sight of the truth that it would be an odd result of her magnanimity to prevent her friend's shaking off a woman he disliked."*

So close does James come in *The Spoils of Poynton* to the dramatic propriety of his greatest work that we can measure precisely in its pages the margin of error between his successes and failures. Though he acknowledges Fleda's excesses, as I have said, he makes them too great to be blinked at, and he spends too much ingenuity on muffling the censure he had reassuringly built into the characterization. Thus, he makes Mrs. Gereth a surrogate for the reader's objections only so that he may allow the girl to check them. The older woman's complaints against Fleda's "systematic . . . idiotic perversity" admittedly present a "showy side of the truth"; but in their argument, Mrs. Gereth is made to be self-defeating. When she says, "Any one but a jackass would have tucked you under his arm and marched you off to the Registrar," the unprejudiced reader is expected to remember that this is precisely what Owen did not do. Remembering this lends credence to Fleda's contention that Owen's love for her could not be built on. But James is sidestepping in this way the larger question of Fleda's contribution to the weakness of Owen's desire.

Of all Fleda's motives, both tenable and suspicious, the one which goes furthest against the grain is her belief that Mona

* It is never certain in the book that Owen does dislike Mona. For once, an ambiguity is functional. In one of their arguments, Owen sounds very much as if he were appealing for Fleda's agreement that the marriage would take place if only Mona would recognize his constancy ("Was it—I, pray, who perpetrated the wrong? Ain't I doing what I can to get the thing arranged?"). In his notebook James makes this clearer than in his novel: "[Fleda] sees that Owen is ashamed of his disloyalty to Mona" (*Notebooks*, p. 216). James might have gone further in making Fleda acceptable had he made Owen's tie to Mona less repellent.

requires justice. Since Mona is a monster, to James as well as to Mrs. Gereth, this moral scruple verges on the quixotic. It is as irrelevant to the issues of love and freedom that validly concern Fleda as Hoffendahl's order is to the issues of justice and art that concern Hyacinth Robinson. In both cases, James creates figures so quixotically honorable that in the long run their honor makes them ludicrous. But in Fleda's case, unlike the case of any character we have thus far met, there lies beneath the posturing, the fearful withdrawals, the self-delighting superiority to the bad world, an authentic kernel of virtue upon which empires might be built. What we want to see now is how James built his empire and how he succeeded in securing firm foundations.

But first we should review the faulty architecture and hollow materials that damage works already surveyed. In the Jamesian house, character is architecture, his fictional structure being the progress of a soul. In novels thus far discussed, James either cannot distinguish between progress on the one hand or stasis and retrogression on the other, or, contemplating an equivocal instance, he declines to clarify the merits of the case. Thus, the governess and the Newmarch narrator are not certainly judged, while Milly, Fleda, and, to a lesser degree, Hyacinth and Newman have defects that almost cancel their virtues. Moreover, instead of building these qualifications into their characterization, James celebrates these heroes for the very qualities that provoke suspicion.

Eliot famously said that James couldn't be violated by ideas, but the author's immunity to theoretical generalizations didn't extend to optative assertions. James's passionate conviction of what the world should be left him open to violation by character; when any of his personages speaks for one of his ideals, James has difficulty "detecting" him. These ideals cluster about three large subjects, and James was more or less likely to write well as he was more or less able to contemplate the subject disinterestedly.

Of these subjects, sex has thus far received most extensive treatment as a problem area, but the emphasis has been biographical. Critically, what seems crucial is not the actual state of James's feeling about sex but its consequence in his fiction. Possibly James felt as discomforted by this subject as many readers think, but his books are disturbed by it only when they communicate discomfort without valid cause. Insofar as James admires Fleda Vetch because he sympathizes with her sexual terror, he embodies a private response that is not likely to meet wide approval. Insofar as he admires her because she will not use sex for public advancement, she is every bit as good as James thinks her, and we must applaud the fineness of her distinction.

In novels like *What Maisie Knew* and *The Ambassadors* James dramatizes sexual enslavements, threatening to reduce man to his private parts, in a manner not incompatible with affirmation of sexuality in *The Bostonians* and *The Golden Bowl*. In the first pair James shows that sex can threaten man's capacity for self-direction and responsible behavior, just as in the second pair he shows that responsible behavior must take account of sex. In his best work, James's characters are searching for personal freedom, which occasionally includes freedom from sex. In his worst books, freedom from sex is confused with the larger freedom. On these occasions, James is parochial, with all the limits in wisdom that that implies.

Partiality also dogs his attitude toward society. Like sex, society is necessary to human development, though it may encourage a development subversive of value. This paradox so disturbed James that he sometimes sought refuge in a gross exaggeration of one of its terms. Thus, in *The Sacred Fount* he tries to depict society as literally cannibalistic; but even here he cannot forget what he also knows: that society is grand. James perceives sex or society truly only when he emphasizes rather than exaggerates one of its potentialities (as in *The Wings of the Dove*) or, better, when he gives each its due.

But although James can give society its due, at bottom he is ascetic. His moral opposition to worldliness goes even deeper than his understanding of its advantages. As a result, the ideal Jamesian gesture is renunciation; but in his work there are renunciations of different sorts. Again, James is sometimes parochial, seeming to admire renunciation *per se*. Thus he can love Newman, Hyacinth, Milly, and Fleda for gestures of rejection in which the reader finds egotism more exquisite and no more moral than what it rejects. Only in Fleda's case do we discern even a hint of asserted ideals; but without asserted ideals, renunciation is only a peculiar form of self-expression. As we shall see, in *What Maisie Knew* and *The Ambassadors* James could establish an important distinction between giving up the world selfishly and giving it up in witness of a higher good.

In short, James had to recognize the moral ambiguity of each of his three primary subjects (sex, society, renunciation). More importantly, he had to make ambiguity not a reflection of his own ambivalence but an expression of the subject. This involves coming out from behind what I have called his epistemological relativism. His famous experiments in point of view are partly conditioned by a conviction that all comprehension is inflected by sensibility. But these experiments are also related to a habit of equivocation (cf. the Bellegardes) that suggests a desire *not to decide*. If James was ambivalent, what easier way to operate than through structures that preclude definition. *The Sacred Fount* is open-ended not only in form but in content.

James is successfully ambivalent (without loss of clarity) only when he adopts not the form of a certain perspective but the manner of a certain form: tragicomedy. Tragicomedy—that most indefinable, because most ample, of genres—is truest to the complexity of life. James achieves richness rather than equivocation only when he corrects, through comic criticism of each contestant, his essentially tragic vision of the ultimate defeat of virtue by worldliness.

Part Two

AMBIGUITIES

CHAPTER FOUR

The Private Life and the Public Menace

In one of his few comments on *The Bostonians* (*Notebooks*, p. 47), James projects a "tale relat[ing] the struggle that takes place in the mind of [Verena Tarrant]." Fortunately, when he came to write the book two years later, James abandoned this plan. The very objectivity that he had not intended and that made him deny the novel its place in the New York edition makes *The Bostonians* sharper, wittier, and more amiable than James's typical fiction.

Having decided not to center the action in Verena's mind, James freed himself to speak in his own person. The result is a voice proclaiming that bodies are not to be subsumed within "bodies of doctrine," that the rhythms of life are muffled by the drone of cant. Uneasy at "going behind" in the interests of satire, James sometimes seems embarrassed by his unwonted omniscience. Yet, for all his technical blushing, the platform manner suits him better than one would have expected.

A mixture of delighted skepticism and disdain, *The Bostonians*'s humor can be matched by few other examples of native satire. One has to wait until Nathanael West to find a portrait of idealistic quackery so unyielding in its scorn. Consider, for example, this character sketch of Mrs. Tarrant, Verena's mother, whose stance of bewildered patience belies her opportunism:

> She was queer, indeed—a flaccid, relaxed, unhealthy, whimsical woman, who still had a capacity to cling. What she clung to was "society," and a position in the world which a secret whisper told her she had never had and a voice more audible reminded her she was in danger of losing. To keep it, to recover it, to reconsecrate it, was the ambition of her heart; this was one of the many reasons why Providence had judged her worthy of having so wonderful a child. Verena was born not only to lead their common sex out of bondage, but to remodel a visiting-list which bulged and contracted in the wrong places, like a country-made garment.

Mrs. Tarrant's bewilderment is the result of a sudden transference from the world of high-minded abolitionism (she is the daughter of a libertarian saint) into her husband's seedy ambience of mesmerism, spiritualism, and irregular liaisons. Mr. Tarrant had "been for a while a member of the celebrated Cayuga community, where there were no wives, or no husbands, or something of that sort (Mrs. Tarrant could never remember), and had still later (though before the development of the healing faculty) achieved distinction in the spiritualistic world. (He was an extraordinarily favored medium, only he had had to stop for reasons of which Mrs. Tarrant possessed her version.)"

These sly hints measure the proximity of sordid fact to Mrs. Tarrant's ingenuous conscience. A like invulnerability is what she most admires in Mr. Tarrant: "She knew he was an awful humbug, and yet her knowledge had this imperfection, that he had never confessed it—a fact that was really grand when one thought of his opportunities for doing so. He had never allowed that he wasn't straight. . . . Even in the privacy of domestic intercourse he had phrases, excuses, explanations, ways of putting things, which, as she felt, were too sublime for just herself; they were pitched, as Selah's nature was pitched, altogether in the key of public life."

The key of public life, to change the metaphor, is the key to quackery's success: public displays of reformist zeal before an audience rewardingly anxious for its titillating moment of moral pretense. Having tried his hand, and other unexpected organs, at "two dollar . . . sitting[s]" for Cambridge ladies, Mr. Tarrant believes he has stumbled on a more lucrative service: advocacy of female rights. Throwing himself into this reform movement with equal fervor, he remains impelled by the same covetousness: a desire to be "known":

> The newspapers were his world, the richest expression, in his eyes, of human life; and, for him, if a diviner day was to come upon earth, it would be brought about by copious advertisement in the daily prints. He looked with longing for the moment when Verena should be advertised among the "personals," and to his mind the supremely happy people were those (and there were a good many of them) of whom there was some journalistic mention every day in the year. Nothing less than this would really have satisfied Selah Tarrant; his ideal of bliss was to be as regularly and indispensably a component part of the newspaper as the title and date, or the list of fires, or the column of Western jokes.

With their selfish lust for fame operating behind a mask of humanitarianism, the Tarrants typify James's Bostonians. Blather as they may about human rights, the reformers are concerned only with personal privileges. Talk as they will before sober Boston audiences, they really speak the language of Matthias Pardon, the prematurely white-haired, baby-faced journalist without whose notice their activities would be stillborn: "He regarded the mission of mankind upon earth as a perpetual evolution of telegrams; everything to him was very much the same, he had no sense of proportion or quality; but the newest thing was what came nearest exciting in his mind the sentiment of respect. He was an object of extreme admiration to Selah Tarrant, who believed that he had mastered all the secrets of success. . . ." Though Pardon falls in love with Verena and asks her to marry him, James remarks dryly: "his passion was not a jealous one, and included a remarkable disposition to share the object of his affection with the American people."

The pursuit of publicity via the route of moral reform involves a total contempt for the personal needs of life: passion, love, a family's developmental warmth. Thus Matthias can easily pardon encroachments on his love affair; when Verena falls into the hands of Olive Chancellor, he offers to yield his claim, provided that he can get what, in a more explicit age, we are likely to call "a piece of the action." Mrs. Farrinder, the doyenne of women's rights, is described by James in a long paragraph, the conclusion of which ("She had a husband, and his name was Amariah") reveals her marriage to be a footnote to her biography, her husband a casualty under a cascading load of verbiage. Miss Birdseye, the symbol of all-purpose revolution, is reported to have a grand passion tucked away in her embattled past, though James urges us to doubt "that she could have entertained a sentiment so personal. She was in love . . . only with causes, and she languished only for emancipations."

Because these would-be reformers ignore life's fundamental facts—the divisions, needs, and troubled alliances between the sexes—their plans are irrelevant. Unlike most of the other books we have thus far examined, *The Bostonians*, with great and often hilarious detail, records a life-threat that is common. So accurate are James's caricatures that frequently they suggest a startling contemporaneity: "[Mrs. Tarrant] had lived with long-haired men and short-haired women, she had contributed a flexible faith and an irremediable want of funds to a dozen social experiments, she had partaken of the comfort of a hundred religions, had followed innumerable dietary reforms, chiefly of the negative order, and had gone of an evening to a *séance* or a lecture as regularly as she had eaten her supper." Though our contemporaries attend rallies rather than séances, and their dietary reforms include commodities never before considered edible, this account prevents substantial revision. Here are no wicked French aristocrats, but shadowy rites; in *The Bostonians* James displays his most no sophomoric conspirators, no socialites engaged in fiendish precise social observation.

But great novels cannot be made from human decor, however precisely painted or entertainingly arranged; they require great characters. With Olive Chancellor, who lives the disease which the others symbolize, *The Bostonians* makes its nearest approach to greatness. In her, James satirizes the rerouting of life into hypocritical channels of arid protest. Morbid, asexual Miss Chancellor is the spiritual sister of Milly Theale, Fleda Vetch, and the governess. We have only to recall James's conflicting attitudes about that sterile sorority to understand, in one stroke, the freedom from sentimental timidities that distinguishes *The Bostonians*.

"The most secret, the most sacred hope of her nature was that she might . . . be a martyr and die for something." But whereas most Jamesian characters who court defeat are thereby admirable to their author, Olive Chancellor is accurately mocked by him. Though she possesses a Jamesian "fine consciousness," she puts it to ridiculous uses: "She had erected it into a sort of rule of conduct that whenever she saw a risk she was to take it; and she had frequent humiliations at finding herself safe after all." Her life is an endless prospect of suffering, for suffering "was always, spiritually speaking, so much cash in her pocket."

Financially secure, Olive spends herself purchasing pain. Unable to bear pleasure, she greets all intrusions of the mitigating with a smile that "might have been likened to a thin ray of moonlight resting upon the wall of a prison." James's failure to specify the illness of Milly Theale raises unfortunate questions. His neglect of etiology in Olive's case aptly serves his satiric purpose. Blocking our understanding, he limits our sympathy: since we don't really become intimate with the stresses that make Olive grotesque, we are only repelled by their manifestations. She is nature's joke: "There are women who are unmarried by accident, and others who are unmarried by option; but Olive Chancellor was unmarried by every implication of her being. She was a spinster as Shelley was a lyric poet, or as the month of August is sultry."

Nor is Olive any closer to the springs of her behavior than we are. In everything, she is self-deceived. The book's first speech is delivered by Mrs. Luna on Olive's "rectitude" ("Nobody tells fibs in Boston"), and Olive herself takes pride in her absence of tact. But in actuality, Olive is a liar who ennobles her schemes by pretending to base them on principles. Olive hates her money, so she decides to set herself against her own class; she hates her sexuality, so she decides to set herself against marriage. Out of self-declared humanitarian zeal, she becomes a connoisseur of poverty. "She had an immense desire to know intimately some *very* poor girl," in order, she thinks, to experience the ordeals against which she is protected by money and status. Yet despite her high-minded motivations, Olive is, like all other people, impelled by libido—which is why her former efforts at friendship have ended in defeat: "There were two or three pale shop-maidens whose acquaintance she had sought; but they had seemed afraid of her,

and the attempt had come to nothing. She took them more tragically than they took themselves; they couldn't make out what
she wanted them to do, and they always ended by being odiously
mixed up with Charlie. Charlie was a young man in a white over-
coat and a paper collar; it was for him, in the last analysis, that
they cared much the most."

Verena Tarrant cares mostly for women's rights. Coupled with
her incredible sexual innocence, this makes her Olive's destined
prey. When the wealthy Bostonian insists that their cause requires them to live as virginal roommates, Verena is momentarily perplexed but soon acquiescent. Yet the very scene in
which Olive makes her proposition reveals the speciousness of
her commitment: " 'Do you live here all alone?' [Verena] asked
of Olive. 'I shouldn't if you would come and live with me!' . . .
'I must stay with my father and mother,' she said. 'And then I
have my work, you know. That's the way I must live now.' 'Your
work?' Olive repeated, not quite understanding. 'My gift [of
feminist rhetoric],' said Verena, smiling. 'Oh yes, you must use it.
That's what I mean; you must move the world with it; it's
divine.' "

Though there is a touch of malice in James's perception of the
lesbianism underlying Olive's convictions, his discovery is remarkable. Its prescience places James among those who, from
angles as different as those of Marx and Freud, challenged the
simple-minded nineteenth-century conception of the disinter-
estedness of belief. Olive's ideas are the result of displaced sexual
energy, which is why Verena, at their first interview, "felt that
she was seized, and she gave herself up, only shutting her eyes a
little, as we do whenever a person in whom we have perfect confidence proposes, with our assent, to subject us to some sensation."
A Zeus in hoop skirts with an oratorical Ganymede, "Olive had
taken her up, in the literal sense of the phrase, like a bird of the
air, had spread an extraordinary pair of wings, and carried her

through the dizzying void of space." Yet, as Matthias Pardon un-
knowingly reveals, when seeing the two ladies in colloquy on a
bleak Boston stoop: "You seem to have started a kind of lecture
out here. . . . You ladies had better look out, or you'll freeze
together!"

Freezing would have been Verena's fate had not James provided as Olive's antagonist a hot-blooded young cousin from the
South. Basil Ransom, as his name suggests, functions to rescue
Verena from the dangerous cant of which she had been the innocent conductor. Realizing that her cause is merely the latest
of mob delights, Basil determines to save Verena for a life of
privacy and love. In a scene that shows James's superlative gift
for melodrama, Basil enters the arena in which the maiden is
being offered to the foot-stomping mob and dooms Olive to the
public exposure she had so long feared; but not before he exposes
the pretensions of the other Bostonians. When Verena begs him
to wait until her lecture concludes, Basil replies, " Not for worlds,
not for millions, shall you give yourself to that roaring crowd. . . .
You are mine, you are not theirs." "Do you want us all mur-
dered by the mob," Mrs. Tarrant screams. "They can have
their money," Verena pleads; "can't you give them back their
money?" "Verena Tarrant," the old woman shrieks, "you don't
mean to say you are going to back down?"

Olive wanted Verena's body; the others wanted her profitable
gift: their cause was merely an obfuscation. Basil has rescued
Verena not only from sexual perversion but from all methods of
exploiting the private soul for public gain. As the lovers make
their frantic exit, James denies that Verena will live happily ever
after, but she will live.

For James, *The Bostonians* is an unusually amoral novel. Basil
Ransom wins not through superior ethics but by the power of
life itself: the bedrock of all morality. Olive is not bad, she is only

twisted. Freed from the necessity of making finicky moral choices, *The Bostonians* is the first Jamesian novel we have encountered in which epistemological relativism does not cloud the scene. No quixotic moral gestures bid us strain our normal commitments; the relevant dichotomy is not good vs. evil but health vs. unhealth. Even in the more attractive decisions of his other heroes (Newman's mercy, Fleda's selflessness) there is a taint of the arbitrary, the jejune. It can be said of *The Bostonians* that no reader, whatever his beliefs, can disapprove of James's loyalties; in that sense, the book is universal.

This wide relevance is earned for James by the clarity of his opponents. In *The Sacred Fount*, *The American*, and *The Princess Casamassima*, James found himself in opposition to the *haut monde*, and as we have seen he could not place himself unambiguously against it. In *The Bostonians*, the *haut monde* consists of one sad lesbian and a crowd of pretentious New Yorkers which James had no difficulty disdaining. In *The Wings of the Dove* and *The Spoils of Poynton*, James presents a pair of waifs too nearly bodiless to be embraced. Basil Ransom and Verena Tarrant (with her flaming hair) are the first Jamesian characters we have encountered who fill out their forms. Allowing for reticence, both personal and period, James does create their romance, which has the merit, unlike Newman's love for Claire, of actually providing the novel's plot.

Still, despite the admirable clarity and zest of this picture of life fighting perverse exploitation, there is some blurring about the edges in *The Bostonians*. To begin with, James himself was less devoted to life than to art. Whereas this devotion was not necessarily damaging, it did provide, as in the prefaces, a means of evading thematic perplexities through an otherwise legitimate concern for problems of craft. That James chose to be so openly exclamatory shows how free from internal stress he was while writing the book. Yet the novel is littered with signs of embarrassment at authorial intrusion that hint at some deeper problem.*

Though James's position is firm, as the novel progresses it begins to waver. Becoming increasingly sympathetic to Olive, he also becomes increasingly derisive about Basil. Such shifting sympathies might have deepened and complicated the book, but James does not abandon his essentially melodramatic structure or his preference for Basil's ideas. As a result, satire doesn't modulate into a less committed stance, nor is melodrama replaced by more formal maturity; rather a melodramatic satire begins to fling our laughter back in our faces and to invite partisanship at the same time that it seems to be changing sides.

Initially, Olive is ludicrous: though even Basil had recognized her tragic potential, James neither justified her nor permitted us to become her intimate. But as the plot narrows to focus on her personal rather than ideological battle with Ransom, James starts to produce a familiarity that, in so pitiful a case, breeds anything but contempt. Gradually James evinces a growing sympathy for the butt of his jokes, almost as if he regrets his earlier treatment. We hear of her melancholy headshaking "that was not devoid of sweetness," of her spasmodic utterance "which was not without its pathos." Later, the mood behind these left-handed rhetorical concessions builds up to a number of scenes approaching tragic intensity.

When Olive serves merely to typify the Bostonians, James

---

* These occur throughout the novel. I merely cite three sorts: (1) After an obviously thematic response of Basil to Mrs. Farrinder: "I am but the reporter of his angry *formulae.*" (2) During a genre sketch of Basil's lodgings: "If the opportunity were not denied me here, I should like to give some account of Basil Ransom's interior. . . ." (3) When faced with the necessity of analyzing Olive's feelings: "I know not what may have been the reality of Miss Chancellor's other premonitions. . . ." James's occasional air of not being able to see into his characters is annoyingly inconsistent in a novel whose satire is normally omniscient. The feigned ignorance shows how much technical reluctance James had to overcome to make his point and thus how passionately he is likely to have felt about it.

treats her with unambiguous derision. But as the tension increases and she is besieged by Basil's sexual weaponry, James
starts presenting her, as it were, from within her beleaguered
fortifications, unavoidably causing the reader to feel some doubt
about his first response. Perhaps the initial sign of this shift is
the affecting scene in which Olive confronts Verena after one of
her clandestine outings with Basil. The scene begins with Olive's
amusing attempt to hide her anger. But James also spends so
much time detailing her fear that the poor woman becomes more
recognizably a tormented soul and less the easily dismissed sport
of nature. In the midst of the girls' altercation (Olive: "You attach importance [to him]; otherwise you would have told me."
Verena: "I knew you wouldn't like it. . . ."), Olive suddenly
makes a startling confession: "Have you noticed that I am afraid
to face what I don't like?" This shock of recognition, the first
evidence that Olive comprehends anything of her profound duplicity, immediately raises her above the level of mere sham.
Then when Verena responds with utter incomprehension ("Verena could not say that she had. . . ."), our sympathy is subtly
but firmly shifted from the healthy simpleton to the twisted
sufferer.

Toward the end of the novel, James begins displaying Olive
in scenes of genuine power. We see Olive sitting in darkness with
Verena, having denied her maid's request that she may be permitted to light the lamp: "[Olive] wished to keep the darkness.
It was a kind of shame." We hear breaking from her lips "a shrill,
unfamiliar, troubled sound, which performed the office of a
laugh, a laugh of triumph, but which, at a distance, might have
passed almost as well for a wail of despair." In the last scene,
James returns to his original satiric tone when speaking of Olive,
but though he obviously means us to remember, when she march-
es off to face the angry crowd, that she has obtained her longed-
for martyrdom, these earlier scenes have created a pity for the

girl which inspires in some readers a complementary distaste for Basil.[42]

On the other hand, though Basil is nearly a stock hero ("the eyes especially, with their smouldering fire"), James sometimes adopts toward him a tone of mockery that performs the admirable service of neutralizing cliché but also, in collusion with the sympathy shown Olive, has the effect of casting doubt on his ultimate superiority. To start with, James underlines similarities between the antagonists. Thus, although Basil is to be James's spokesman for conservative values, both politically and sexually, we are sometimes reminded that Olive is also conservative: "though Olive had no views about the marriage tie—except that she should hate it for herself—that particular reform she did not propose to consider—she didn't like the 'atmosphere' of circles in which such institutions were called into question." "In spite of her wanting to turn everything over, and put the lowest highest, she could be just as contemptuous and invidious, when it came to really mixing, as if she were some grand old duchess." The primary effect of these remarks surely mocks Olive. Secondarily, they tend to deny any real ideological conflict between her and Basil. This, in turn, makes their fight purely personal, in which case we can admire Basil only insofar as his behavior is attractive to us. It is precisely here that James's depoliticizing has a harmful consequence. For, no less than Olive, Basil is seeking to annex Verena Tarrant because he loves her. I do not think that James meant us to take their claims as equally meritorious, but the question needn't have come up. As things stand, it comes up rather forcibly.

James uses precisely the same bird imagery to describe Olive's and Basil's pursuits of Verena ("Verena had had [with him] no such sensation since the first day she went in to see Olive Chancellor, when she felt herself plucked from the earth and borne aloft"). Moreover, by making Basil insist so ruthlessly on Verena's leaving before her last speech, James creates an imputation of cruelty that complicates our response to the ending far beyond any demands of dramaturgical freshness. Olive tells Verena their relationship will involve renunciation, and so does Basil. At moments like these, the book seems a battle which is fundamentally a draw.

More serious than these equations between the combatants, which after all might be attributed to evaluative sophistication, is a stream of jokes at Basil's expense that is gratuitous, if not downright silly. After conservative speeches which are cogent, judging by plot and characters as well as James's expressed viewpoint, James makes comments like the following: "I know not exactly how these queer heresies had planted themselves, but they had a longish pedigree" or "I shall have sketched [here] a state of mind which will doubtless strike many readers as painfully crude." This latter comment suggests that James is not so much mocking Basil because of his own conviction as in order to offset the opposition which he knows Basil's ideas (like his own embodied in the action) must inevitably produce. Indeed, as we all know, *The Bostonians* irritated his public into a fatal contempt for James's future productions. Nevertheless, James overextends himself.

The last half of the novel's action depends upon Basil's reluctance to woo Verena until he has the means to support her. I do not think that this is likely, even today, to strike the reader as a contemptible motive, yet James derides Basil's sense of propriety. "I shall perhaps expose our young man to the contempt of superior minds if I say that [the girl's position] seemed to him an insuperable impediment to his making up to Verena. His scruples were doubtless begotten of a false pride, a sentiment in which there was a thread of moral tinsel, as there was in the Southern idea of chivalry; but he felt ashamed of his own poverty, the positive flatness of his situation. . . ." The question raised by this passage (at whom is the satire directed: the "superior minds" or Basil?) points to James's constitutional inability to see a subject as admitting of only one interpretation: what I have called his epistemological relativism. For this reason, *The Bostonians*'s satiric mode is uncongenial, and such a passage shows James's reluctance to pronounce on manners. Yet surely something more specific is at work here too, for the merest fictional novice knows it is unwise to take too many potshots at one's hero.

In a passage which might with justice be cited as the main utterance of the book, James's unsteady tone seems even more telling. Ransom is declaring to Verena that he hopes to save her from

> the most damnable feminization! I am so far from thinking . . . that there is not enough woman in our general life, that it has long been pressed home to me that there is a great deal too much. The whole generation is womanized; the masculine tone is passing out of the world; it's a feminine, a nervous, hysterical, chattering, canting age, an age of hollow phrases and false delicacy and exaggerated solicitudes and coddled sensibilities, which, if we don't soon look out, will usher in the reign of mediocrity, of the feeblest and flattest and the most pretentious that has ever been. The masculine character, the ability to dare and endure, to know and yet to fear reality, to look the world in the face and take it for what it is—a very queer and partly very base mixture—that is what I want to preserve, or rather, as I must say, to recover. . . .

In a novel full of "hysterical, chattering, canting" ladies, whose other males are an androgynous prattler, a quack confidence man, and a young beau who needs his mother to propose marriage, who can doubt that these sentiments are James's? Yet this is how James glosses the speech: "The poor fellow delivered himself of these narrow notions (the rejection of which by leading periodicals was certainly not a matter for surprise) with low, soft earnestness," etc. One editor tells Basil that his work is "three hundred years behind the age," but when he finally places an essay the recipient periodical is named the "Rational Review." Some of James's equivocation here may be an anticipation of audience response, but we must still ask ourselves why, having anticipated such a response, James did not either give up the project or operate with his customary independence.

One can only surmise that the ambivalence was, to a degree, internal. The books we have thus far discussed give ample support to such a surmise. Olive and Basil polarize three separate issues. He stands for stoical acceptance of life; she for an irresponsible commitment to social reform. He stands for normal sexuality; she for "one of those friendships between women which are so common in New England." He stands for the rights of privacy; she is willing to make an ally of Matthias Pardon. In only the last of these dichotomies is James's position ever secure. As we saw when comparing "The Aspern Papers" and *The Sacred Fount*, James had an abiding contempt for publicity and a fervent commitment to privacy: this is virtually the only commitment unambiguously in force throughout the whole of his career. Toward sex and reform (since reform involves society), James's attitudes were less settled.

When Basil represents James's skepticism about reform—that is, early in the novel where he acts literally as James's point of view—he is treated with complete respect (cf. *The Princess Casamassima*). When, later in the novel, his values become objectified in sexual aggression, James betrays his sometimes unfortunate timorousness before the primacies of flesh. When Olive represents the presumption of reform—at the beginning of the novel where she is James's principal target—James is unambiguously derisive. When, later in the book, she is progressively besieged by Basil's sexual power, James seems more and more to sympathize with her.

Nevertheless, I regret that analytical necessity has tended to throw the emphasis of this discussion upon the book's flaws, for clearly *The Bostonians* is a success. Despite local ambiguities important for the light they shed on James's sensibility, the book is admirably open, wonderfully funny, and humanly attractive. Though James may blur the relative merits of his antagonists in the manner I have outlined, on one issue he never sways: men and women are unique in their gifts and privately precious to each other for that reason. Even Miss Birdseye, a combination of futile busybody and selfless reformer, is ultimately valuable because she has not, like the more recent Bostonians, lost sight of her undeniable self; "Miss Birdseye, for all her absence of profile," Ransom eventually decides, remained "essentially feminine."

For all its vestiges of James's queasiness about sex and instinctive indifference to politics, *The Bostonians*, both in the vigor of its prose and in the orientation of its theme, stands on the side of life. Its special pleading (all suffragettes were not sexually twisted) is the inevitable price of satire, and with satire so brilliant the price is not high. Its disdain of the real issues which its characters parody may, from some point of view, be counted a deficiency, but we must remember that James is precisely not concerned with issues but only with their doctrinal threat to life.*

---

*This is a difficult point to keep in mind when reading the book, but it is essential. James is not considering the pros and cons of the suffragette movement. Rather it serves to symbolize the irrelevancy of any doctrine to fundamental realities. Insofar as this particular doctrine is concerned, James's criticisms are equally general. His views on sexual relations are certainly arguable. (Indeed, as I have shown, they embarrass James.) Nevertheless, he is clearly uninterested in testing whether fundamentally domestic values might not be enhanced by certain refinements in the relations between the sexes. As cannot be repeated too often, James had no interest in ideas.

But in *The Bostonians* this is not, as in the case of *The Princess Casamassima*, a deficiency. In the later book we are invited to regard ideas as cues for a serious, thematic debate, much of which is taking place in the sensitive but alas undemonstrated intellect of the hero. In *The Bostonians* ideas function merely as rationalizations. Basil may be said to be motivated not so much by ideas as by a revulsion against those swirling about his head. The ideological vacancy of *The Princess Casamassima* is thus inconsistent with its theme; that ideas can be irrelevant is, on the other hand, what *The Bostonians* is all about.

Only once again in James's career did he write a book so fundamentally committed to human possibility, and *The Golden Bowl*, astonishing as it may be, is a far more problematical work. The essential James is not perceptible in *The Bostonians*, but its achievement is so high, its testimony to a rare side of his genius so comforting, that we may forgive its faults. Without it we would lack assurance that, fly as he would into the rarefied late prose and moral dilemmas, like all great writers, James was rooted to the earth.

CHAPTER FIVE

The Beautiful Striver and Her Tragic Mistake

The Portrait of a Lady is an even finer example than *The Bostonians* of James's critical intelligence. Since society is here represented either by paragons who worship the heroine *or* by wicked impostors, James is free from his nagging ambivalence toward the great world. Working in a romantic mode, he is impelled to affirm love and thus to criticize the sexual timidity so appealing to him in characters like Fleda Vetch. In contrast to his troubling involvement with the protagonists of *The Princess Casamassima* and *The Wings of the Dove*, James stands, in *The Portrait*, apart from his heroine. Thus, he can expose in Isabel Archer the moral pretension and false perception that inadvertently damage some of his other protagonists. Isabel admittedly fails to see, and the gap between her vision and the book's events is not bridged by rhetoric. When James turns the searchlight of his irony into the abyss, the reader can fully measure the extent of Isabel's fall.

As numerous critics have contended, *The Portrait of a Lady* and *The Wings of the Dove* commemorate James's cousin, Minny Temple, by translating her vigorous but doomed zest for life into a confidence betrayed by worldly evil. Studying them, as we do, in reverse order, we can see the considerable superiority, in honesty and poise, of the earlier book. Whereas James doesn't acknowledge Milly's flaws and so drains *The Dove*'s plot of credibility, *The Portrait*'s logic is precisely the connection between Isabel's flaws and the fate for which they ironically prepare her. Isabel's self-deceptions, unlike Milly's, are attributed to their rightful source: self-interest. She is not, like the dove, supremely good, but only fresh and charming. Milly gets her man, in death, where her virtue remains spotless and his becomes the fruit of a ghostly union. Isabel gets her man too; but her failure in marriage is the accurate judgment of her ambiguity, and the child which the Osmonds bear is mortal.

Since it combines profound analysis with mature art, *The Portrait of a Lady* has sometimes been regarded as James's masterpiece. Though it is the best book we have thus far discussed, it is not so good as the best of James; neither as sharp and powerful as *What Maisie Knew* nor as wise and clear-headed as *The Ambassadors*. Like *The Bostonians*, which it resembles in satirical force and soundness of assertion, *The Portrait* is blurred by ambivalence. Its meaning is qualified (not contradictory, as in *The Sacred Fount* or "The Turn of the Screw," or bogus, as in *The American*, *The Dove*, or *The Princess*), but the qualification is serious. Isabel is surely responsible for her fate, but is she principally responsible? On the answer to this question depends our final evaluation of the heroine, and this is precisely what readers have found it so difficult to agree about.[43]

The disagreement is nicely stated in Philip Roth's *Letting*

Go, where contradictory judgments of Isabel are used to establish distinctions between Roth's characters. Gabe Wallach, who is Roth's version of a Jamesian observer, is arguing with Libby Herz, the lady of this book. Libby finds Isabel foolish and blameworthy: " 'She's practically frigid, at least that's what it looks like a case of to me. She's not much different finally from her friend, that newspaper lady. She's one of those powerful women, one of those pushers-around of men—' 'I've always found her virtuous and charming.' 'Charming? . . . For marrying *Osmond*?' "[44] Libby puts the question well. If Isabel employs her freedom so badly, isn't her fate self-condemning? That figures in a novel written eighty years later can so argue Isabel's case offers impressive evidence of the centrality of James's theme. Unfortunately, James had trouble because it was central.[45]

Part of *The Portrait of a Lady* establishes Isabel as the author of her ruin, but another part shows that Isabel was the victim of a plot. Ultimately, this melodramatic fact is compatible with a tragic reading: Isabel also chose her betrayers. But tragedy and melodrama give formal recognition to classically opposed explanations of failure, and though James does demonstrate that Isabel's error was tragically inevitable, he spends too much of the novel's last third trying to evoke in her behalf the pity reserved for victims. As a result, he suppresses the emotionally purged comprehension with which tragedy treats the self-maimed, and courts the simplifications of melodrama.

James stood outside Isabel, but not entirely. Thus, in his New York edition preface, he celebrates his adherence to her point of view. To the older James, the forty-second chapter containing Isabel's reverie was his greatest triumph. For all its superbly pictorial language however, the chapter comes closer to being the book's main flaw. In it, James's assumption of Isabel's consciousness enhances, if it does not produce, his damaging equivocation about causality.

If *The Portrait of a Lady* were exclusively tragic, this chapter would correspond to the heroine's recognition scene, a description that has been traditionally applied to it. Though the chapter does partially fulfill such a function, much of its analysis seems calculated instead to justify Isabel. For example, she is permitted to formulate her cruel disillusionment in the following manner:

> It was not her fault—she had practised no deception; she had only admired and believed. She had taken all the first steps in the purest confidence, and then she had suddenly found the infinite vista of a multiplied life to be a dark, narrow alley with a dead wall at the end. Instead of leading to the high places of happiness, from which the world would seem to lie below one, so that one could look down with a sense of exaltation and advantage, and judge and choose and pity, it led rather downward and earthward into realms of restriction and depression where the sound of other lives, easier and freer, was heard as from above, and where it served to deepen the feeling of failure.

On the next page, Isabel acknowledges her complicity but quickly judges Osmond's to have been greater. Though we see that Osmond's behavior cruelly disappointed Isabel, James doesn't trouble to remind us that the disappointment was somehow deserved. When rejecting Lord Warburton, Isabel had proclaimed her determination not to separate herself "from the usual chances and dangers, from what most people know and suffer"; yet marrying Osmond was a bid for separation. In that sense Isabel is fittingly made to pay for her own self-deception.

In the forty-second chapter however, Isabel is featured as a victim; Osmond's evil, clear enough before this, is turned through imagery into negative proof of her virtue. James attributes to Osmond an "evil eye" and egotism "hidden like a serpent in a bank of flowers." Passages such as a revealing description of Isabel's morally opportunistic motives ("She would launch his boat for him; she would be his providence; it would be a good thing to love him") are organized in a manner that makes it impossible to know whether Isabel admits their validity. After the sentence just quoted, for instance, the consideration of virtue's ironic fruits modulates into a recollection of Osmond's venality. But though Isabel's "cheek burn[s]" at the thought that Osmond got her money because she "had . . . married on a factitious theory," she is "able to answer quickly enough that this was only half the story."

Surely it is half the story; *The Portrait* is great because Isabel's situation is complicated. But in a chapter whose avowed purpose is explication, one detects an attempt not to clarify or even restate earlier motivations but to raise questions of comparative guilt that veil the issue. Osmond's wickedness has no bearing on Isabel's responsibility. After all, as she herself maintains, she chose him. Her later recognition that the marriage was a prepared trap kills her false notions of freedom and dramatizes the ironic fact that she was so easily betrayed because she presumed total self-direction. As a result of chapter 42 however, we are invited to forget that irony in proportion as we remember just how grossly Isabel had been tricked.

This damaging partiality to Isabel is caused by an ideological affinity which makes the detachment James does manifest all the more impressive. Though he sees that Isabel's moral idealism covers a fear of life, he shared this attitude too fully to be harsh toward her. In his treatment of Isabel, James comes closer to Olive Chancellor, whose idealism is merely rationalization, than to the governess, who may or may not be false; but there is a trace of his ambivalence about the governess in both figures. Despite James's tendency to equivocate, Isabel is a greater creation than Olive because she is less of a case; but because James was trying to depict a more universal heroine, his moral idealism restrained his genius for satire. This inability to conceive of a "big" novel about a "small" heroine is the most significant cause of James's ambiguity in *The Portrait of a Lady*.

It has long been recognized that *The Portrait* bears to other novels a relationship more telling than that usually designated by the concept of influence. F. R. Leavis has argued that James virtually rewrote *Daniel Deronda*.[46] Though other contemporary English novels have also been mentioned, few critics deny that Eliot's book was an important model. The other work whose bearing on *The Portrait* seems undeniable is *Madame Bovary*. Recalling these prototypes, we can see where James's novel runs aground.

In his enthusiastic essay on Flaubert's masterpiece James had one serious reservation: "Emma Bovary, in spite of the nature of her consciousness and in spite of her reflecting so much that of her creator, is really too small an affair. . . . Why did Flaubert choose, as special conduits of the life he proposes to depict, such inferior . . . specimens?" [47] Emma is even smaller than James supposes; and to the degree that she reflects Flaubert, she exists to purge him. *Madame Bovary* is the greatest example of the sort of cold satire that James could not produce. *The Portrait* is a larger work than *Madame Bovary*, whose perfection seems, by contrast, a bit self-satisfied. Just as its heroine is more admirable, her fall is more complex, less easily wrapped up and thrown away by a mind too intelligent to share her folly. Nevertheless, *Madame Bovary* is more courageous. Without flinching at Emma's inanity and selfishness, Flaubert can still inspire our concern. Not pity. Emma evokes that frightened solicitude one feels for his own childish fancies. She is the primal ego, the great "I want" doomed by the paltriness of life to frustration and an inevitable longing for death. Yet, for all that, and for all Flaubert's involvement, he wastes no tears.

With his ampler intellect, James shrank from Flaubert's pitiless comprehension. He found in *Daniel Deronda* exactly what he missed in *Madame Bovary*. Whereas Flaubert had traced the decline of a petty voluptuary, Eliot had comprehended the fate of a girl intelligent enough for "tragedy [to] have a hold upon."[48] Leavis believes that the comparison between James and Eliot works entirely to the latter's advantage and that Isabel is inferior to Gwendolyn Harleth because she is portrayed, too chivalrously, by a man. In one respect though, James's heroine is treated with less sentimentality. *Daniel Deronda* concludes in a regeneration to which, however we may wish to ignore it, the novel clearly moves, whereas James avoids any comforting reform of Isabel's character. But Eliot is undoubtedly more merciless in her depiction of Gwendolyn's egotism and less disposed than James to place the blame for her marriage on the shoulders of others. Thus, for the resistible economic necessity that forces Gwendolyn to marry Grandcourt, James substitutes the plot whose ingenuity seems to justify Isabel. He therefore goes further than Eliot in advocating his heroine, but he joins Eliot in disdaining a heroine, like Emma Bovary, who makes no strong appeal to our admiration.

In *The Portrait of a Lady*, the model of Gwendolyn Harleth served to protect James from the threat of Emma Bovary. It wasn't, as James asserts in his preface, merely a matter of selecting a heroine large enough to sustain a long tragic action. For him, the subject of romantic presumption could not be confronted without mitigation; his fool of passion had to be slightly divine—not shallow like Emma, or even greedy though intelligent, like Gwendolyn Harleth. James's heroine had to be grand: Isabel Archer, the beautiful striver. James got his grandeur, thus a bigger book, but at the cost of that very skepticism which made him appreciate *Daniel Deronda* and *Madame Bovary* in the first place.

Nevertheless, Isabel ranks with her sisters in folly. When we look at her "brother" however, we see just how damaging is James's pursuit of virtue. Sickly, spectatorial, a witty bachelor devoted to the cousin he loves but cannot marry, Ralph Touchett is transparently the Jamesian prodigy of intellect who merely touches life (recalling Hyacinth Robinson and Milly Theale). He is also so irresponsible as to be destructive. Here as elsewhere in *The Portrait*, James portrays his subject with unusual—but qualified—candor.

Very early in the book, James warns us that though Ralph's attitude toward Isabel "was contemplative and critical, [it] was not judicial." Like Isabel herself, Ralph prefers to indulge his imagination rather than his judgment, so long as he can thereby enhance his sense of possibility. Too sick to enter life himself, he figuratively lives off Isabel, a fact which he admits without acknowledging its effrontery.

The fortune which he provides her contributes to her downfall. In the very scene where Ralph arranges the bequest, James establishes his error. "You speak," his father tells him, "as if it were for your mere amusement. . . . Doesn't it occur to you that a young lady with sixty thousand pounds may fall a victim to the fortune-hunters?" "That's a risk," Ralph replies, "and it has entered into my calculation. I think it's appreciable, but I think it's small, and I'm prepared to take it!" Ralph prepares to risk Isabel's life with a complacency based on his willful misrepresentation of her character. Constantly encouraging Isabel's foolish self-confidence, he alarms even her. "Spread your wings; rise above the ground," he urges her. "I wonder if you appreciate what you say," she retorts. "If you do, you take a great responsibility. . . . I'm afraid. . . . A large fortune means freedom, and I'm afraid of that. It's such a fine thing, and one should make such a good use of it. If one shouldn't one would be ashamed. And one must keep thinking; it's a constant effort. I'm not sure it's not a greater happiness to be powerless." "For weak people

I've no doubt it's a greater happiness. . . ." "And how do you know I'm not weak?" "I don't know what you're trying to fasten upon me," on another occasion Isabel asserts with double significance, "for I'm not in the least an adventurous spirit. Women are not like men." When Ralph admits the vicarious satisfaction he takes in her career, as a way of arguing against her engagement, she rightly accuses him of being parasitic: "Don't amuse yourself too much, or I shall think you're doing it at my expense."

But in his death scene, when presumably Ralph and Isabel are confronting the whole truth of her career, James works to make us forget what we know about Ralph even more ingeniously than he worked, in the forty-second chapter, to make us forget what we knew about Isabel. In a wash of sentiment, Ralph's sin is effaced. Remaining are his love for her and their joy at the moment of parting in being able to acknowledge this important bond. Looking closely at the scene however, one sees that Ralph is still living off Isabel; he admits that he lingers just to hear her confess her misery, the details of which he seems indecently avid for. Yet despite Ralph's characteristic behavior, James once more has recourse to Osmond's undoubtedly blacker villainy to evade the truth: "Is it true—is it true?" Isabel asks. "True that you've been stupid? Oh, no." "That you made me rich—that all I have is yours?" "Ah, don't speak of that—that was not happy. . . . But for that—but for that—! . . . I believe I ruined you." " 'He married me for the money,' she said. She wished to say everything; she was afraid he might die before she had done so." But everything is being ignored. As soon as Ralph acknowledges the truth, James has Isabel change the subject. Eloquent proof that the trick is effective can be found in the nearly universal absence of negative criticism concerning Ralph's role.[49] James faces in *The Portrait of a Lady* the ubiquitous self-interest that requires one to redefine "good" and "evil," but in Ralph's death scene, he drowns our clamorous memories of the man's egoism in a deathbed hush. This scene is the book's unique lapse into Dickensian sentimentality.

Happily, it *is* unique. Aside from this scene and those moments, as in chapter 42, when James tries to flee his own insights, *The Portrait of a Lady* clearly criticizes the ambiguity of moral idealism. Like other works, say *The Wild Duck* or *Huckleberry Finn*, in which a writer moves against his own deep pieties, *The Portrait of a Lady* is energized by a fundamental tension. As in Twain's masterwork, the vessel contains more household gods than the author can transport. Yet, though he hides some in out-of-the-way chapters, the boat is not lightened; residual loyalties start to drag it down. Twain's ship remains afloat, despite the diminishing power of its chief passenger, because the surroundings are so buoyant. *The Portrait of a Lady* sails, for all its lurching, because its main character stays on course. Despite the ambiguity we have traced, Isabel Archer is one of the most complex and fully realized figures in world literature.

Furthermore, her complexity does not confound James's judgment. In *The Portrait of a Lady*, ambiguity resides not in the author but in the character; it is Isabel's ambiguity that James criticizes. Still, "poor human-hearted Isabel" appeals to our sympathy. She is not, like the governess, good *or* bad or, like Milly, good *and* bad despite James's intention; Isabel's virtues and failings are logically related and humanly appealing. She offers herself to our sympathy through her moral fervor, whose underside is life-denying, and her innocent optimism, whose ironic result is collusion with evil.

From her first appearance, Isabel takes the center of our attention with the same confident assurance that causes her to swoop up Touchett's barking little dog. Her eye "denote[s] clear perception," her manner is pert though dignified, and she is "very fond of [her] liberty." With her come the expansive demands of youth and of a young nation; and if she is a trifle too assertive or self-confident, we admire the fresh power of her imaginings: "Her imagination was by habit ridiculously active; when the door was not open it jumped out of the window. She was not accustomed to keep it behind bolts." Though she lets her imagination move freely, she confines her person. In her grandmother's house, she spent much of her childhood in a solitary room, cut off from the street "by bolts which a particularly slender girl found it impossible to slide," and by a door which blocked her vision of the street with sidelights covered by green paper. Even after she is old enough to slide the bolt, she refuses; "she had never assured herself that the vulgar street lay beyond."

Isabel's youth had trained her to ignore life's harsh realities. Her irregular household seemed to her "a bustling provincial inn kept by a gentle old landlady who sighed a great deal and never presented a bill." When her Aunt Lydia comes to her rescue, advising her to sell the house, she proudly announces her ignorance of money matters. Nor does she understand vice. Her maid's elopement "with a Russian nobleman" staying at Isabel's hotel seemed to her "a romantic episode in a liberal education." But her education had not been liberal; her "much-loved father" (with his "taking manner"—people said "he was always taking something") "had an aversion to [pain]."

Realizing she lacks knowledge of evil, and desirous, in her typically American way, of knowing what she must shun, Isabel feels impelled to seek the very unhappiness she so feared during her romanticized childhood. That is one reason why she rejects Lord Warburton: " 'I can't escape unhappiness,' said Isabel. 'In marrying you I shall be trying to.' " Warburton misunderstands, assuring Isabel that he can provide unhappiness too. What he cannot provide are those moral tests that endear adversity to a girl whose hunger for virtue is at least equal to her yearning for pleasure. She wants to be happy (being young, she believes in this last and most potent of dreams); but she also wants to be good, and she knows that virtue, like the prehensile thumb, attains vigor through counterforce and exercise. As she tells Ralph, she wants to front experience but not to "drain . . . the poisoned . . . cup."

For all her outrageous faith in her ability to judge, she is exhausted by standing always at attention: "A swift carriage, of a dark night, rattling with four horses over roads that one can't see," she tells Henrietta, "that's my idea of happiness." But her idea of virtue is diametrically opposed: "I try to judge things for myself; to judge wrong, I think, is more honourable than not to judge at all. I don't wish to be a mere sheep in the flock; I wish to choose my fate and know something of human affairs beyond what other people think it compatible with propriety to tell me."

Because she is female, this daughter of Emerson and Thoreau is all the more heroically self-reliant in asserting her freedom despite restrictive nineteenth-century mores and the subtle proprieties of the old world. But, as she had told Ralph, "Women are not like men." Isabel has reversed her sexual role, and she will suffer an appropriately sexual tragedy. "Like the heroine of an immoral novel," Henrietta warns, "you're drifting to some great mistake." But Isabel is not immoral. Long as she does to yield in the darkness, while riding in a carriage (of assignation?) on a road she can't see, she insists on plotting her course, mapping her progress toward virtue, like the good, typically Jamesian heroine she is.

Torn between appetite and morality, between feeling and rational restraint, Isabel cannot distinguish pain from joy. This confusion is nearly the first thing we see in her. When Mrs. Touchett probes her attachment to the Albany house, Isabel says, " 'I'm extremely fond of it.' 'I don't see what makes you fond of it; your father died here.' 'Yes; but I don't dislike it for that,' the girl rather strangely returned. 'I like places in which things have happened—even if they're sad things. A great many people have died here; the place has been full of life.' 'Is that what you call being full of life?' " Isabel's greatest wish at Gardencourt is an encounter with its ghost, but she ignores the ghost's significance. As Ralph tells her, "It has never been seen by a young, happy, innocent person like you. You must have suffered first. . . ." "I'm afraid of suffering," Isabel returns, "but I'm not afraid of ghosts. And I think people suffer too easily."

Eager to meet life, James's little soldier is ignorant both of the battleground and of the weaponry massed against her. What is worse, with part of her soul she wants to be shot, for a wounded veteran has had both the opportunity and the badge of heroism. To James's credit, he clearly sees that Isabel's simultaneous desires for enriching happiness and educative suffering pervert her feminity. This virgin huntress turns on any normal man peering at her with desire, because desire might cheat her of suffering: "Deep in her soul—it was the deepest thing there—lay a belief that if a certain light should dawn she could give herself completely." But the light must be darkness, the carriage on the blackened road. When Warburton stares at her with a passion so pure that his eyes burn "as steadily as a lamp in a windless place" or when Caspar implores her "with clear-burning eyes like some tireless watcher at a window," Isabel turns away; in Caspar's case, actually burying her own eyes in her hands. She cannot bear to *see* passion. It terrifyingly demands the surrender she desires but which her virtue, in both senses, cannot countenance.

As soon as Warburton gives the slightest sign of wishing to propose, Isabel becomes too "agitated" to speak with ease; this admirable opportunity seems instead "a vast cage." Caspar, to whom she is more susceptible, repels her with his "hardness of presence . . . his way of rising before her. . . . She wished him no ounce less of his manhood, but she sometimes thought he would be rather nicer if he looked, for instance, a little differently. His jaw was too square and set and his figure too straight and stiff:

these things suggested a want of easy consonance with the deeper rhythms of life." To Isabel, satisfaction comes "of having refused two ardent suitors in a fortnight." It provides the "enjoyment . . . found in the exercise of her power. . . . She had tasted of the delight, if not of battle, at least of victory; she had done what was truest to her plan." Isabel's plan—to sally forth, taste difficulty, and thus display her heroism—will not permit her to get close to a man. She cannot enter the other arena of life, where a woman's heroism is less significant than her pliancy, her ability to love.

The Portrait of a Lady is a greater novel than any we have discussed because James fathoms his heroine. He tells us that Isabel is ignorant of her true self: "The depths of this young lady's nature were a very out-of-the-way place, between which and the surface communication was interrupted by a dozen capricious forces." He tells us that her "taste played a considerable part in her emotions." He admits, in passages of ruthless analysis too long to quote here, every ambiguity and contradiction which the action reveals, thus demonstrating a consistency of insight greater than we have witnessed in his other books. From time to time, James begs the reader not to be too critical, asks us to share his own love for Isabel. But these interjections (which culminate in the terminal obfuscation we have already discussed) serve only to show how fully aware James is of Isabel's shortcomings. "With all her love of knowledge," James finely admits, "she had a natural shrinking from raising curtains and looking into unlightened corners. The love of knowledge coexisted in her mind with the finest capacity for ignorance." James here sees that people like Isabel do not see.

Despite warnings from Henrietta, from Mrs. Touchett, and from Ralph, Isabel persists in her folly. Merle characterizes herself as a vessel which is "shockingly chipped and cracked . . . very well for . . . the quiet, dusky cupboard . . . but when I've to come out and into a strong light—then, my dear, I'm a horror." Osmond himself confesses he is pure "convention," but in the "dry account" of his career which he presents, Isabel's "imagination supplie[s] the human element which she was sure had not been wanting." Isabel cannot guess the opportunism of Merle and Osmond because it is so like her more moral version. Her family's opposition serves only to strengthen her choice by making it more irrevocably personal. Desiring, above all, to admire herself, she will not admit that she has made a mistake.

Isabel's "nature had, in her conceit, a certain garden-like quality, a suggestion of perfume and murmuring boughs, of shady bowers and lengthening vistas, which made her feel that introspection was, after all, an exercise in the open air, and that a visit to the recesses of one's spirit was harmless when one returned from it with a lapful of roses. But she was often reminded that there were other gardens in the world than those of her remarkable soul, and that there were moreover a great many places which were not gardens at all—only dusky pestiferous tracts, planted thick with ugliness and misery." The triumph of this novel is James's realization that anyone who needs to think of his soul as a garden is thereby more certain to inhabit the swamp.

Isabel begins her search for maturity in a setting only slightly to the east of her Edenic childhood: Gardencourt, a civilization so harmonious that "the wide carpet of turf that covered the level hill-top seemed but the extension of a luxurious interior." But this superlative mixture of the natural and the cultivated is too bland for her. Like Warburton, it offers no challenge. The dusk which "would not arrive for many hours," in the book's splendid opening, gathers around Isabel when she leaves Gardencourt for Florence. From an ample lawn peopled by witty, loving men, she moves to "an olive-muffled hill" on which figures gather as if bidden by a painter to compose a scene. When she returns to Gardencourt to see Ralph die, the "day is dark and cold . . . with dusk . . . thick in the corners. . . ." Darkness encroaches throughout the book, as "Osmond . . . one by one . . . put[s] out the lights." Darkness is what Isabel has always wanted: to evade herself, to provide the right atmosphere for yielding. When Osmond begins to inspire what other men have frightened, "her imagination . . . [hangs] back: there was a last vague space it couldn't cross," James tells us, "a dusky, uncertain tract which looked ambiguous and even slightly treacherous like a moorland seen in the winter twilight. But she was to cross it yet."

Isabel enters the swamp, where she will catch a disease, because her character impels her. But subtly, unerringly, Osmond does his share. With his erudition, he appeals to her desire for improvement, her need to discern limitations of the sort that time can remove: "It would have annoyed her to express a liking for something he, in his superior enlightenment, would think she oughtn't to like; or to pass by something at which the truly initiated mind would arrest itself. . . . She was very careful therefore as to what she said, as to what she noticed or failed to notice; more careful than she had ever been before." Mixing the censure of his example with the flattery of his facile tongue, Osmond appeals to Isabel's ambivalence. Similarly, his situation—that of a supreme but impoverished teacher—permits her to "surrender to him with a kind of humility . . . and a kind of pride; she was not only taking, she was giving." To match her intellectual ambitions is Osmond's refined aestheticism; to match her sexual timidity is Osmond's cold reserve; to match her shame at an undeserved inheritance is Osmond's need for cash: he will relieve her of all her burdens.

What he lacks, her imagination fills in. As Ralph reflects, "it was wonderfully characteristic of her that, having invented a fine theory about Gilbert Osmond, she loved him not for what he really possessed, but for his very poverties dressed out as honors. Ralph remembered what he had said to his father about wishing to put it into her power to meet the requirements of her imagination. He had done so, and the girl had taken full advantage of the luxury."

Isabel's adventures have been leading up to Osmond's proposal, just as her ordeal will date from her acceptance. By means of a cunning display of art, these facts are reflected in the proposal scene when Isabel is discovered sitting alone in a vulgar room, reading "a volume of Ampère." To Osmond, the yellow upholstery, purple walls, and orange sofas are "ugly to distress"; but to Isabel, reading the father of electrodynamics, the room is perceived through "a strange pale rosiness . . . diffused . . . by . . . a lamp covered with a drooping veil of pink tissue-paper . . . on the table beside her." When Osmond enters, he makes no move as aggressive as Warburton's or Goodwood's at similar moments. Rather, he is "deeply respectful," declaring himself "in a tone of almost impersonal discretion, like a man who expected very little from it but who spoke for his own needed relief."

> The tears came into her eyes: this time they obeyed the sharpness of the pang that suggested to her somehow the slipping of a fine bolt—backward, forward, she couldn't have said which. The words he had uttered made him, as he stood there, beautiful and generous, invested him as with the golden air of early autumn; but, morally speaking, she retreated before them—facing him still—as she had retreated in the other cases before a like encounter. "Oh don't say that, please," she answered with an intensity that expressed the dread of having, in this case too, to choose and decide. What made her dread great was precisely the force which, as it would seem, ought to have banished all dread—the sense of something within herself, deep down, that she supposed to be inspired and trustful passion. It was there like a large sum stored in a bank—which there was a terror in having to begin to spend. If she touched it, it would all come out.

For once, Isabel does not retreat; she cries in her consciousness of stirred passion. But is the bolt opening or closing; will she now enter life or be even more irrevocably shut away from it? Osmond's words "invest" him with a mellowness soon to be materially enhanced, while Isabel fears her release of passion as one fears the expenditure of hoarded treasure. Ironically, treasure is all Osmond wants.

Isabel is responsible for her error in the sense that one is responsible for one's soul. Osmond's responsibility comes closer to what one usually means by "guilt." Isabel's ambivalence, literally beyond her control, damages herself; Osmond's planned duplicity damages another. It is true that Osmond mistakes her temporary amiability for ultimate usefulness, so that, as Isabel admits, one can feel a certain sympathy for him when he discovers his error. But this sympathy is much less strong than the anger we feel at his brutal exploitation.

Yet terrible though he is, Osmond is simply the most decisive of those seeking to exploit Isabel. Though James tries to soften the truth, Ralph makes use of her too. Merle announces that she "only know[s] what to . . . do with [people]," as she prepares to "put [Isabel] in [Osmond's] way," but the presumably impersonal Mrs. Touchett, who began it all, had her selfish motive as well: "If you want to know, I thought [Isabel] would do me credit. I like to be well thought of, and for a woman of my age there's no greater convenience, in some ways, than an attractive niece." Even Caspar and Warburton, in their amorous desire to annex Isabel's person, consider chiefly themselves.

Of all Isabel's satellites, only Henrietta cares for her.* Despite

---

* Isabel's eyes "*denote* clear perception"; they don't have it. Henrietta's eyes "rest . . . without impudence or defiance, but as if in conscientious exercise of a natural right, upon every object [they] happen . . . to encounter." They are like buttons; they secure. And they see through everything, as Ralph realizes when he meets her.

James gave too little credit to Henrietta in his New York preface. Actually, she is a virtual seer who gets most of the key speeches concerning Isabel's character. Unfortunately, most critics have followed James's false lead in treating her.

The contrast between Henrietta and Isabel raises one other point which should be remembered in passing. Henrietta's orderly progress toward marriage, together

her confessed prejudices (unlike Isabel's rationalizations), her chauvinism (in place of Isabel's zest for European culture), Henrietta is open to other people; what her prejudice blinds her to, her warmth corrects. Unlike Isabel, she prospers. Isabel never supposes that Henrietta will marry Bantling, but Henrietta immediately predicts Isabel's bad choice. And when Henrietta announces her engagement, Isabel is simply surprised that she would move to England. What Isabel fails to see is that Henrietta loves Bantling despite his nationality and his faults: "He's not intellectual," Henrietta admits, "but he appreciates intellect. On the other hand he doesn't exaggerate its claims. I sometimes think we do in the United States."

Because Isabel exaggerates the claims of intellect, it is richly fitting that the truth of her ordeal be placed before her by the scatterbrained Countess Gemini. Consistent with James's theme, Gemini provides the illumination for selfish reasons. She tells Isabel the truth out of boredom and because she desires to see Osmond checked. Not only did Isabel choose the wrong man; in some sense, she didn't choose him at all. Gemini reveals that Isabel was married by Osmond for her money and given away by Merle for Pansy. When Merle delivers the final blow—that the money itself came through Ralph's vicarious ambition—Isabel's world is "illumined by lurid flashes." Now James has finished showing that Isabel walked in darkness, that her desire to yield herself was indeed stronger than her desire to judge and control. But whereas she might have yielded to the light of Warburton's or Goodwood's passion, she sought instead the darkness of Osmond's sterile deceit. The ghost she had wished for at Gardencourt has come at last; the "haunting . . . terrors" of her midnight

---

with her obvious love for Bantling, is meant to serve as an unflattering counterpart to Isabel's history. James is much more devoted to normal sexuality in this novel than in any of his other early books except *The Bostonians*. In Merle's relationship to Osmond, he adumbrates his later theme of the enslavements of sex.

vigil have taken on flesh. Imagining Madame Merle is "suddenly, and rather awfully [like] seeing a painted picture move."

With her hopes shattered beyond recall, Isabel remains the beautiful striver. Now realizing her mistake, she lives to keep faith with it. Osmond had cemented their attachment, when she announced her world tour and forestalled their engagement, by controlling his avidity and by asking her to stop off in Rome to visit Pansy. It is to Pansy that Isabel now turns in an effort to redeem the past. Behind the promise she makes the young girl, however, stands the same personality that made the original mistake. "I can't publish my mistake," she tells Henrietta; "I'd much rather die." When Henrietta faults her consideration for Osmond, at last Isabel tells the truth: "It's not of him that I'm considerate—it's of myself."

Isabel has matured, become a lady; but she hasn't changed. Neither Ralph nor Henrietta can persuade her to leave Osmond, to opt for pleasure over heroism. Furthermore, as usual, Isabel finds in honor an escape from passionate importunity. When Caspar begs her to come away with him, she feels the lure. But for her, passion is like drowning; to maintain her freedom, which is her life, she must "beat with her feet, in order to catch herself, to feel something to rest on. . . . His kiss was like white lightning, a flash that spread, and spread again, and stayed. . . . But when darkness returned she was free."

The finale of *The Portrait of a Lady* is James's finest achievement in the book, the one bit of plotting, as I have said, which is braver than Eliot's dramaturgy in *Daniel Deronda*. Nevertheless, it has come in for a good deal of criticism. As Arnold Kettle contends, ". . . what Isabel finally chooses is something represented by a high cold word like duty or resignation, the duty of an empty vow, the resignation of the defeated . . . in making her choice she is paying a final sacrificial tribute to her own ruined conception of freedom."[50] Insofar as James tries to make the final choice seem noble, Kettle's criticism is sound. James's fondness for quixotic renunciations is an objectionable sentimentality. In that sense, the ending of the book is consistent with both the melodramatic attempts at exculpation diffused through its last chapters and the implausible but profoundly Jamesian conclusions to *The American* and *The Wings of the Dove*. But the other novels violate characterization to achieve a pale moral glow, whereas Isabel's choice is absolutely necessary. To the degree that James admires it, we must fault him. To the degree that Isabel's choice reflects her blindness and incapacity, it is a considerable achievement for James to have faced her doomed consistency. However much he may have feared the revelation, he reveals through Isabel Archer more of the dark side of his values than he reveals in any but his strongest books.

Since the revelation is strong and since the dark side of Isabel has been discovered rather recently, critics have tended to exaggerate it. In fact, Isabel is no more dismissible than any other tragically blind protagonist. There will always be readers for whom Hamlet and Gatsby are callow fools and for whom Macbeth and Thomas Sutpen are merely venal. Despite her shortcomings, which James so profoundly depicts, Isabel remains endearing in her desire to be both happy and good. In her failure we find an implication more wide-ranging than any we have thus far encountered in James: since virtue and pleasure are often separated in the world, for the person who can admit neither the world's double appeal nor his own ambivalence, defeat is inevitable.

We have seen enough of James to imagine what great resistance he had to overcome in order to articulate such a theme with so little sentimental obfuscation. The wonder is not that *The Portrait of a Lady* is slightly blurred but that it is so clear.

Part Three

COMPLEXITIES

CHAPTER SIX

Comic Criticism

To a Jacobite, the Depression might have seemed a national en-actment of Isabel Archer's personal drama, in which expansive hopes ironically constrict the future. No wonder that when James was rediscovered the dark side of his fiction seemed especially per-tinent. But those who emphasized his immersion in the de-structive element frequently neglected his shield of urbane intelligence. At his best, James's buoyancy is indissoluble. He has the ability to create pathos, but no high tragic tone; a knowl-edge of selfish deceit, but no vision of total destructiveness. Disappointments and disillusionments abound in his fiction, but there are few final catastrophes. When James simulates tragedy, he is unconvincing. What leads Hyacinth Robinson to the ex-treme act of suicide remains undramatized, while his defeat seems suspiciously like victory. As much may be said against Milly's early death or Newman's empty-handed return from Paris.

During the first stage of the James revival, Jacques Barzun rightly maintained that James was melodramatic rather than tragic.[51] Moreover, when grandiose heroes fight phantom villains and virtue is itself dubious, Jamesian melodrama confesses its origin in sentimentality. The moral gestures in such works are either bogus (*The American, The Princess Casamassima*) or ambiguous (*The Sacred Fount, The Wings of the Dove, The Spoils of Poynton*). When James asks that we respond to them with high tragic feeling, he solicits an emotion he has not inspired.

Unlike *The Wings of the Dove, The Portrait of a Lady* nearly succeeds in being tragic, yet what one takes from that novel is less a sense of Isabel's waste than of the superlative mind that understood how that waste came about. As in *Paradise Lost*, to which it often alludes, we rejoice in the author's intelligent comprehension of a fall not wholly unfortunate. Despite its ambivalence, *The Bostonians* vibrantly laughs at the self-serving reformist cant that ironically complements social injustice. Like most of James's failures, *The Spoils of Poynton* is best when it is comic.

Hostile critics frequently accuse James of unconscious self-parody but, at his best, the parody is intentional. James's forte is critical comedy in which he allows his intelligence to scrutinize his ideals. He lets himself see that the relativity of truth must prohibit arrogant belief, not dignify it. He lets himself satirize the great world plausibly, without ambivalence or exaggeration. He acknowledges that escapes through renunciation or asceticism are unviable and even unadmirable. Though devoted to provincial honesty, goodness, and moral stamina, he acknowledges that such virtues can be destructive as well as naive. As *The Portrait of a Lady* shows, the moral dream is a kind of death wish. At his soundest, James dispersed that dream with laughter.

But this laughter accommodates tears. Jamesian comedy of

manners—despite affinities with other examples of its Anglo-Saxon mode—is especially compassionate. *The Europeans* recalls Jane Austen, but it is less astringent. *The Awkward Age* reminds us of *Vanity Fair*, but it is not so bitter. In James's masterpieces—*What Maisie Knew* and *The Ambassadors*—he achieves a comedy so complex that laughter seems indistinguishable from pity.

However, *The Europeans*, James's first successful comedy, isn't pitying because its plot invites few strenuous emotions. Rather, we are asked to smile kindly at the very international imbroglio that James treated melodramatically in *The American*. Written a year after the weaker book, *The Europeans* reverses more than its action. When Christopher Newman tried to buy his way into the cultured Bellegarde family, they wickedly rejected him so that his virtue could shine by contrast; but James's love for European elegance made the contrast blurred. By mocking both national styles, *The Europeans* becomes as clear as the spring weather through which it transpires. In it, James sees what it would take him years to see about *The American* (that even aristocrats will sell themselves when they need money). Moreover, he admits, as he never admitted in *The American* and other novels of its type, that American virtue has its ridiculous, self-defeating side.

As James's principal representative of European life, we have the Baroness Eugenia, who is grand and stylish, but also theatrical and portentous. When we first see her, looking into a mirror, she is too busy to pay attention to her brother's Boston sketches. Where Felix finds charming sights in abundance, Eugenia finds only the grotesquely incomprehensible. To her jaundiced eye, people entering a streetcar suggest "the scramble for places in a lifeboat at sea," while a charmingly generic scene of red-brick Boston houses near a white New England church is "the ugliest thing she had ever" witnessed. Ironic here at the expense of the usually sacrosanct, James mocks her artful transformation of the Wentworths' simple guest cottage:

She began to hang up *portières* in the doorways; to place wax candles, procured after some research, in unexpected situations; to dispose anomalous draperies over the arms of sofas and the backs of chairs. The Baroness had brought with her to the New World a copious provision of the element of costume. . . . There were India shawls suspended, curtain-wise, in the parlor door, and curious fabrics, corresponding to Gertrude's metaphysical vision of an opera cloak, tumbled about in the sitting-places. There were pink silk blinds in the windows, by which the room was strangely bedimmed; and along the chimney-piece was disposed a remarkable band of velvet, covered with coarse, dirty-looking lace.

Nevertheless, when compared to Eugenia's cultivation, the Wentworths seem callow. Showing her about the house, Mr. Wentworth diffidently boasts, "The house is very old . . . George Washington once spent a week here," to which Eugenia crushingly replies, "Oh, I have heard of Washington. . . . My father used to tell me of him." The Americans are also naively censorious: "The idea that his niece should be a German Baroness, married 'morganatically' to a Prince had . . . given [Mr. Wentworth] much to think about. Was it right, was it just, was it acceptable? . . . The strange word 'morganatic' was constantly in his ears; it reminded him of a certain Mrs. Morgan whom he had once known and who had been a bold, unpleasant woman." Throughout the book, James offers other examples of ludicrous provinciality, but his main satiric point in *The Europeans* is that continental avarice is matched by American priggishness.

The book's first prominent exponent of this American foible is Mr. Brand, the Wentworths' lay minister. In love with Gertrude, an apostate from Wentworthiness, Brand is continually baffled by the girl's moral indifference. Coming upon her sister Charlotte and learning that Gertrude has decided to spend Sunday in the garden, Brand "smile[s] down on [Charlotte] from his great height" when the latter expresses concern about Gertrude's restlessness: "I shall be very glad to talk to her," he avers. "For that I should be willing to absent myself from almost any occasion of worship, however attractive." But when Gertrude appears, she seems quite as perverse as Charlotte had feared. "Your sister," Brand intones, "tells me you are depressed." "Depressed?" the girl marvels; "I am never depressed." " 'Oh, surely, sometimes,' replied Mr. Brand, as if he thought this a regrettable account of one's self."

With such a suitor, it is no surprise that Gertrude prefers the wind in the trees to the whisperings of courtship. Only with Felix can she enjoy love. But so far from being cast down by his loss, Brand rejoices at his opportunity to be magnanimous. When Mr. Wentworth balks at giving his daughter to her frivolous relative, Brand intercedes on the lovers' behalf: "Charlotte thought he looked very grand; and it is incontestable that Mr. Brand felt very grand. This, in fact, was the grandest moment of his life. . . ." Scaling even further heights, the spurned lover declares, "I should like, in my ministerial capacity, to unite this young couple"; but this bit of altruism is too much even for the upright Mr. Wentworth: " 'Heavenly Powers!' murmured Mr. Wentworth. And it was the nearest approach to profanity he had ever made."

This comedy is not only buoyant and shrewd; it is liberating. For the first time in his novels, James acknowledges that renunciation and moral heroism can be ridiculous. We have only to compare the minister with other Jamesian rivals in love to recognize the special freedom of this book's satire.

However, despite all the evidence she witnesses that Puritans dispense only moral capital, Eugenia determines to sell her wares. Knowing the Wentworth Arcady contains a single worldly soul— Mr. Acton, who had been to China—Eugenia marks him out for prey. But she is mistaken, and it is through her error that James reaches the highest pitch in his laughter at both European and American folly.

Half-recognizing Acton's fastidiousness, Eugenia still reasons that his love of honesty might suit her well: "One could trust him, at any rate, round all the corners of the world; and, withal, he was not absolutely simple, which would have been excess; he was only relatively simple, which was quite enough for the Baroness." What Eugenia forgets is that Acton, like the Wentworths, is proud of his simplicity. When, in American fashion, her worldly friend brings her to meet his mother, in European fashion, Eugenia overdoes things. Unfortunately, Acton deems her sociable exaggerations, exaggerations *tout simple*. "She had struck a false note. But who were these people," Eugenia muses in a blend of pique and astonishment, "to whom such fibbing was not pleasing?"

Temporarily foiled by Acton's priggishness, Eugenia amuses herself in flirting with the Wentworths' young heir, Clifford, who has been sent home from Harvard for having liquor on his breath. But when she finds, to her chagrin, that Clifford's wild oats were no more adventurous, she decides to cast him away. The great comic explosion in *The Europeans* occurs when Acton, whose ardor has neutralized his fear of Eugenia's dishonesty, pays an evening call, thus forcing Eugenia to hide Clifford in an adjacent room. Eventually, in his embarrassment at having been relegated, Clifford crashes into the tête-à-tête, thus giving Acton a chance to escape the romantic involvement he didn't really desire.

James mocks Eugenia's byzantine mannerisms, but he also exposes in Acton what he blinked at in similar figures like Fleda Vetch: that self-serving fastidiousness which is fear of life masquerading as morality. As F. W. Dupee was the first to realize, Acton merely uses Eugenia's lies as "excuses for avoiding an entanglement which his egoism, his prudence, and his attachment to his mother render embarrassing."[52] He is, as Richard Poirier cleverly says, " 'action' with the 'I' left out."[53] Even his initial interest in Eugenia was egoistic. He flirted with her to prove that of all his group he alone might attract a cultivated European: "You detest them for the dull life they make you lead," he tells her during their love scene. "Really, it would give me a sort of pleasure to hear you say so."

On native grounds, James feels no patriotic defensiveness in *The Europeans*, while the book's light mood lends his criticism a unique relaxation. Thus, Europeans are not evil, but only refined and self-seeking; Americans are not supremely virtuous, but only simple and stiff. Yet Eugenia feels provinciality's appeal, while James is also conscious that Americans are kind and pleasant, despite their inhibitions. In *The Europeans*, as F. R. Leavis says, James is "feeling towards an ideal possibility that is neither Europe nor America";[54] thus he avoids the ambiguity inevitable when so judicious a man is forced to take a simple position.

Insofar as *The Europeans* is a committed work, its commitment is to love. Between the poles of Eugenia's blatant egotism and the inverted variety of Brand and Acton, James places Gertrude and Felix, people who seek a natural mixture of self-satisfaction and giving. It is Felix and not Eugenia who knows how to enjoy life, and it is Gertrude who comes to share this knowledge. When Felix appears she thinks him an Arabian Nights prince, whereas to the other Wentworths, his arrival is only "an extension of duty, of the exercise of the more recondite virtues . . . [but not] an extension of enjoyment." Felix rescues Gertrude from the joyless Wentworth world by teaching her the value of natural egotism. Gertrude is, at first, a bit dubious when he proposes that Charlotte should marry Brand: " 'It seems as if it would make me happy,' said Gertrude. 'To get rid of Mr. Brand, eh? To recover your liberty?' Gertrude walked on. 'To see my sister married to so good a man.' Felix gave his light laugh. 'You always put things on those grounds; you will never say anything for yourself. You are all so afraid, here, of being selfish. I don't think you know how,' he went on. 'Let me show you!' " And he does. Immediately after this conversation, Gertrude sends Brand packing: " 'You are trying . . . to lower yourself.' 'I am trying for once to be natural!' cried Gertrude, passionately. 'I have been pretending, all my life; I have been dishonest; it is you that have made me so!' Mr. Brand stood gazing at her, and she went on, 'Why shouldn't I be frivolous, if I want? One has a right to be frivolous, if it's one's nature. No, I don't care for the great questions. I care for pleasure—for amusement.' " To get the full significance of this climax one must recall that its author, himself so vigilant against egoism, would one day embody freedom in Fleda Vetch and virtue in Milly Theale.

In the romantic world of *The Europeans*, however, abnegation is foolish while self-assertion is blessed. Yet, unlike the lovers who flee a cold North in Keats's "Eve of St. Agnes," Felix and Gertrude can find no permanent home, for James was no visionary. Though they periodically return to Boston after their marriage, they do not remain there, and James cannot say where they went. Even to imagine their fulfillment within a social context, he had to set the novel in a pastoral Boston forty years before his own time. *The Europeans* is the loveliest embodiment in James's fiction of a positive ideal. His more characteristic works show that society either banishes the natural self or exploits it.

"The Siege of London" makes the latter point with relative lightness. Oddly neglected, this witty high comedy is one of the most neatly ironic of James's novellas, while despite the thin plot, it is also one of his more complex. Mrs. Headway, its American heroine, is a divorcée seeking to become respectable by entering British society. Unfortunately, her past threatens to exclude her: "She got divorces very easily, she was so taking in court. She had got one or two before from a man whose name [Littlemore] had forgotten, and there was a legend that even these were not the first. She had been exceedingly divorced! . . . She was a charming woman, especially for New Mexico; but she had been divorced too often—it was a tax on one's credulity; she must have repudiated more husbands than she had married."

As James tells us in his preface, he wrote "The Siege of London" in order to present a more realistic and morally sound version of its situation than existed in the Dumas play that had given him his plot. In "Le Demi-Monde," the adventuress is blocked in her design to marry a French nobleman by a former lover's denunciation; but James rightly believed that Dumas's approval of the lover's action was social conservatism masquerading as morality. In James's version, the former lover, Littlemore, does not behave this basely. Moreover, he is only one of several people watching Nancy make headway, and James satirizes, through an ample cast, not only the *arriviste*'s temerity but the conservative smugness of those seeking to oppose her.

As a further complication, James criticizes the sort of morally pretentious, sexually timid fear of Mrs. Headway that he is elsewhere so sentimental about. And he manages to do this without ambiguity by attaching the errors not to his spokesman, Littlemore, but to a second of Nancy's admirers, Waterville. Like Winterbourne in the more famous story "Daisy Miller," Waterville is an American who has become too Europeanized. Thus, although he finds himself attracted by the beautiful Mrs. Headway, he worries, in European fashion, about the effrontery she displays in doing battle against caste. Throughout the story he vacillates. When she responds to him favorably, he is disposed to forget his objections; when she is too busy to neutralize his disapproval, he expresses his personal chagrin by styling himself the defender of society. Baffled by his conflicting reactions, Waterville can only watch the lady with passionate interest; so when her intended mother-in-law invites him to a weekend party in Nancy's honor, Waterville goes "down to Longlands with much the same impatience with which, in Paris, he would have gone, if he had been able, to the first night of a new comedy."

Shunned by her, Waterville tells himself he is affronted by the blatancy of Nancy's siege: "There was something in Mrs. Headway that shocked and mortified him, and Littlemore had been right in saying that she had a deficiency of shading. She was terribly distinct; her motives, her impulses, her desires were absolutely glaring." But when he takes full measure of the massed fortress of Longlands, Waterville begins to pity the woman who must scale its walls, just as he begins to realize that they are not admirably impregnable: "All those people seemed . . . wrapped in a community of ideas, of traditions; they understood each other's accent, even each other's variations. Mrs. Headway, with all her prettiness, seemed to transcend these variations; she looked foreign, exaggerated; she had too much expression; she might have been engaged for the evening. Waterville remarked, moreover, that English society was always looking out for amusement and that its transactions were conducted on a cash basis. If Mrs. Headway were amusing enough she would probably succeed, and her fortune—if fortune there was—would not be a hinderance." In *The Europeans* the natural extricates itself from both venality and moral pretension; in "The Siege of London" its fate is more dourly conceived: the natural becomes a commodity. "Nancy knew of course that as a product of fashionable circles she was nowhere, but she might have great success as a child of nature."

Mrs. Headway becomes ultimately threatening to Littlemore, as she had been to Waterville, because she puts society in a bad light: "She appeared vaguely to irritate [Littlemore]; even her fluttering attempts at self-culture—she had become a great critic, and handled many of the productions of the age with a bold, free touch—constituted a vague invocation, an appeal for sympathy which was naturally annoying to a man who disliked the trouble of revising old decisions, consecrated by a certain amount of reminiscence which might be called tender." Though her pushiness is deplorable, society provides no strong opposition. Sir Arthur Demesne, her target, was "pleased . . . to believe he was romantic; that had been the case with several of his ancestors, who supplied a precedent without which he would perhaps not have ventured to trust himself." Lady Demesne is right to be worried about her son's future, but her attempts to get the truth about Mrs. Headway out of Waterville and Littlemore offend against the very propriety she purports to symbolize. Nancy, however, understands propriety and thus snares her dilatory aristocrat because of those very manners that made him hesitate in the first place. Luring Littlemore to her hotel room, she arranges for Sir Arthur to interrupt them. Announcing that Littlemore will oblige her fiancé with any information he could wish concerning her past, she coolly retires. Faced with such a compromising opportunity, the proper Britisher must, of course, decline to prosecute his inquest.

Nancy triumphs through the system which regards her with horror, while Littlemore learns that it is not so different from her as he had thought. Throughout the tale, Littlemore's sister, an American who had successfully besieged London with the armor of respectability, begs him to stop Mrs. Headway. At last, Littlemore realizes that his sister, and by implication Lady Demesne, are not superior: "It had the queerest effect . . . to see his sister playing the same tricks as Nancy . . . !" Ultimately, he comes to understand that Waterville also fell below his pretensions; his irritating moral censure was based only on unrequited love.

Like *The Europeans*, "The Siege of London" turns transatlantic opportunism into an exposé of the very idea of society. *Washington Square* is also satiric in tone, but it treats a more private situation, and it enriches its comedy with pathos. In some ways, this little book is James's most balanced production. Notoriously slight, famously denied a place by James in the New York edition, *Washington Square* has always been underestimated. Since it first appeared, critics have tended to sentimentalize its meaning (a process completed by the interpretation dramatized in "The Heiress").[55] Dr. Sloper is usually deemed a melodramatic villain, Catherine (until her last moment) seems no more than a pitiable victim, and the plot, as one critic asserts, forces us to conclude that "though her father's judgment is correct, . . . he creates for Catherine a harsher and sadder life than she would have had" with her beloved fortune hunter.[56] In fact, Catherine and her father are complicated both in themselves and in their relationship, and James in no way encourages the poignant notion that Catherine might have been better off with Morris Townsend.

Morris is dreadful. James's prose settles this question beyond dispute. Had any doubt about Catherine's chances with him lingered in our minds, James dispels it when Morris meets Lavinia at a restaurant he selects for one of their councils of romantic warfare. Though the lady bubbles with plans to help Morris get both the girl and her fortune, Townsend is annoyed at even having to consider the problem: "He was in a state of irritation natural to a gentleman of fine parts who had been snubbed in a benevolent attempt to confer a distinction upon a young woman of inferior characteristics"; to assuage his annoyance, he gorges himself on a bowl of oysters. Lavinia, who was dismayed at his choice of so crass a setting for their tête-à-tête, is shocked to see a love-sick swain gormandizing. When they are through, Morris makes the poor fool pay for her tea—a nicely comic forecast of his plans for Catherine. Townsend could have married the girl with her mother's money, but "he had a perfectly definite appreciation of his value, which seemed to him inadequately represented by the sum. . . ."

With his knowledge of the world, Sloper unerringly types Morris. But when he declares his opinion "the result of thirty years of observation," his sister reminds him that the important "thing is for Catherine to see it." "I will present her with a pair of spectacles!" he predicts, ignoring the fact that tampering with Catherine's vision is also what Morris had planned.

Like Robert Acton, Dr. Sloper is as selfish as his more blatantly dangerous antagonist. Esteemed as a doctor and a wit, Sloper himself values only success or cleverness. Though he earned his fortune from ladies, both as husband and practitioner, "he had never been dazzled . . . by any feminine characteristics whatever; and . . . his private opinion of the more complicated sex was not exalted. He regarded its complications as more curious than edifying, and he had an idea of the beauty of *reason*, which was, on the whole, meagrely gratified by what he observed in his female patients." After the death of his wife, who had been an exception to his idea of the sex, and his son, who was to have re-created the father's splendor, Sloper is thrown back on his distinctly unclever little girl. To him, Catherine is doubly useless for being a woman with no saving remnant of masculinity. His judgment of Morris is abetted by his knowledge of the world, but it is founded on his contempt for Catherine. Since he himself has so little regard for her, he cannot imagine that Morris would want her except for the money.

As it happens, Sloper is right. Nevertheless James wants us to condemn him—not for underestimating Townsend's ability to give pleasure, or for damaging Catherine's opportunities, but for the motives which make him seek to protect her. Had Sloper been truly concerned with Catherine's welfare, something might be said in his behalf. Instead, he is concerned only with the position guaranteed him by her docility. Thus, when Morris, trying to make himself agreeable, asks, "Is there nothing I can do to make you believe in me?" Sloper replies, "If there were, I should be sorry to suggest it, for—don't you see?—I don't want to believe in you." Though, to a solicitous parent, Catherine's plan would be, at most, self-destructive folly, Sloper regards it as "treason." Unable to argue credibly on grounds of concern, he continually appeals to Catherine's sense of duty, once even predicting— cruelly, to so loving a daughter—that her marriage will cause his death.

The ironic self-regard behind Sloper's behavior is almost acknowledged in one of the most violent outbreaks in James's fiction. On the European journey with which Sloper has thought to break the girl's romance, he is infuriated by a constancy of which he would not have thought her capable. Though she never mentions Morris and behaves dutifully toward her father, Sloper becomes convinced that nothing has changed. One cold, sharp evening, taking his daughter to "a hard, melancholy dell, abandoned by the summer light," the Doctor determines to test her. "Does he write to you?" he asks. "Yes, about twice a month," she mildly replies. "I am very angry," he blurts out, to which she replies, still more mildly, "I am sorry." Sloper is infuriated: "You try my patience . . . and you ought to know what I am. I am not a very good man. Though I am very smooth externally, at bottom I am very passionate; and I assure you I can be very hard." The full implications of his confession are lost on Sloper, and though Catherine momentarily thinks he means to kill her, she herself makes little of the wild scene. Later, it has its effect.

Insofar as *Washington Square* is satiric, it views Sloper and Townsend in much the same way that *The Europeans* views its antagonists: as obverse cases of selfishness. Catherine's protector thinks no more of her than the young man who wants only her fortune. However, though James maintains his witty manner until the end, *Washington Square* darkens and deepens as it progresses.

Since Catherine is precisely the dullard her father thinks, the novel initially treats her romance as a comedy. But we gradually see that Morris's feigned kindness—the first she has ever known— brings forth unsuspected strength of character. Determined to marry Townsend while maintaining her father's love, Catherine waits with great delicacy and patience for the old man to change his mind. Sloper's obstinacy, then, ultimately shows her that he is unable to love. The spectacles with which Dr. Sloper meant to clarify her vision of Townsend also enable her to see him: "From her own point of view the great facts of her career were that Morris Townsend had trifled with her affection, and that her father had broken its spring. . . . Nothing could ever undo the wrong or cure the pain that Morris had inflicted on her, and nothing could ever make her feel toward her father as she felt in her younger years."

Though he cannot acknowledge the fact, this unintended result of Sloper's campaign robs him as well as Catherine. As we can see from the violent irrationality with which he opposed her marriage, the old man, despite his contempt, needed his daughter. But like the narrator of "The Aspern Papers," Dr. Sloper loses the love of a homely but large-souled woman because of a proud obsession with his own ideas. So clear is James's derision that he can risk showing that Sloper's conceit was self-punishing.

All his life, Dr. Sloper has undervalued the one person who might have mitigated his domestic disappointment. Having determined that Catherine was poor compensation for the loss of his wife and son, the Doctor's judgment insured its own accuracy, beating the girl into passivity before his cold disregard. Sloper is surprised by the constancy with which she had clung to Morris. Lavinia had warned Dr. Sloper that his knowledge of Catherine was deficient: "If you regard Catherine as a weak-minded woman you are particularly mistaken!" The girl herself has intimations of her strength before the occasion arises for testing it. When Morris, as selfishly blind as Dr. Sloper, complains that she is timid in waiting for her father's consent, Catherine replies, "I don't think I am—really!"

Faced with Catherine's insistence that she broke off her engagement, the Doctor has no way of assuring himself that she is lying. Out of the twisted intensity of his disdainful love, he makes her promise that she will not marry Townsend after he dies, only to be surprised by her response: " 'I can't promise,' she simply repeated. 'You are very obstinate,' said the Doctor. 'I don't think you understand.' 'Please explain, then.' 'I can't explain,' said Catherine; 'and I can't promise.' 'Upon my word,' her father exclaimed, 'I had no idea how obstinate you are!' She knew herself that she was obstinate, and it gave her a certain joy." And it ultimately gives her the power to make her contention come true; when Morris returns to woo her, she does reject him.

Neither Dr. Sloper nor Morris Townsend understands the woman over whom they contend. Townsend sees her only as money, Sloper only as blighted expectations; neither sees what she is: a firm point of love. Yet through his misunderstanding, each man forces her further into that final self-communion which constitutes her modest victory. Ironically, they, who are stronger, lose more.

To James's honor, *Washington Square* neither simplifies its characters nor sentimentalizes their significance. The book's casuistical situation is merely the vehicle for James's ironies, which condemn both the charming, venal Townsend and the upright, egotistical Dr. Sloper. In Catherine's tight triumph, James portrays one of his most convincing examples of the power of integrity; yet his narration carefully avoids taking us into the girl's sensibility and thus blocks a sentimental identification. Shunning melodrama, James makes Catherine stolid, Morris at-

tractive, and Dr. Sloper intelligent. Commenting on his material
with witty clarity, James shows in *Washington Square* the difference between complexity and equivocation upon which the
present study is based.

But to appreciate this distinction fully one should compare
Washington Square with a work like "The Turn of the Screw."
Just as *The Europeans* disperses the international fantasy prominent in *The American,* so *Washington Square* clears up the
problem of moral arrogance that James seems unable to face in
the ghost story. Like the governess, Dr. Sloper determines to
protect his young charge from evil by forcing her to acknowledge
that she is in its grip. In the process, like the governess, he proves
himself no less threatening than his antagonist, and he is capable
of more definitive damage.

Washington Square dramatizes what required a critical revision to unearth in "The Turn of the Screw": zeal to protect
innocence from danger ironically includes the thrill of seeing
innocence menaced. Like the governess in the face of the ghosts,
Dr. Sloper wants to learn that Morris is wicked and that Catherine is possessed in order to vindicate his own wisdom: " 'It seems
to make you very happy that your daughter's affections have been
trifled with' [his clairvoyant sister asserts]. 'It does,' said the Doctor; 'for I had foretold it! It's a great pleasure to be in the right.'
'Your pleasures make one shudder!' his sister exclaimed." Like
the governess, Dr. Sloper seems to take obscene delight in the
spectacular value of the innocent's plight:

> "Say it amuses you outright. I don't see why it should be such a
> joke that your daughter adores you," [his sister complains].
> "It is the point where adoration stops that I find it interesting to
> fix."
> "It stops where the other sentiment begins."
> "Not at all; that would be simple enough. The two things are
> extremely mixed up, and the mixture is extremely odd. It will

produce some third element, and that's what I'm waiting to see. I wait with suspense—with positive excitement; and that is a sort of emotion that I didn't suppose Catherine would ever provide for me. I am really very much obliged to her."

But whereas James condemns Dr. Sloper despite his accuracy, James complicates our evaluation of the governess by involving us in the effort to make certain that she combats an external threat.

Whereas the governess is guilty if there are no ghosts, Sloper's guilt in no way hinges on a misjudgment of Townsend. In *Washington Square*, James confronts the arrogance of asserted morality, though in "The Turn of the Screw" he seems disposed to champion the assertion if it can be proved correct. The later work suggests that James's commitment to the possibility of victorious moral action grew slightly protective as he more and more came to question the possibility of certain judgment. But in the earlier book, he was able to see how closely the moral vision approached immorality even when its judgment was impeccable.

As I have said, the governess's real sin is her refusal to accept life's multiplicity. Having been brought up to believe that beauty is somehow incompatible with goodness, she insists that the lovely children must have been corrupted. In obverse fashion, Dr. Sloper believes that anyone as plain and dull as Catherine must surely be unlovable. The governess destroys Miles by hounding him until he corroborates her vision, but the corroboration never convinces us that she was right. Catherine acknowledges her father's accuracy, but this does not lessen his egotism. However, unlike Miles's, Catherine's innocence triumphs over worldliness, both by refusing to confess her abasement to Dr. Sloper and by refusing the amends which Morris hypocritically offers. In this, the novel achieves its final freedom from the sentimentality characteristic of James's weaker fiction. For Catherine's renunciation is no inverted moral victory snatched from defeat, but rather a spirited self-assertion against denials of her human dignity. It is the one such moment in James that the common reader would cheer.

Despite its small scope, *Washington Square* faces the theme of tyrannical moral vision with more honesty than James often achieved. By demonstrating the malignity that may underlie "good intentions," James accomplished a first-rate cautionary tale, while his high-spirited prose kept the lesson from being heavy or facile. Moreover, in Catherine's final gesture, James conceived his first plausible expression of the judgment that purity must make against the world.

CHAPTER SEVEN

Innocence Exposed

More significant examples of James's capacity for unsentimental criticism dramatize the judgment that the world might make against purity. In several comic novellas and in *The Awkward Age* James shows that overzealous pursuit of virtue is itself a vice and that innocence is a mixed blessing. Admitting what he seems anxious to deny in *The Spoils of Poynton* and *The Wings of the Dove*, James turns the defects of their heroines into his subject. With Isabel Archer and Olive Chancellor, James approaches a critique of innocence, but he muffles his censure. Moreover, in the latter case, Olive's involvement with a cause James despised made him conceive of her as pathological, thus limiting her relevance. The telegraphist of "In the Cage," Euphemia de Mauves, Laura Wing, and Nanda Brookenham are instead perfectly normal representatives of a type James particularly admired. In exposing them, he showed notable courage.

As is commonly accepted, the telegraphist resembles two of

James's most problematical heroes: the governess and the narrator of *The Sacred Fount*. Like them, she observes vice from a
disadvantaged position, and her attempt to protect others is
vitiated by self-interest. But whereas the other figures are too
shrouded in mystery to validate judgment, we can easily criticize
the girl. Two obvious distinctions suggest the superior freedom
of "In the Cage." "The Turn of the Screw" and *The Sacred
Fount* are first-person narratives, involving an unavoidable degree of authorial identification; "In the Cage" is clearly ironic
because James narrates from the protagonist's viewpoint but not
in her voice. The others involve us in questioning the protagonist's adversaries; "In the Cage" is solely concerned with how
and why the telegraphist believes what she does. Doubtless, most
of her customers do toss themselves around as freely as their
shillings, but our judgment of her is not made dependent on our
judgment of them. As a result, "In the Cage" is precisely that
comedy of misperception which is blocked in *The Sacred Fount*
by a "distraught, disintegrating parable."[57]

Like "The Siege of London," this novella has been unfairly
neglected; and since James placed the tale in the New York
edition alongside *What Maisie Knew* and "The Pupil," most
critics who have treated "In the Cage" see it as a study of vanquished sensitivity.[58] In fact, "In the Cage" is satiric, not celebra-
tory. Working in Cocker's grocery, among hams and cheeses, the
postal clerk dreams herself a confederate of the "class that wired
everything, even their expensive feelings." A mere office-worker
beneath that class's notice, she regards her position as a special
privilege: "It had occurred to her early that . . . she should know
a great many persons without their recognising the acquaintance." The telegraphist is a spy delighting in clandestine
knowledge, like the Newmarch sleuth, whose opening note this
resembles. But whereas James's adoption of the first-person prevented him from telling us how the narrator's needs informed

his project, he provides the necessary background in the girl's case.

Before the story opens, the telegraphist's family had had a reverse in fortune, with the inevitable sequel of drink for the less industrious and hard work, presumably culminating in marriage, for her. Unfortunately, her social station had turned up no one more feasible than a certain Mr. Mudge, whose appeal is accurately suggested by his name. With hams and postage stamps on one side and Mr. Mudge on the other, it isn't surprising that the girl begins to dream. The subjects of her excursions are socialites whose wickedness offsets her virtue. This propensity for a lower-class girl to believe vile things of her betters is also exhibited by the governess; but whereas James seems to have forgiven her prototype, he mocks the telegraphist's indignation.

Throughout the story, a friend named Mrs. Jordan, equally cast down, tries to entice the girl into her own profession: flower arranging for the rich. Claiming that her post entails superior knowledge of the favored class, the telegraphist refuses to surrender her advantage. Mrs. Jordan may be on speaking terms with the right people, but the girl is intimate with their vices. With their profligate wiring "twist[ing] the knife in her vitals," the impoverished girl takes an exquisite revenge: "In private [she experiences] a triumphant vicious feeling of mastery and ease, a sense of carrying their silly guilty secrets in her pocket, her small retentive brain, and thereby knowing so much more about them than they suspected or would care to think. . . . She was rigid . . . on the article of making the public itself affix its stamps, and found a special enjoyment in dealing to that end with some of the ladies who were too grand to touch them."

Everything is subordinated to her ludicrous fixation. If a fellow clerk falls in love with her, this opportunity merely serves to extort from him additional hours at the cage's public end. If she is intimate with her fiancé, it is only to inspire with her stories "the particular prostration in which he could still be amusing to her." "Dimly struck with the linked sweetness connecting the tender passion with cheap champagne," Mudge thinks of opening a grocery in a fashionable neighborhood; but his fiancée has a subtler definition of profit.

Becoming infatuated with the dashing Captain Everhard, the telegraphist begins to pay special attention to the prodigious, and frequently pseudonymous, correspondence which he shares with Lady Bradeen. Her passion rising, the girl starts to haunt his street at three in the morning, "the hour at which, if the ha'penny novels were not all wrong, he probably came home for the night." Success crowns her perseverance in one of two hilarious scenes that make "In the Cage" a masterpiece of mockery.

Causing the bewildered dandy to stroll in the park with her, the perfervid girl stages a parody love scene, the passion of which is befuddling to him, the humor invisible to her. In what could be his only approach to a declaration, the poor man pledges her to remain at the post office (she had dramatically announced that she would leave). Thrilled by his interest, she promises, in order to bind them together, to remain in the cage.

The second scene is a sequel. In the interim, the girl has been crowing about her knowledge, which includes awareness of an important telegram that will determine the outcome of his affair with Lady Bradeen. Despite the telegraphist's assumption of a deep tie with the Captain, she has not heard from him since their night in the park. One day he flies into the post office, passionately pursuing the incriminating wire. Now she has her chance. Deciding that his distant manner is a ruse to conceal their complicity, she behaves like the Knightsbridge operator he seems to consider her. There ensues her demonstration of feigned denseness, all too superbly enacted, which is doubly funny because it is superfluous. As later events prove, the telegraphist doesn't understand this occasion any more than she understood his feelings in the park. But she exposes her own motives in a way which makes the reader fathom her invincible pettiness: "It came to her there, with her eyes on his face, that she held the whole thing in her hand, held it as she held her pencil, which might have broken at that instant in her tightened grip. . . . 'You say "about the time you speak of." But I don't think you speak of an exact time—*do* you? . . . It wasn't delivered? . . . I see—I see. . . . And you have no clue? . . . Oh the last of August? . . . Oh the same as last night?' " And on and on, while Captain Everhard turns white with anger, which is as deep an emotional response as she ever has from him. Lady Bradeen is his real master, and though the telegraphist has been trying to spare him from vice, her behavior facilitates the very marriage she thinks he has feared. At that, she has to learn the results of her efforts, despite her vaunted clairvoyance, from Mrs. Jordan.[59]

By itself, "In the Cage" is a gay, pitiless satire of the sort of person who slavers indignantly over gossip columns, simultaneously satisfying prurience, morality, and a bruised social consciousness. In the context of James's work, it is a delightful critique of a type more usually celebrated: a social outcast—by reasons of birth, inexperience, and prudery—whose efforts to "save" the world are really self-aggrandizing. The telegraphist not only clarifies what is obfuscated in the Newmarch narrator, she reverses the sentimental contemplation of such a figure that James achieved with Hyacinth Robinson.

Nevertheless, like Olive Chancellor, the telegraphist is something of a special case. Two earlier novellas look coldly at moral fastidiousness in more representative situations. "Madame de Mauves" and "A London Life" exhibit the same impartiality toward the respective merits of innocence and worldliness that *The Europeans* displays toward Americans and continentals. "Madame de Mauves" is poised in its presentation of both dichotomies.

Published in 1874, thus James's earliest success, "Madame de Mauves" combines liveliness of commentary with dramatic verve. Its protagonist, Bernard Longmore, a typical Jamesian vacillator, becomes infatuated with an American woman married to a French nobleman. When a friend informs Longmore that Euphemia de Mauves is unhappy, Longmore's chauvinism produces instant belief. " 'What else is possible,' he asked himself, 'for a sweet American girl who marries an unclean Frenchman?' " Yet this question, whose rhetoric so flatters himself, suggests only part of his reaction to the Baron. "The Baron was plainly not a moral man," the young American muses, but "poor Longmore, who was, would have been glad to learn the secret of his luxurious serenity."

Because of Longmore's inexperience, one suspects that his initial view of the de Mauves is oversimplified—a possibility to which Longmore himself becomes increasingly sensitive. How partial therefore were early critics of "Madame de Mauves" who saw the married couple precisely in Longmore's callow terms.[60] Reading the story as a celebration of American virtue in unholy alliance with French lubriciousness is not permissible even on artistic terms, since it ignores the irony of the prose. More importantly, James's initial description of Euphemia dispels the belief that she is simply a heroine.

As several critics have pointed out, Euphemia is an early version of Isabel Archer.[61] Like Isabel, "she found it easier to believe in fables, when they had a certain nobleness of meaning, than in well-attested but sordid facts." But in the second chapter of the novella, James explores this characteristic idealism with none of the protectiveness he exhibits in the novel. Euphemia's dream, which James attributes to "primitive logic," is that one day she should marry a nobleman, since, though her notions of the breed are based merely on "ultramontane works of fiction," she is certain that "blood . . . of the very finest strain" must insure happiness. This dream is not vulgarly romantic, however, for Euphemia wishes her lover to be ugly and poor: "His ugliness was to be nobly expressive, and his poverty delicately proud. Euphemia had a fortune of her own, which, at the proper time, after fixing on her in eloquent silence those fine eyes which were to soften the feudal severity of his visage, he was to accept with a world of stifled protestations." Unfortunately, Baron de Mauves is poor but handsome; still, "a very few days reconciled her to his good looks."

Like Isabel's, Euphemia's marriage is a scheme for the suitor's advantage concocted by a presumed friend. But whereas James uses this fact to wring sympathy for his beautiful striver, he makes it the crowning indication of Euphemia's folly. This convent-bred American adores the Baron's sister only because she is an aristocrat, but as James wittily remarks: "A certain aristocratic impudence Mademoiselle de Mauves abundantly possessed, and her raids among her friend's finery were quite in the spirit of her baronial ancestors in the twelfth century,—a spirit which Euphemia considered but a large way of understanding friendship,—a freedom from small deference to the world's opinions which would sooner or later justify itself in acts of surprising magnanimity." This magnanimity Mademoiselle de Mauves displays by delivering Euphemia to "a thoroughly perverted creature . . . overlaid with . . . corruptions."

Seeing her first fancy shattered, Euphemia retreats into a second. As she tells Longmore, she "wished [she had been] the daughter of a poor New England minister, living in a little white house under a couple of elms, and doing all the housework." Though she cannot achieve this Puritan delight, she comes very close, with effects on a pleasure-loving French husband that one can imagine. The harassed nobleman tries to get her off his back by dropping her into Longmore's bed, but the young man's timidity (aided by the lady's rectitude) prevents this relief. Longmore "had hoped that when he fell in love, he should do it with an excellent conscience, with no greater agitation than a mild general glow of satisfaction." The proffered affair would be rather strenuous for such a person; nevertheless, sex asserts itself. Repairing to the countryside to consider the Baron's proposition, Longmore's "ideal bliss" in Euphemia's purity begins to evaporate when exposed to the tangy pastoral air. At a charming tavern before a succulent lunch, Longmore begins to hear the call of the flesh: "The homely tavern sounds coming out through the open windows, the sunny stillness of the fields and crops, which covered so much vigorous natural life, suggested very little that was transcendental, had very little to say about renunciation, —nothing at all about spiritual zeal. They seemed to utter a message from plain ripe nature, to express the unperverted reality of things, to say that the common lot is not brilliantly amusing, and that the part of wisdom is to grasp frankly at experience, lest you miss it altogether."

In *The Eccentric Design,* Marius Bewley has used this passage to prove James a proto-Lawrence, which is going rather far, but its existence places "Madame de Mauves" among James's least anti-Lawrentian works.[62] For when Longmore comes upon a couple of adulterers, it is Longmore who is exposed. In the sensuous forest, with the couple's laughter ringing in his ears and the hot sun beating on his brow, Longmore falls asleep. In his dream, the forest becomes bisected by a stream near which he saw the adulterers. On the opposite bank, he spies Euphemia, and though she makes no motion for him to join her, he decides to cross. "He knew the water was deep, and it seemed to him that he knew that he should have to plunge, and that he feared that when he rose to the surface she would have disappeared." To Longmore, plunging into passion threatens him with loss of the beloved. Nevertheless, he is willing to meet the risk, until he sees a boat, which takes him to the other bank. But when he arrives, Euphemia replaces him at the journey's origin. The boatman, of course, is revealed to be Baron de Mauves.

Longmore's passion is equated in his own mind with the mores he condemns. Loving Euphemia would literally place him in the Baron's boat. Still, he decides to seize the day; but Euphemia doesn't give him time to propose, insisting instead that he prove his admiration by returning to America. Despite his passion, this is just the sort of moral substitute desired by the timid young man. In the following description of Longmore's response, James points up its irony through an audacious allusion: "Longmore's imagination swelled; he threw back his head and seemed to be looking for Madame de Mauves's conception among the blinking, mocking stars." The Baron had advised seduction; but it is Longmore who is seduced and impregnated by Euphemia's stiff moralism: the result is a suitably miraculous virgin birth.

And death. In America, where he worships her memory, Longmore hears that the Baron, a repentant husband now rejected by his wife, has shot himself. Several critics have complained that this ending, with its unmistakable criticism of Euphemia (even moral persons should be charitable), makes "Madame de Mauves" ambiguous.[63] But, as I have shown, the tale is consistently critical of Euphemia and Longmore. In addition, the ending is carefully prepared for, not only in the recently emphasized parallel between Euphemia and her sister-in-law, whose vengeance on disappointed hopes has an equally fatal result.[64] Early in the tale, before Euphemia's marriage, her future mother-in-law gives her some advice. Telling the callow girl that a young innocent's misery would grieve her, the old lady asserts: "Whatever befalls you, promise me this: to be yourself. The Baronne de Mauves will be none the worse for it. Yourself, understand, in spite of everything,—bad precepts and bad examples, bad usage even. Be persistently and patiently yourself, and a De Mauves will do you justice!" Euphemia evidently took the advice, though the old lady could scarcely applaud its consequences. By rejecting adultery, Euphemia retains her American virtue, which so intrigues her husband that he falls in love with her. Then she denies him what he had disdained. Longmore provides Euphemia with her means of vengeance.

In addition to its other accomplishments, "Madame de Mauves" manages to expose Euphemia without minimizing for a moment her adversaries; whereas in stories like "The Turn of the Screw" James uses the adversary's presumed wickedness to excuse if not advocate an innocence that is really predatory. In "A London Life" worldly wickedness is even more adroitly displayed with no greater qualification of the story's satirical point. The heroine of "A London Life," Laura Wing, is an orphan forced to live with her stylishly immoral and fashionably mismatched sister. Like the telegraphist, Laura lives in "a house of telegrams; they crossed each other a dozen times an hour, coming and going, and Selina in particular lived in a cloud of them. Laura had but vague ideas as to what they were all about; once in awhile, when they fell under her eyes, she either failed to understand them or judged them to be about horses." What they are about she cannot long ignore, for her brother-in-law, Lionel, anxious for allies in his divorce proceedings against Selina, becomes the girl's unwanted tutor. This determination by the worldly that innocence abet its schemes provides James's first convincing motivation for innocence to assert itself—since, in such a case, quitting the field has been ruled out. Reappearing in *What Maisie Knew*, this situation exempts the innocent from charges of meddling and self-aggrandizement that cast doubt on other typical heroines. Moreover, Selina attacks Laura in a way that throws our sympathy toward the girl.

When Laura begins to see a fastidious young man named Wendover (cf. Longmore, Waterville, Winterbourne), Selina cynically uses the harmless liaison to throw sand in her sister's eyes; when Laura accidentally encounters Selina and her lover in a museum, Selina springs to the attack, accusing Laura of the impropriety attached to unmarried girls who parade through London with a man and no chaperone. James has great fun with Selina's hypocrisy, culminating in the hilarious scene in which Laura confronts her wayward sibling after a particularly late night. At first, the woman wins the argument through sheer brashness, but soon she cracks under the strain of so many lies: "[Selina] besought [Laura] to save her, to stay with her, to help her against herself, against *him*, against Lionel, against everything—to forgive her also all the horrid things she had said to her. Mrs. Berrington melted, liquefied, and the room was deluged with her repentance, her desolation, her confession, her promises and the articles of apparel which were detached from her by the high tide of her agitation." But despite Selina's graphic badness and Laura's obvious excuses for opposing her, James's main satire is directed at the girl, whom he sees as essentially fatuous, regardless of what might be said in her defense.

In itself, adultery is never a sin to James, yet adultery is all that Selina commits. Thus, Laura's response is disproportionate to the circumstances. Moreover, it stems from an aesthetic rather than a moral commitment. On the second page, James informs us that Laura condemns wrongs chiefly as they violate her image of London's charm. Her main reason for hating Selina's activities is that they threaten to erupt in public scandal; and when Wendover enters her consideration, she fears that a scandal might repel his advances. In addition to its naive and selfish underpinnings, her moral ardor has dubious effects. Berating Lionel while "glowing like a young prophetess," Laura doesn't shrink "from the enjoyment of an advantage—that of feeling herself superior and taking her opportunity." When confronting Selina, Laura wonders "was it the asseveration of her innocence that she wished . . . or only the attestation of her falsity?"

Like Longmore, Laura feels the appeal of relaxed values and pleasures. Because of this and because she fears that the Berringtons' divorce will leave her homeless, she throws herself at the dilatory Wendover. Four years later, James was to have the perpetrator of a similar *faux pas* commit suicide, and indeed suicide was the denouement of the anecdote, suggested by Paul Bourget, which gave James the plot of "A London Life."* But in the robust world of this novella such a melodramatic conclusion would disagree with James's tact. Thus, he includes Mrs. Davenant, a stage dowager like the Marquise de Mauves, to act as authorial spokesman and control the plot. This lady, who had always taken a dim view of Laura's stringency, proposes that Wendover honor the girl's request. After characteristic hesitation, the young man agrees, but by that time the shame-faced girl has fled to America. As the last sentence asserts however, London "is far from the banks of the Rappahannock," and the actions of "Berrington *versus* Berrington and Others . . . are matters of the present hour."

Because Laura is the least perverse of James's militant moralists and because her adversaries are sketched with restraint, "A London Life" is one of James's most equable works. No one but F. W. Dupee has thought of talking about *The Awkward Age* in similar terms, but, alone of all its critics, Dupee views the book correctly.[65] In addition to being James's supreme depiction of innocence in *operation* against the world, *The Awkward Age* is unmatched among his novels for its dispassionate scrutiny of rival claims.

But for most readers, the dispassion is felt as heartlessness and the book seems less equable than trivial. Moreover, of James's greatest novels, *The Awkward Age* is exceeded in difficulty only by *The Golden Bowl*; neither book stands a chance of attaining

---

* In "The Visits," referred to in Chapter Three. See James's account of the genesis of "A London Life" in the *Notebooks*.

even that degree of popularity which *The Ambassadors* may be said to possess. As James reports in his preface, the novel was a total failure with his contemporaries, and today, though its virtuosity is often noted, it is not widely admired.[66] The book's donnée is simple enough, though the issues involved are complex. Like *The Spoils of Poynton* (which, however, lost its comic bearings midway), *The Awkward Age* was designed as a comedy about specifically British mores. Noting that British society sheltered its marriageable daughters from inappropriate experience far less rigorously than was habitual on the Continent, James wondered what the fate of the "exposed" young girl might be. The social arrangement which gave James his plot has long since vanished, but its implications concerning education and the proper relationship between innocence and sophistication are still with us.

Objections to the novel based on its presumed triviality of subject require no refutation. But even readers who know that subject does not dictate result in a work of art may object to the byzantine intricacies of the novel's plot—intricacies made all the more confounding by plot's absence in the normal sense. The plot of *The Awkward Age* lies in its speeches and gestures; the book is essentially a play. Both in its ambience and its fabulous wit, *The Awkward Age* is imbued with the spirit of Restoration comedy—particularly the comedy of Congreve, and especially *The Way of the World*. Both works present a ballet of sexual and financial intrigue in which goodness, to survive, must learn the steps. Each contains highly verbal and subtly controlled characters, so that even the fools wear gorgeous motley. Yet despite the relentless artifice, both works trenchantly expose those behind-the-scenes machinations that keep society presentable.

Stylization makes it impossible to call *The Awkward Age* a "realistic" novel. But in the nontechnical sense of the term, which unites James with Howells and Twain despite crucial dissimilarities, *The Awkward Age* is James's most realistic book. Avoiding metaphor (employed in *The Sacred Fount*), melodrama (*The American*), or subterfuge (*The Princess Casamassima*), James portrays high society here in detail and *in extenso*. Apologists for the novel's mannerism sometimes maintain that *The Awkward Age* is also realistic in the technical sense. Thus Dorothea Krook accounts for the oblique dialogue by attributing it to "a homogenous, closely-knit social group, sharing common standards, attitudes, forms of behaviour."[67] Now, in addition to the obvious fact that no such people as James creates ever existed, putative realism isn't likely to excuse obliquity for most readers. The case for James's style may be better made.

As he asserted in a famous lecture, "all life comes back to the question of our speech, the medium through which we communicate with each other; for all life comes back to the question of our relations with one another."[68] *The Awkward Age* embodies this belief, and James might very well have felt that so revelatory a method justified the reader's deepest attention. Though differing in degree of greatness, *The Awkward Age* is no more densely packed in dialogue than *Ulysses* in allusions or *The Sound and the Fury* in consciousness of time. One should accept its means because they objectify James's meaning as perfectly as those of Joyce or Faulkner objectify theirs. To understand *The Awkward Age* one has only to pay the closest attention to what is said. Its characters never lie, unless they confess their lies subsequently, and their obliquities are always temporary. Since their speech, which reveals their inner lives, takes place in the same temporal medium in which they live, sequence is central to the meaning of the novel. Explication must therefore stick more closely to the sequence of events than is usually amiable.

The novel's first book is exposition. Mr. Longdon, an old man who makes his home in the country, encounters the young swell Vanderbank and discusses with him the Brookenhams' domestic problem: the future of Nanda. Longdon is funny by virtue of the same old-fashioned values that make him admirable, and Van, who is subtly dissatisfied with the modern world, immediately adopts the old fellow.

Longdon's devotion to the past is symbolized by an unrequited adoration for Mrs. Brookenham's mother, whose memory he tends like a priest. Book One is named after Lady Julia, but her disembodied spirit hovers over the action with decreasing force as Longdon comes to realize that her granddaughter, who resembles her, is really as admirable, though presumably less pure. But before Longdon forgets a world long gone and accepts modernity, James shows what a feat of tolerance that will be.

The modern world is typified by Mrs. Brookenham's "circle," a group of witty but heartless gossips who treat one another's problems as mere grist for the mill. Will Mrs. Cashmore bolt with one of her innumerable lovers or will she stay home in countenanced mutual adultery with her husband? She does the latter. Has Tishy Grendon the right to be unhappy at her husband's neglect or is she being foolishly ceremonious? She is. Does the Duchess hide her affair with Lord Petherton behind his friendship with Mitchett or is she platonic and disinterested? She isn't. The modern world is dominated by cash, so that Mrs. Brookenham's preeminence is precarious, despite her brilliance, because of her limited means. Forced to maneuver, she obtains a civil service post for her dim-witted husband (through methods we are free to suspect) and trains her eldest son to sponge off his friends (a lesson he learns so well that he succeeds in annexing the indecisive Mrs. Cashmore). But she is defeated by her romantic daughter, who will not let herself be sold.

As Longdon sees midway through the book, "society . . . can never have been anything but increasingly vulgar. The point is that in the twilight of time . . . it had made out much less how vulgar it *could* be. It did its best, very probably, but there were too many superstitions it had to get rid of. It has been throwing them overboard one by one, so that now the ship sails uncommonly light." Though the debased modern world has abandoned Longdon's pieties, it has not abandoned his traditional manners. Though its familiarity breeds essential contempt for life, its respect for wit, charm, and "good breeding" is boundless. Ironically, even in such an ambience, the old ways count. Thus, though the Duchess is sleeping with Petherton, she is determined that her niece, Agnesina (Little Aggie), should know no more about sleep than one learns unconsciously. Enrolling her charge in "Mr. Garlick's class in Modern Light Literature" is as much contact as the Duchess will permit Aggie with contemporaneity. When Mr. Longdon is introduced to her, the girl is engrossed in a volume of "*Stories from English History*" which "leaves the horrors out," while the Duchess trills: "We like to know the cheerful, happy, *right* things. There are so many, after all."

But whereas Longdon is devoted to morality sanctified by tradition, the Duchess is devoted to morality salable in the marketplace. Loose-living men like to marry virgins; such wisdom women like the Duchess have absorbed. Thus Aggie must become a creature of "emphasized virginity . . . [as if] prepared . . . by a cluster of doting nuns, cloistered daughters of ancient houses and educators of similar products." Therefore in Book Two, the Duchess warns Mrs. Brook that her indifference to what Nanda finds out will render the girl unmarriageable. But Mrs. Brook had thought herself safe by singling out Mitchy, who is both in love with Nanda and utterly indifferent to her possible sophistication. Mitchy, however, knows that Nanda loves Van. "You really have never suspected?" he asks when the mother shows her astonishment. Despite the magnitude of her surprise, Mrs. Brook quickly recovers to predict the book's outcome: "He may 'like' Nanda as much as you please: he'll never, never, . . . he'll never come to the scratch. And to feel that as *I* do . . . can only be, don't you also see? to want to save her." Brilliant as she is, Mrs. Brook also foresees what saving Nanda will require: "I'm not proud *pour deux sous*. And some day, on some awful occasion, I shall show it."

In Book Three, Longdon asks Mitchy why Van is a bachelor; when Mitchy cites poverty as the cause, Longdon determines to provide Van's wherewithal. Meanwhile, having assumed that Nanda won't marry Mitchy and that Van won't marry Nanda, Mrs. Brook determines to insure her daughter's future by means of Longdon. In Book Four, Van tells Mrs. Brook that Longdon is interested in Nanda's welfare, and, to test him, she suggests that the interest might also be turned to his advantage. But when Van shrinks from so venal a plan, Mrs. Brook makes him promise to work on Nanda's behalf—which he does.

At an estate which Mitchy has rented for the weekend, Van meets Nanda in the garden. While they discuss their mutual involvement in Mrs. Brook's world, Nanda forthrightly insists that she can't rise above it: "I shall never change—I shall be always just the same." "It's astonishing," Van muses, "how at moments you remind me of your mother!" "Ah, there it is! It's what I shall never shake off," the girl admits, though she adds that Van has helped to bring her down, in both the spiritual and the domestic sense.

Meanwhile, the Duchess, who wants the wealthy Mitchett for her niece, tells Longdon to propose to Van on Nanda's behalf; since if Nanda is out of the way, Mitchy will marry Aggie by default. When Longdon does propose to settle a fortune on Van if he marries Nanda, Van hesitates as if in consciousness of some prior claim. He confesses that had he loved Nanda no pressure would have been required; and though he spares Longdon's feelings when the latter avows his intention to bribe, Van seems taken aback by Longdon's dubious means. It is not only the bribery (however they rechristen it): "I'm a mass of corruption!" Van protests; to which Longdon replies, "If you're good enough for me, you're good enough, as you thoroughly know, on whatever head, for any one." But still Van refuses to commit himself; the rest of the book shows why, and thereby, how the modern world manages to thrive, despite its corruption.

Mrs. Brook understands Van's reasons quite well, and she states them for us in her conversation. "What dear Van will find at the end that he can't face will be, don't you see? just this fact of appearing to have accepted a bribe," she says, knowing full well that Van will not compromise his precious sense of being in but not of his world. And when Van speculates that, as a sort of recompense, Nanda might get a greater fortune if he doesn't marry her, Mrs. Brook triumphantly proclaims that he now has a moral excuse to dignify his refusal. Attributing to him what she confessed to lacking herself, she sums it up: "He's proud."

Van tries to deemphasize his own responsibility for Nanda's unhappiness by shifting the blame to the heartless lucidity with which Mrs. Brook and Mitchy discuss her fate. But when he accuses her mother of "playing with . . . the idea of Nanda's happiness," the mother retorts, "I'm not playing." At this point, the alert reader should remember that Van and Longdon, especially the latter, are more liable to the charge. When Longdon offered his own good opinion as an answer to Van's doubt that he would be a suitable husband, the pure old man was guilty of something very like arrogance; however benign his intentions, his project *is* a bribe. Ironically, the immoral Mrs. Brook plays her hand more decently.

As she reveals to Mitchy, she could easily bring Van to deny Nanda by informing him, as she rightly suspects, that Nanda knows about the bribe. Such a revelation would stop Van cold, for such a man could never bear his future wife to know he had been bought. Yet she disdains so gross a ploy, for, after her fashion, she is honorable. As in the novellas already discussed,

James shows that virtuous people can bribe and manipulate; but he goes further in *The Awkward Age* to show that the worldly can play fair.

Forbearing to embarrass him, Mrs. Brook gives Van ample time to disprove her judgment. But when she learns that Nanda has eliminated Van's rival, Mitchy, by advising him to marry Aggie and that Van still hesitates, she determines to strike. This she does at Tishy Grendon's party.

One of the nicest ironies in *The Awkward Age* is the "set's" horror at modern French literature. With a cynicism possible only in the depraved, Mrs. Brook's friends despise in fiction what they enact in life. When Van arrives at Tishy's, he finds Nanda alone with one of the incriminating novels. This offends him, the more so when Nanda says she read the book, which Van had given her mother, to make sure that it wasn't too risqué for the susceptible hostess. It was. Soon the guests arrive, among them Aggie, who is now making up for all her lost years of innocence by committing adultery with her aunt's lover. While Aggie and Petherton are romping in another room, Mrs. Brook determines to show Longdon that Nanda must be his. Thus, when Petherton and Aggie run in grappling with the French novel, Mrs. Brook seizes the opportunity to force Nanda's admission of having read it. Here, she overreaches herself. Thinking to give Van incontrovertible proof of Nanda's sophistication, she succeeds only in exposing the Duchess, Aggie, Mitchy, Petherton—and Van, as the owner of an incriminating volume.*

The rest of the novel is denouement. Having publicly called Nanda home, Mrs. Brook is forced to wait until Longdon comes for her. During this period, Nanda is installed in her own draw-

---

* James heightens the irony of the scene when he has Aggie protest that she thought, since the book was Van's, it was innocent. What Mrs. Brook exposes is not so much Nanda to Van as Van and the others to themselves. His cultivated aura of respectability begins to vanish at the exposure of his literary taste; their decorous avoidance of public scandal is shattered in the same stroke.

ing room upstairs, while her mother presides over one emptied in her attempt to insure Nanda's future. That this was her principal motive throughout is made clear in a long conversation with her husband that should answer most questions raised by the plot. Van comes to visit Nanda but goes without seeing her. Realizing that his omission is as open a denial as he will ever provide, Mrs. Brook asks her husband to see that Nanda is apprised of Van's bolting. "Are you in such a hurry she should know that Van doesn't want her?" the dunderhead asks, to which she replies, "What do you call a hurry, when I've waited nearly a year? Nanda may know or not as she likes—may know whenever: if she doesn't know pretty well by this time she's too stupid for it to matter. My only pressure's for Mr. Longdon." And when Edward sighs over his daughter's fate, Mrs. Brook again speaks the truth: "Does she strike you as so poor . . . with so awfully much done for her?" Mrs. Brook admits that she too wanted Van for Nanda; in that way she would have provided for the girl and still have kept her lover close. (She is honest and fair, not good.) Moreover she knows that Van would "like her if he could"; and when Edward asks why Van was unable, Mrs. Brook replies, "It's *me*."

> "And, what's the matter with 'you'?"
> She made, at this, a movement that drew his eyes to her own, and for a moment she dimly smiled at him. "That's the nicest thing you ever said to me. But ever, *ever*, you know."
> "Is it?" She had her hand on his sleeve, and he looked almost awkward.
> "Quite the very nicest. Consider that fact well, and, even if you only said it by accident, don't be funny—as you know you sometimes *can* be—and take it back. It's all right. It's charming, isn't it? when our troubles bring us more together."

This exchange, culminating in her confession that she loved Van, is a miracle of economy, surprise, and power. Despite the

note of bitterness in Mrs. Brook's words, there is an overtone of
lamentation, revealing the waste of her wonderful capacities. To
have been married to such a man, one as incapable of love as of
appreciation! Now we see why Mrs. Brook has needed a circle of
admirers, opportunities to use her intellectual powers—and Van.
Despite her immorality and cold chic, she has been a pearl worn
round the neck of a donkey, and we sympathize with her frustration. That James could make us sympathize is one of his supreme
human as well as artistic triumphs—demonstrating mature compassion where he usually exhibits the censure of a melodramatist.

Yet Mrs. Brook's fate is not tragic, for she lacks the requisite
fervor. More importantly, neither is Nanda's. Nanda doesn't get
Van, but, as Ezra Pound asserted, there isn't any reason why she
should.[69] It is sentimentality, in no way warranted by the action,
to maintain with all critics except Dupee that the book concerns
Nanda's destruction. After all, she only loses a self-divided young
man who doesn't love her, whereas she gains the support of a rich
old one at an age when her future, however bleakly she foresees
it, has not been foreclosed. As Nanda realizes, her mother is the
real loser—of the "set" and of Van.

Thus, when Van visits Nanda on a subsequent occasion, the
girl takes the opportunity to tell him not to forget Mrs. Brook.
Though surely virtuous, this action is less heroic than critics have
made out. Nanda now knows that Van never loved her, just as
she had always known that her mother was her rival. In similar
circumstances (*The Wings of the Dove*) James would try to make
the reader ignore the more innocent rival's sexual interest, but
he doesn't evade this in *The Awkward Age*. Nor does he make
Nanda's renunciation in favor of the other woman into a saintly
act, since Nanda never had anything to renounce.

In their last scene together, Van confesses why he could never
have loved her. "I'm only afraid, I think, of your conscience";
and when she seems puzzled, he gently urges, "Think it over—

quite at your leisure—and someday you'll understand." This, said with one eye on the reader, points to the mystery's key, corroborating Mrs. Brook's explanation of why Vanderbank won't propose. Cherishing the idea of his own innocence, Van can entertain Longdon's offer of salvation but cannot bring himself to marry its means. For if Van accepts a bribe, he will be forfeiting virtue; and if he married a girl so knowing as Nanda, she would realize how pitifully weak was his power to abstain. As Mrs. Brook says, Van would have liked to be rich and adored, but not at the cost of self-esteem. Not to reach the point where one's actions may be publicly condemned is Van's pathetic pretense of innocence. In this, he reveals the ironic significance of Mrs. Brook's "set."

That the set's corruption is a decadent fixation on lost innocence is James's profoundly ironic theme. Though the title seems to apply to girls in general and to Nanda in particular, Aggie exhibits no awkwardness and Nanda very little. It is less young girls than their mothers who are in an awkward position, since young girls, not yet interested in pleasure or money, might become awkwardly censorious. And it is less the mothers who are awkward than the entire *Age*, hovering between a traditional past and a future made bleak by confusion of values and nostalgia for a long-gone certainty. F. R. Leavis and Miss Krook have called the book tragic, but it is rather tragicomic; not only in its tonal mixture but in its cultural implications.

Nowhere is James's refusal to be tragic more apparent than in the very characters who are customarily thought his heroes. Nanda is good because she is guiltless of the egoism, the scheming, and the wantonness of her elders. But she is motivated by the same ironic obsession with innocence, and the errors she commits are even more disastrous. She may appeal to us because of her situation, just as Mrs. Brook repels us with hers; but whereas her mother is witty and accomplished, Nanda is something of a prig. Both Mitchy and her mother agree that she utterly lacks a sense of humor and thus a sense of proportion. Like the telegraphist, her knowledge is defective; for all her protestations of seeing "everything," she never fathoms the power of Mitchy's love. When Mr. Longdon asks if she might consider the man, she not only vehemently denies interest in Mitchy, she "positively enjoy[s] telling [Longdon] there's nothing in it" on Mitchy's part. Therefore, when she foolishly suggests that Mitchy marry Aggie, she fails to understand his motive for compliance. At the end of the book, Mitchy proposes to assuage his marital disappointment with her in the worldly manner, but she predictably refuses. Yet she acknowledges that recompense is due him for the mess she has made of his life.

Mitchy adored her as much as she adored Van. She could not love him for reasons that are ultimately even more unamiable than Vanderbank's: she finds Mitchy ugly. Moreover, as he asserts, Nanda can only love a man who won't love her. "Do you positively *like* to love in vain?" he asks, to which she returns a frank "Yes." Dorothea Krook, who wishes to maintain that Nanda is the book's tragic heroine, asserts that her "perversity" here proves that her ambience has been infectious, which it surely was.[70] Miss Krook, however, wants us to take the infection as a reminder that otherwise Nanda is invulnerable; but as the girl herself says, she had "become a sort of drain-pipe with everything flowing through." Indeed her shamed sense of having been corrupted is a negative force. For it leads to the grotesque error of believing in Aggie's counterfeit innocence and of recommending that, for the betterment of his soul, Mitchy trade his fortune for false coin.

Despite his generous and decorous nature, Mr. Longdon is equally blameworthy. His attempt to reform the age through Vanderbank is as mischievous as Nanda's attempt to reform Mitchy. No more than the other characters, Longdon is nostalgic for a prelapsarian past, but he learns from Nanda that the present deserves to be met on its own terms. Ezra Pound accused James of "a long tenzone . . . a long argument for the old lavender" in the figure of Longdon;[71] but James is far more critical of Longdon than Pound suggests. Mildred Hartsock puts the matter well: "The irony in the portraiture of Longdon is that he begins with judgments as superficial as those of Van or the Duchess; he is sentimentally drawn to Nanda because of her physical resemblance to her dead grandmother whom Longdon loved. But, as Nanda's honesty forces him to look at old ways, he comes to love and respect her for what she is. . . . The aspect of Longdon with which James identifies is his openness to new experience."[72] In short, Longdon grows beyond Van, who, though younger, is more atavistic.

Tragedy concerns conflict between mutually exclusive truths; *The Awkward Age* is a tragicomedy about conflicting falsities. Neither group deserves our approval; neither the "set" with its elegant indifference, nor Nanda and Longdon with their disastrous attempts at salvation. Therefore, *The Awkward Age* is the first work in which James fully abandons his dream that virtue might restore a golden age—if only for a saving remnant. In *The Sacred Fount* he rebounds from this confession, just as, after his greatest portrayal of impotent innocence (*The Ambassadors*), he would create his most miraculous embodiment of virtue in triumph (*The Wings of the Dove*). But *The Awkward Age* was an essential first step in bringing James to the amoralism of *The Golden Bowl*. That astonishing near revision of his entire sense of life is based not only on his willingness to scale innocence down but on his ability to face the secondary power of everything he most valued. *The Awkward Age* brought James very far in that direction, but its good characters are still magically unscathed— through the characteristically invoked power of money. In another series of masterpieces James came closer to seeing that innocence could not be spared. "Daisy Miller" makes a good transition from the critiques of innocence to the contemplations of its defeat because it shows that virtue is itself ruinous.

With ample justification, "Daisy Miller" has always been one of James's most popular tales. Despite the contemporary misinterpretation which has made it a chapter of literary history, it is also one of James's most widely understood.[73] For "Daisy Miller" is the simplest, clearest expression of James's knowledge that innocence can be guilt. Daisy herself is guilty of the social innocence that makes her frivolous and the sexual innocence that makes her a flirt. Nevertheless, she is less culpable than those who persecute her. Her story is really about them.

From its beginning, the novella focuses on Winterbourne. Before we become involved in his questioning of Daisy's character, we are invited to question his: "He was some seven-and-twenty years of age; when his friends spoke of him, they usually said that he was at Geneva, 'studying.' When his enemies spoke of him they said—but, after all [James coyly remarks], he had no enemies." Winterbourne is James's definitive portrayal of the fastidious young man who won't reach for a woman until someone certifies her safety. He is Acton with his specious worldliness, Vanderbank with his ironic nostalgia, Longmore, Waterville, and a host of others. In his case, however, James exposes the whole range of flaws of which the others are specializations.

Winterbourne's concern for innocence stems from sexual reserve. Like Waterville, the tide of his opinion ebbs and flows with the motions of Daisy's virginal regard. When arriving at Rome and finding her involved with Giovanelli, Winterbourne's censure is inspired by her apparent indifference: "He had perhaps not definitely flattered himself that he had made an ineffaceable impression upon her heart, but he was annoyed at hearing a state of affairs so little in harmony with an image that had lately flitted in and out of his own meditations; the image of a very pretty girl looking out of an old Roman window and asking herself urgently when Mr. Winterbourne would arrive." Actually, Daisy's flirtation with Giovanelli is an even more pertinent sign of her interest; but, ironically, the man who worries that she may be a coquette needs a more open declaration before he declares himself. Winterbourne was "rather annoyed at Miss Miller's want of appreciation of the zeal of an admirer," James wryly records, "who on his way down to Rome had stopped neither at Bologna nor at Florence, simply because of a certain sentimental impatience."

This sentimental impatience is weaker than Winterbourne's anxiety for his reputation. His pedantic deference to his aunt, like his collusion with Mrs. Walker, shows how deeply he needs the world's esteem. When Mrs. Walker purports to advise Daisy, for the girl's welfare, against strolling with Giovanelli on the Pincio, Winterbourne does not reject her high-handed manner, any more than he criticizes the brutal way in which she snubs Daisy, an invited guest at her own party. Like Lady Demesne in "The Siege of London," Mrs. Walker is improper while upholding propriety, but Winterbourne cares too much for her acceptance to point that out. In his obsession with respectability, Winterbourne allies himself with a bunch of jabbering old women capable of dissecting Daisy's reputation while the "vesper-service was going forward in splendid chants and organ-tones in [an] adjacent choir" of St. Peter's.

Ultimately, Winterbourne is guilty of a failure of feeling. In no other example of this type is James so clear on that point. Having sold his soul to a fashionable world, Winterbourne, like Waterville or Vanderbank, can no longer trust his instincts— "and his reason could not help him." Faced with a woman full of the usual contradictions, Winterbourne desperately reaches for "the formula that applied." Yet he cannot find it. The more his heart inclines toward her, the more he "find[s] himself reduced to chopping logic."

In part, "Daisy Miller" recalls "The Turn of the Screw," whose ambiguity it avoids. Like the children, Daisy is a baffling mixture of innocence and seductiveness. Yet Winterbourne, like the governess, cannot love her because of her ambiguity. But whereas James suggests that the governess's hostility might be only a reaction to external evil, James shows that Winterbourne's suspicions, however responsive to facts, are unquestionably perverse. Thus, Winterbourne literally kills the girl he loves in an effort to purify her.

Daisy dies of Roman fever, but James shows that the fever is a response to Winterbourne. When the young man confronts Daisy with her Italian in the Colosseum, Giovanelli assures the girl that they will be safe if they return home before midnight—a preventive measure which has no physical basis. More significantly, Daisy decides to let herself be infected because of Winterbourne's cruel treatment. When she challenges him to admit whether or not he had thought her engaged, he replies, "I believe that it makes very little difference whether you are engaged or not!" At that point, after "fix[ing]" his eyes "through the gloom," Daisy decides to remain in the air made fatally cold by his contempt. After her death, when Winterbourne learns of her final state, he confesses his responsibility: "I was booked to make a mistake. I have lived too long in foreign parts."

The America for which Winterbourne finally yearns is a symbol of Edenic possibility, a place where love was perfectly innocent and sex benign. It is the America of *The Europeans* and not of the other novels and tales. The bulk of James's fiction is laid in a fallen civilized world, where love is threatening to the fastidious soul. In stories discussed in this chapter, James admits how wrong are those who feel threatened. Laura Wing and the telegraphist are hysterical virgins; the former, we are told, will likely grow up. Vanderbank is sterilized by nostalgia for his own lost innocence, just as Longmore is impotent (except when the sap rises in the forest). Love of innocence can literally kill, as Baron de Mauves and Daisy Miller discover. For a writer too devoted to innocence, even to the degree of fearing sex *per se*, these admissions must have been hard to make. That he was able to make them in tales so witty and shrewd indicates the fundamental strength of James's genius.

CHAPTER EIGHT

The Pupils

With the last three novels we have considered, *What Maisie Knew* and *The Ambassadors* share crucial virtues that set them above James's inferior books. Like *The Europeans* and *Washington Square,* each novel dramatizes both the threat of worldliness and the foolishness of moralism. In a book like *The Wings of the Dove,* James tries to deny that his heroine may be self-seeking, while in one like *The Sacred Fount* he casts too oblique a glance at society's evil. But the moral pretension of Maisie's governess and Strether's employers is lucidly mocked, and the selfishness of Maisie's parents or the lovers' duplicity in *The Ambassadors* is portrayed in candid detail.

But, like *The Awkward Age* (in contrast, say, to *The American* or *The Princess Casamassima*), these novels show that innocence will not remain uncompromised. Debarred by its own logic from accommodation to the world, if it succeeds it also vanishes. So Maisie must learn what Nanda Brookenham learns—that life

will soil her—whereas Newman and Hyacinth can pull their gar-
ments back from the mud, the latter purifying himself even
through the debacle of his suicide. As she loses innocence, Maisie
loses everything; but she does not wanly renounce life. For her,
as for Catherine Sloper, renunciation is a public announcement
that her integrity has been violated, not a dubious expression of
charity toward her enemy, like Milly Theale's, or a self-delighting display of magnanimity, like Newman's. Strether's renunciation more nearly resembles that of Nanda Brookenham: both
acknowledge an incapacity for life. But whereas we must infer
this about Nanda, Strether himself is aware of this implication,
so that *The Ambassadors,* in this way, admits even more fully
than *The Awkward Age* the flaw in cherished innocence.

Another virtue which these novels share is their candid treatment of sex. *What Maisie Knew* offers James's most tenable
indictment of its threatening imperiousness, while *The Ambassadors* is James's most notable attempt since *The Bostonians* to
affirm its claims. Finally, each novel controls the pathos of the
protagonist's ordeal with a comic tone that precludes sentimentality. We are never permitted to forget that Maisie's virtue is
being eroded by maturation, just as we are never permitted to
forget that Strether's innocence makes him a fool. For this reason,
we are all the more likely to sympathize with Maisie (than with
the mysteriously invulnerable Milly) or to feel affection for
Strether (who is not, like Isabel, wept over for having fallen
into a trap).

Maisie's fierce wit and *The Ambassadors*'s gentle irony are, in
fact, supreme instances of Jamesian tragicomedy, but neither this
nor their combination of major themes earns them preeminence
among James's works. Rather, they are his masterpieces because
their plots most clearly articulate his vision. More even than
The Portrait of a Lady, the most structurally comparable of
James's novels, these two books are *Bildungsromans.* Because

James sticks so close to Maisie's or Strether's process of education, we are brought into intimate contact with the things they learn. Moreover, because he gets inside them he can make them persuasive examples of the one Jamesian value that does not often merge with its parody.

As we have seen, Jamesian virtue can be too much like prudishness or self-display, Jamesian innocence too much like ignorance voluntarily maintained for self-enhancement. But in a character like Catherine Sloper, James was able to conceive of a more authentic ideal. Avid for love and apt pupil of life, Catherine is also distinguished by her willingness to serve. But because James does not adopt her point of view, Catherine's marvelous capacity is not the most prominent feature of *Washington Square*. In *What Maisie Knew* and *The Ambassadors* James does focus on his protagonist's power of love, and that makes these books James's most convincing presentations of value. Having taken the measure both of worldliness and morality, James portrays value not as a tendency to reject the world in the name of virtue but as the ability to fight for the fullest realization of earthly possibility. The fight may be doomed, but man can aim no higher. Maisie and Strether, defeatedly but inspiringly, pay their tribute to life.

The pattern of their tribute is contained in one of James's best novellas, though "The Pupil" does not identify worldliness with sex, and Morgan Moreen pays for his innocence more tragically than Maisie or Strether. Like the larger works, this story presents an unusually intelligent and loving innocent who conceives too highly of life's possibilities. It is therefore a good introduction to the novels.[74]

Naturally selfless and honest, Morgan Moreen was unluckily born into a family of *parvenus*. The more they climb, the more ashamed he becomes of their ignoble ambitions; the more they fall, the more Morgan suffers neglect as well as shame. Morgan's mother is introduced wearing "soiled *gants de Suède*," a detail that nicely suggests both her affectation and her ludicrous failure to live up to it. Stroking her son with a "practised but ineffectual hand," she forces him into "curious intuitions and knowledges," despite his tender years.

Therefore, when Morgan's parents, in a rare moment of concern, hire a tutor for their son, the boy gives to Pemberton all the love that formerly lacked an object. Unfortunately, the tutor is not so single-minded. James's opening description tells his story: "The poor young man hesitated and procrastinated." Despite his sensitivity to Morgan's "far-off appeal," Pemberton is only a hired hand. Poor scholar that he is, he must keep his eye on the main chance. To Morgan, he is life itself; but to Pemberton, Morgan is, at best, an opportunity. As things turn out, the opportunity is more moral than financial.

Desiring status and knowledge, as adults will, at first Pemberton believes that "living with [the Moreens] would really be to see life"; but what they show him of life is pathetic and sordid. Nevertheless, though they take advantage of his service and offer nothing in return, Pemberton feels "a fantastic . . . sympathy" with them. For he is as desirous of moral position as they are of social position. Despite their different goals, the Moreens and Pemberton are closer to each other than either is to the child placed in their care. Thus, the ironic point of "The Pupil" is the unexpected similarity between the moralist and the worldling. Each is devoted to self-interest. Morgan is different.

During their walks consecrated to intimacy, Morgan tries to make Pemberton confess that he is not being paid so that some remedy might be found. But Pemberton believes that it would not be "decent to abuse to one's pupil the family of one's pupil" and responds to Morgan's loving solicitude by telling "severely correct" lies. Though he has privately concluded that he "had simply given himself to a band of adventurers," his initial "romantic horror" becomes something more "soothing . . . it pointed a moral, and Pemberton could enjoy a moral." While Morgan suffers over his tutor's ill-treatment, Pemberton remains silent so as to enjoy the delights of martyrdom. Like Christopher Newman, he keeps his scars to himself; but in this case, James shows that apparent magnanimity can really be self-serving. To feel himself eminently proper though victimized, Pemberton has to deny Morgan's concern.

Unsurprisingly, when a better job offers itself, Pemberton is tempted to leave Morgan, though he knows the child's situation to be dreadful. And though Morgan is totally dependent on his friend, he urges the young man to go.

During the tutor's absence, Morgan begins to sicken under repeated indignities and lack of care, giving his mother her great chance. Using the child's illness as an excuse, Mrs. Moreen recalls Pemberton, reminding him that "he had created for himself the gravest of responsibilities." Though the motive behind her assertion is cynical, she is basically correct. Even though the Moreens have thrust Morgan at him, Pemberton's avowed superiority and declared concern have made Morgan his. But what is he to do with the child?

> He could neither really throw off his blighting burden nor find in it the benefit of a pacified conscience or of a rewarded affection. . . . It was all very well of Morgan to count it for reparation that he should now settle on him permanently—there was an irritating flaw in such a view. He saw what the boy had in his mind; the conception that as his friend had had the generosity to come back he must show his gratitude by giving him his life. But the poor friend didn't desire the gift—what could he do with Morgan's dreadful little life? Of course at the same time that Pemberton was irritated he remembered the reason, which was very honourable to Morgan and which dwelt simply in his making one so forget that he was no more than a patched urchin. If one dealt with him on a different basis one's misadventures were one's own fault.

In his professions of superior concern and high capacity, Pemberton had not reckoned with the fervor of childish faith. Alert to moral rewards, Pemberton was less selfless than he had seemed. So, when he is asked to live up to Morgan's pure conception of loyalty, he can only hesitate.* Once more he takes the lad on one of those walks in which his honesty does not match his pupil's. Then, making neither commitment nor disavowal, the tutor returns Morgan to his parents in a mood of expectancy. When Mrs. Moreen offers to give him the child and takes Pemberton's silence for acquiescence, Morgan has "a moment of boyish joy" in the promised relief. But though Pemberton feels that he should say "something enthusiastic," again he hesitates. Unable any longer to believe that his tutor cares more deeply than his parents, Morgan dies, as Mrs. Moreen hurls at his betrayer, "You walked him too far, you hurried him too fast!"

By showing Morgan the limits of adult love, Pemberton did drag the boy into maturity before he could build maturity's defenses. Against his parents' open neglect, Morgan was armed; but what can protect a child against temporizing and ambiguity. As with the boy's body, Pemberton had pulled Morgan's soul only "half out of his mother's hands."

Nevertheless, both the tone and the conception of Morgan's story warn against easy indignation. Sad though it be, "The Pupil" is also gaily and wittily narrated. The Moreens are not monsters but rather charlatans. After their fashion, they even love the child, though they cannot deal with him either through cash or understanding. Nor is Pemberton wholly to be condemned. Impoverished, unmarried, himself scarcely weaned from childhood, the poor young man could hardly be expected to assume so great

---

* In this hesitation, seeking relief from his dilemma, Pemberton almost begins to look forward to the child's death. The passage from which I have quoted ends with the following sentence: "So Pemberton waited in a queer confusion of yearning and alarm for the catastrophe which was held to hang over the house of Moreen."

a responsibility. The claims of innocence are too austere. By dramatizing this theme, "The Pupil" passes beyond praise or blame and thus beyond melodrama. What happened had to happen. Morgan's tribute to the possibility of love could not be supported by anyone other than a child.

Maisie's power of love is also too great for those around her, but she does not die of the gift. Rather, James takes her to the threshold of adolescence where she gains the power to free herself from those who have mocked her capacity. And though the ideal she represents proves unviable in the world of the novel, it remains inspiring to the reader.

Maisie stands for absolute commitment based not on self-interest but on admiration for its object. Such commitment is blocked in her parents and step-parents by the impersonal demands of sex. Doubtless, the sharpness with which James satirizes sex in this novel springs from the perturbation that also gives us Milly Theale and the governess. But in *What Maisie Knew* such perturbation results in overt satire, not covert advocacy; James portrays sex as a force that unites people only momentarily, creating few permanent bonds. The prodigious round of mating that we witness merely exaggerates James's point for comic effect. If man allows himself to be ruled by his glands, he can turn into just the grotesque mixture of irresponsibility and frustration represented by Maisie's parents. Even more than the characters in *The Awkward Age*, who conceal their affairs behind decorous arrangements of reputation, the Faranges graphically enact the squalor of loveless coupling.

Ironically, their very virtues serve their vice. Maisie's mother is witty and lovely, but her wit is employed to score against her husband for his infidelities, while her beauty facilitates her own. With eyes "like Japanese lanterns swung under festal arches," Ida is a sexual amusement park; to one of her lovers, she directs a "face that was like an illuminated garden, turnstile and all, for the frequentation of which he had his season-ticket." As the metaphor suggests, her romances are short-lived; rushing from one to another, "she was always in a fearful hurry, and the lower [her] bosom was cut the more it was to be gathered she was wanted elsewhere." Little wonder that when she finally takes leave of Maisie, after years of neglect, she is off to South Africa for some rest. Maisie's father is also a parody of indiscriminate mating, who is finally seen in the embrace of a "frizzled poodle" of a woman whose only attraction is money.

With such people who have the sexual habits of flies, life contains few elevated pleasures. As a result, the Faranges are coarsened. Beale's most prominent features are a set of predatory teeth and a rough beard with which, on rare occasions of parental display, he "rakes" Maisie's cheek. When Ida surprisingly grabs the child to her maternal bosom, Maisie feels as if she had been "thrust with a smash of glass into a jeweller's shop-front."

When such roughness eventuates in divorce, "the child was provided for," as the book begins with a characteristic flash of irony; but this phrase sounds more comforting than it should. Because Beale cannot return Ida's dowry, Maisie is used to liquidate his debt. Though he is "bespattered from head to foot . . . the mother's character had [also] been damaged . . . [since] the brilliancy of a lady's complexion (and this lady's, in court, was immensely remarked) might be more regarded as showing the spots." As a result, each parent gets half the child that neither wants, while James wryly alludes to the judgment of Solomon. Such "justice" suits a world in which "beauty" is bait for vice, "freedom" the power to indulge one's whims, and where everyone seeks to "square" others the better to take with ease.

However, though her parents do nothing for her, Maisie tries to be a dutiful daughter. Unfortunately, in such circumstances, her loving determination has the effect of making her "a ready vessel for bitterness, a deep little porcelain cup in which biting acids could be mixed." Passed back and forth between their lips, Maisie is forced to brim over with infamies. Soon, however, she comes to realize that she can protect them by seeming too stupid to report what they have said. In the name of love, she is forced to lie; but this is only the first occasion when she will have to express her virtue through means that seem to deny it.

When her father hires and marries her governess at the same time that her mother marries the handsome Sir Claude, Maisie's good intentions are more cruelly traduced. As quickly as the Faranges tired of one another, they tire of their new spouses with even greater haste. Never having known the peace of a stable home or reciprocated loyalty, Maisie attempts to attach herself to her step-parents; but all she accomplishes is a new liaison. Heartbreakingly, the innocent child brags of having brought Mrs. Beale and Sir Claude together, but what she has done is help them to bed.

Nevertheless, Maisie continues her efforts to serve. When, for example, she and Claude collide with Ida in the comic Kensington Garden scene and Ida consigns Maisie to her newest lover so that she can enjoy a quarrel with Claude, Maisie tries to make the new lover admit a deep attachment to Mrs. Farange. In a subsequent scene, when her father offers insincerely to take her away with him, she pretends to refuse only in order to "let him off with all the honours—with all the appearance of virtue and sacrifice on his side."

But though Maisie remains remarkably selfless despite the ruthlessness with which she is handled, her character suffers erosion. Not only does she learn to lie and scheme, when all she wants is to be candid and giving, she learns to like the intrigue that swirls about her head. Pretending to be ignorant so as not to have to tell wicked stories, she "spoiled [her parents'] fun, but she practically added to her own. She saw more and more; she saw too much."

The "too much" that constitutes what Maisie knew is her insight into the speciousness of both people who propose themselves as alternatives to her heartless parents. First, like Morgan Moreen, Maisie is given a hired guardian, the governess Mrs. Wix, who, like Pemberton, promises to provide the love that her parents have so terribly denied her. But even more lucidly than Pemberton, Mrs. Wix is shown to be only a different kind of opportunist.

Greasy, impoverished Mrs. Wix first looms as a repellent figure. As the dereliction of her parents increases, however, Maisie gradually finds herself ignoring the old woman's ugliness out of gratitude for her affection. But though Mrs. Wix protests her commitment and proclaims her virtue, her loyalty is shifty and her morals dubious. Literally and figuratively cockeyed, her "moral sense," like her "straighteners," is a mechanism designed to help others "recognise the bearing, otherwise doubtful, of her regard." Remove either spectacles or system and her inner deficiency becomes clear. One of Mrs. Wix's eyes may be fixed on others; the other is fixed on herself. Though she counterfeits disinterest, she is almost as selfish as more worldly characters.

James first hints at this irony when Mrs. Wix appears at Beale's, armed with Sir Claude's photograph, to announce that, since Ida has remarried, Maisie now has a home. When the child seizes on the evidence of such hope, there ensues a "struggle between [Mrs. Wix's] fond clutch of it and her capability of every sacrifice for her precarious pupil." Later, with wild comedy, Mrs. Wix makes a more tangible play for Sir Claude.

After Beale and Ida have unmistakably "decamped," Claude hustles the child across the English Channel, hoping to gain time and, eventually, Maisie's acquiescence to forming a *ménage* with him and her stepmother. Unexpectedly, Mrs. Wix arrives, and astonishingly she offers herself as a better alternative. Leave Mrs. Beale, the old woman advises with "infinite variety," and come away with her:

"Here I am; I know what I am and what I ain't; but I say boldly to the face of you both that I'll do better for you, far, than ever she'll even try to. I say it to yours, Sir Claude, even though I owe you the very dress on my back and the very shoes on my feet. I owe you everything—that's just the reason; and to pay it back, in profusion, what can that be but what I want? Here I am, here I am!"— she spread herself into an exhibition that, combined with her intensity and her decorations, appeared to suggest her for strange offices and devotions, for ridiculous replacements and substitutions.

No wonder that during this performance Sir Claude makes a face that "was to abide with his stepdaughter as the very image of stupefaction."

Even the upright Mrs. Wix bends before the force of passion, though she is too ludicrously ugly to represent its appeal. Moreover, she uses her morality to advance her ridiculous suit. Like Dr. Sloper and the governess, Mrs. Wix fills a child's head with evils out of presumed concern for its moral health. But though the evidence for self-interested morality is dubious in "The Turn of the Screw," Mrs. Wix is an even clearer example than Dr. Sloper that a moral warning, even when correct, may be given principally for the advantage of the donor.[75]

Sir Claude, the other possible source of Maisie's safety, is also impelled by passion; but, young and attractive as he is, he knows more than Mrs. Wix of how passion may compromise. Maisie's growing knowledge about Claude provides the book's central drama.

Because she is a child and thus judges things by their look, Maisie immediately loves Sir Claude, just as she had loved Mrs. Beale, because he is beautiful. Soon her love is deepened by his kindness to her. Despite his many involvements with women, Claude confesses a particular affection for children. "I'm a family-man," he avers, and when Mrs. Beale asks him why he never married a family-woman, Claude provides an explanation that the novel labors to support: "There *are* no family-women—hanged if there are! None of them want any children—hanged if they do!" Because of his beauty, Claude has long been the object of implacable, unstabilizing desire; but, though he enjoys sex, he is drawn to the steady, disinterested affection that is characteristic of Maisie. To Claude, the little girl is always "old man" or "old boy"; only with her can he feel comfortable and safe.

Though she is too young to fathom these motives, Maisie is thrilled by his preference and does all she can to recompense his kindness. As always, her good intentions bear ironic fruit, yet she willingly lies to protect Sir Claude and Mrs. Beale so long as he is the unconscious beneficiary of her deceit. When, however, she discovers that he wants her to lie, she is distressed at "the first small glimpse of something in him that she wouldn't have expected."

Maisie's distress increases when she begins to learn that Claude himself is living a lie. Too young to have adopted a code of sexual ethics that James has already mocked in the character of Mrs. Wix, Maisie never objects to Claude's promiscuity, which, insofar as her innocence comprehends it, seems merely the sign of his undeniable appeal. But during one of their conversations, when Maisie is confessing her childish fear of her mother and Mrs. Beale, she makes a shocking discovery about Claude's attitude toward the ladies. When he echoes her dread of Ida, Maisie innocently asks, "Why, then, did you marry her?" to which he puzzlingly replies, "Just because I *was* afraid." "Even when she loved you?" "That made her," Claude insists, "the more alarming." For Maisie, who has had so little of it, being loved is a blessing. For Claude, who has experienced love in its adult form, the blessing is mixed. Maisie is too young at this point in the book to understand what Claude is trying to tell her. Later, she will learn that adults, unlike children, are capable of wanting what they do not will and of doing what they cannot approve.

Though she has not yet comprehended this important fact of life, she begins to show its effects. In order to see more of Sir Claude, Maisie agrees to spend as much time as possible at Mrs. Beale's house, since Claude is now more often to be found there than at home. But this decision, as Claude points out, has the effect of throwing Mrs. Wix out of a job. Seeing that Maisie's love of him threatens to dilute the very disinterested loyalty that constitutes her appeal, Claude responds to Maisie's suggestion "with the first faint note of asperity she had ever heard him sound."

Maisie must gradually learn that her beloved Claude is the slave of passions that shame him. He, on the other hand, admires her integrity of feeling because he has this capacity for shame. The remainder of their relationship is a contest between Claude's desire to keep Maisie's virtue intact and his desire to keep her person in his company. Eventually, he will acknowledge that the two objectives are incompatible and will therefore help her to free herself from the net of egotism in which she has been struggling.

Actually, the climax comes about as much through Maisie's developing grasp of the situation as through his. Because she understood Mrs. Wix's designs on the young man and because Maisie's love could admit no contradiction, the child had always resisted her governess's criticism of Claude's weakness. As the action nears its conclusion, Maisie begins to see that Mrs. Wix was right. During a tense moment when they are fleeing their entanglements, Maisie notices Claude ogling "a young woman . . . [who] sweep[s] past them on her way to the dining-room, leaving an impression of a strong scent which mingled . . . with the hot aroma of food." And at an even more crucial moment in their flight to Boulogne, "she seemed literally to see him give . . . up . . . *her* affairs" while he stands gazing at the "fine stride and shining limbs of a young fishwife."

Out of her great love, Maisie had been willing to lie, to repudiate Mrs. Wix, and to accept the precarious role of stepdaughter to a high-living ne'er-do-well despite her long-starved need for safety. All this seemed possible because Maisie had believed in Claude's fidelity. Like Morgan Moreen, however, she must learn that good intentions are not enough. Claude is not free to love her. Moreover, any love he feels could work her enslavement. When she learns this, Maisie fights to get free.

After Claude establishes the child and Mrs. Wix at Boulogne, he returns to England, so Maisie hopes, in order to settle his affairs. Presumably, he will break with Mrs. Beale, satisfying both the governess's antipathy to an adulterous household and the child's distaste for a relationship he wants with only part of his soul. But, to her surprise, Mrs. Beale precedes Sir Claude back to France, while, to her horror, the woman is quickly able to bribe and flatter Mrs. Wix into abandoning her objections to Mrs. Beale's relationship with Sir Claude. Now Maisie sees that she must rely totally on herself, for even the moralistic Mrs. Wix can be bought.

Putting on the hat with which Mrs. Beale had sought to bribe *her*—the most lady-like garment she has ever owned—Maisie goes with Claude to a kind of assignation, though it takes place in the morning and is accompanied by coffee and buns. In a poignant parody of seduction, Maisie attempts to woo Claude with her innocence, hoping to free him from a commitment that shames him into lies. Her project frightens her by its effrontery, but at the same time she senses a new sort of power:

his fear was sweet to her, beautiful and tender to her, was having coffee and buttered rolls and talk and laughter that were no talk and laughter at all with her; his fear was in his jesting postponing perverting voice; it was just in this make-believe way he had brought her out to imitate the old London playtimes, to imitate indeed a relation that had wholly changed, a relation that she had with her very eyes seen in the act of change when, the day before in the salon, Mrs. Beale rose suddenly before her.

Understanding in a flash that he is afraid to tell her that Mrs. Beale has ensnared him again, Maisie also understands that she can use this fear, as it were, to rival Mrs. Beale. It is at this point in the novel that Maisie is in clearest danger of becoming manipulative and egotistic, like the adults.[76]

However, though she does want Sir Claude, she opposes his lover not out of jealousy but in order to give Claude a chance to separate his preferences from his passions. This she does, impetuously, as, strolling back to their hotel, they spy a train pulling out for Paris. Offering, as a sign of her total disinterest, to run away without luggage, and understanding in the precociousness of the moment the very French of which she had always been so poor a pupil, Maisie invites Claude to board the train. But whereas she can relinquish the security granted by her governess as well as her obligation to the woman, he cannot give up Mrs. Beale, though he is less obligated to than fearful of his paramour.

Had Claude acceded, Maisie's triumph would have been compromised; appealing to emotion—though not the same emotion inspired by Mrs. Beale—it should have imitated the latter's manipulation of Claude's will. Now that Maisie sees how little Claude had been tempted, she decides to appeal to him in the form of a proposal, so as to make his response premeditated and thus significant. Though Maisie knows that she can keep the man she so loves by agreeing to live with him and Mrs. Beale, she also knows that Claude himself does not want this. Were he able, he would repudiate his lover. Thus she gives him one last chance to do so, telling him she will wait, as he considers her plan, near the statue of the Golden Virgin, a sign of the purity and freedom that enable her even to conceive he might imitate her behavior.

Wanting to agree with a plan whose purpose he understands, Claude is unable to do so. All he *can* do is pay tribute to her belief in him by insisting that she not be turned into a convenience. When they return to the hotel and find that Mrs. Wix has thought better of her collusion with Mrs. Beale, Claude announces that the child cannot be used to legitimize his love affair but that she must be permitted to depart with the woman who, under the circumstances, is most capable of caring for her. Mrs. Beale rages against his decision, making perfectly good points against Mrs. Wix, but Claude remains steadfast. Then, exchanging glances with "the eyes of those who have done for each other what they can," Maisie and Claude say goodbye.

Trapped as he is by sexual desire, Claude could no more support Maisie's life than Pemberton, trapped by circumstance, could support the life of Morgan Moreen. But he can liberate in Maisie something far deeper than the moral sense—a combination of prudery and self-interest—that Mrs. Wix had so tried to inculcate. When Maisie refuses to be made use of, Claude greets her stubbornness with "a kind of ecstasy." For he sees in the child a self-respect that he is good enough to appreciate, though too old to possess.

However, though Claude insists it would be wrong to go on abusing Maisie's innocence, how has her innocence sustained her? By this time, she is almost mature; will maturation maintain her integrity and freedom any more than it has maintained that of the other characters? And what of her life with Mrs. Wix? Surely, the woman is at the moment a more suitable guardian than Claude or Mrs. Beale, but has she not been discredited for the long haul? The last sentence reminds us that Mrs. Wix's capacity for understanding is, even at her age, far inferior to that of her pupil. And so we close the book, wondering, along with the governess, at what Maisie knew, and wondering even more what her knowledge can possibly do for her. In *The Ambassadors*, by presenting a man who learns Maisie's lesson later in life and thus with more equanimity, James shows us.

The Ambassadors is James's rueful study of a man who had reached middle age without comprehending life's moral ambiguity. Like Maisie, Lambert Strether must understand that beautiful and gifted adults can sacrifice integrity to passion; like Maisie and Morgan Moreen, he must see through representatives both of worldliness and morality. But whereas Morgan is killed by his discovery and Maisie's casts her into a sort of limbo, Strether adjusts to his disillusionment, even going so far as to support the morally ambiguous figure who was its cause. This gesture—not only the novel's symmetrical structure or rich metaphors—places *The Ambassadors* at the summit of James's wisdom. Except for Maggie Verver (who will be considered in my conclusion) no other Jamesian protagonist comprehends life with such poise. And when Strether concludes his education by confessing that poise is too difficult to maintain, James criticizes him for his moral nostalgia. In weaker books, James cannot decide whether the world is good or bad; in *The Ambassadors* he shows that it is simultaneously both. In weaker books, James advocates an innocence less sound than he intends; in *The Ambassadors* he shows that innocence is childish. In no other novel does James make such peace with things as they are.

This adjustment is precisely what Strether was kept from by his tradition. Reared in ascetic, moralizing Woollett, whose taste for righteousness he epitomizes, Strether is nevertheless intelligent enough to recognize something arid in the virtues of his past. Sent by Mrs. Newsome to bring her son home, Strether takes the job as much to join in Chad's worship of Paris as to return the young man to the Woollett way. This is why he is so anxious to avoid Waymarsh at the port of debarkation, for Strether's friend represents all he most wishes to leave behind.

Though Strether is already aware of Woollett's shortcomings at the beginning of the novel, subsequent events provide further enlightenment. Not only is Woollett too simple-minded to appreciate Madame de Vionnet and the wonderful education she has given Chad, its moral simplicities are insincere. Mrs. Newsome may be as invulnerable as some "iceberg in a Northern sea," but when her compatriots reach Paris they instantly melt.

Waymarsh is so frightened of Europe that he passes through the Continent like "a person established in a railway coach with a forward inclination." Nothing he sees there measures up to his high-pitched American values. Yet, as James wittily shows, Waymarsh is oddly susceptible to what he pretends to deplore. Shortly after we meet him, he takes up with the pointedly named Miss Barrace.

The Pococks, Chad's sister and brother-in-law, are even funnier examples of Woollett's shallow rectitude. Sent out by Mrs. Newsome when Strether shows signs of a dangerous sympathy to Chad's temptress, Sarah and Jim are certain that the woman is a whore. But Jim can't wait to enjoy the very vices from which he is presumably trying to save his relative. Scarcely off the boat, he wishes to make a start by finding his way to the Varieties, and when Strether confesses to an acquaintance with them, Jim responds with "a play of innuendo as vague as a nursery rhyme, yet as aggressive as an elbow in his side." While Mr. Pocock indulges his salaciousness at the nineteenth-century Follies, his wife becomes involved in the job of replacing Miss Barrace at the center of Waymarsh's attention. Like Mrs. Wix, the Woollett contingent is far less moral than moralistic.

When Strether understands this, as a result of having discovered Waymarsh's affair with Mrs. Pocock, he decides to avenge himself on the meanness with which they view Madame de Vionnet by supporting their loss of moral superiority. Thus, in a comic parody of his famous "live" speech, he encourages Waymarsh to pursue his lady. "*Let* yourself," Strether breathes with more boldness, "go—in all agreeable directions. These are precious hours—at our age they mayn't recur. Don't have it to say to yourself at Milrose, next winter, that you hadn't courage for them. . . . Live up to Mrs. Pocock!" and when Waymarsh concludes this scene by repeating his earlier advice that Strether quit venal Paris, our hero is happy to perceive a diminution in his friend's "old intensity."

But Strether goes too far in mocking Woollett. At the end of the novel we learn that his friends have understood far better than he the basis for Chad's liaison with Madame de Vionnet. What Strether must now free himself from is not, as critics have generally contended, his ascetic, inexperienced past but the loyalty toward worldly Paris he too simply forms by way of reaction.[77] During the scene with Waymarsh, he knows what he is advising; during the more famous scene that it parodies, Strether does not understand his key term. This is what his adventure must teach him. When he first visits the apartment of Madame de Vionnet, he nearly swoons before its combination of history and loveliness; in their last interview, he smells blood in the history and discovers that the loveliness includes duplicity and waste. The "vast bright Babylon" that shimmers before Strether on his second morning in Paris "seemed all surface one moment [and] . . . all depth the next." The depth is what Strether must fathom.

Because he does so reluctantly, the book achieves humor. Resembling Morgan and Maisie in his desire to think only the best of those he admires, Strether's capacity for self-deception is greater. In the manner of children, Morgan and Maisie cannot shield themselves from the brute force of facts. Too honest to hide behind Woollett's moral armor, Strether is nevertheless able to construct his own. But whereas Woollett's presumptions are censorious and self-righteous, Strether's are loving and appreciative. As a result, we sympathize with him because his errors are well intentioned; but they are errors, and we cannot see how bravely candid a book this is until we understand how James mocks Strether's folly.

To begin with, James shows us that Strether has gone over to the enemy before he even knows what it is like. Not only does he wish to avoid Waymarsh at dockside, but this wish is "instinctive." When he meets Maria Gostrey, he confesses his origin in so plaintive a manner that she responds, "You say that . . . as if you wanted one immediately to know the worst." Though he has avowedly tasted little pleasure in life, he begs that Maria win him to its cause: "Is it really an 'order' from you?—that I shall take the job? *Will* you give yourself up?" "If I only could! But that's the deuce of it—that I never can. No—I can't." "But you want to at least?" "Oh, unspeakably!" "Ah then, if you'll try." Strether will try, so hard that in the first chapter, before anything has happened, he already intimates that he shall never marry Mrs. Newsome.

This fervent desire to become worldly explains the speed with which Strether denounces Woollett's attitude toward Chad and Madame de Vionnet. His preparation for apostasy is suggested by his first bout of theatergoing, in which, before a spectacle concerning "a bad woman in a yellow frock who made a pleasant weak good-looking young man in perpetual evening dress do the most dreadful things. . . . Strether . . . was vaguely anxious over a certain kindness into which he found himself drifting" toward the gentleman. When just such a gentleman steps from the play into Strether's box, he takes the fact thus shockingly introduced in the same spirit of aesthetic appreciation with which he viewed the drama. From Chad's good looks he infers his good morals, and from Chad's good morals he infers that Madame de Vionnet must be mentor rather than mistress. As yet, he cannot understand that she may be both, that good looks may imply only good manners, and that art is an abstraction from reality.

Strether has the soul of an artist, but James reveals how bitter-sweet a fact that can be, with what cause for embarrassment as well as pride when art is all admiration without negative capability. Having lost his youth and his son through deficient powers of involvement, Strether determines to love life—Paris, Chad, Madame de Vionnet—as he feels he should have in days when he was distracted by his "double consciousness." Deliberately simplifying things, Strether courts affirmation, shuns qualifications, begs to be awakened by those earthly powers that mock reason. To him, Chad is "the young man marked out by women . . . and . . . the dignity, the comparative austerity . . . of this character affected him almost with awe."

In this reverential mood, he enters Gloriani's garden, the great postlapsarian world, "a nursery of young priests" indulging in black rites within an atmosphere "too thick for prompt discrimination." But Strether does not wish to discriminate and so takes the diplomats and *demi-mondaines* for worshipers at a cult, without wondering what they worship. Face to face with Gloriani, Strether forgets his intimation of depths, just as he ignores the depths in Paris, to open "for the happy instant, all the windows of his mind . . . letting this rather grey interior drink in for once the sun of a clime not marked in his old geography." When the sun enters, he is dazzled, feels ashamed for being innocent in a world where innocence is guilt. So he passes from being awed by Chad to identifying with him, even to envying him, and to sanctifying his adoration with a testimonial to a worldliness he does not understand. "Live," he tells little Bilham, to which Bilham responds with ironic kindness. Yes, Bilham says, Chad is quite as wonderful as you'd like to believe. But Bilham also says, "You're not a person to whom it's easy to tell things you don't want to know. Though it *is* easy, I admit—it's quite beautiful . . . when you do want to." This warning is lost on Strether, but it is by means of such warnings that the reader understands what is happening.

Wanting so much for the world to be as innocent as he is and thus epitomizing his creator, Strether wastes his remarkable intelligence dodging painful evidence—as James's even more remarkable intelligence now permits him to understand. In zeal to establish the purity in James's handling of point of view, critics have underestimated the more significant consistency with which the author stands apart from his hero. Thus, when other characters give Strether damaging information, James says, "He wondered what they meant, but there were things he scarce thought they could be supposed to mean, and 'Oh no—not *that!*' was at the end of most of his ventures." Lest the point be lost, James casts the action forward, as he does repeatedly throughout the book, to warn the reader against accepting Strether's current convictions: "This was the very beginning with him of a condition as to which, later on, as will be seen, he found cause to pull himself up; and he was to remember the moment duly as the first step in a process." James summarizes:

> No one could explain better when needful, nor put more conscience into an account or a report; which burden of conscience is perhaps exactly the reason why his heart always sank when the clouds of explanation gathered. His highest ingenuity was in keeping the sky of life clear of them. Whether or no he had a grand idea of the lucid, he held that nothing ever was in fact—for any one else—explained. One went through the vain motions, but it was mostly a waste of life. A personal relation was a relation only so long as people either perfectly understood or, better still, didn't care if they didn't. From the moment they cared if they didn't it was living by the sweat of one's brow; and the sweat of one's brow was just what one might buy one's self off from by keeping the ground free of the wild weed of delusion.

Ironically, Strether's orders force him to care about Chad's personal relations, but his desires water his delusions until he chokes in a veritable jungle of weeds.

First, he wants to maintain his delusion about Chad. When Miss Gostrey warns, "He's not so good as you think," Strether gives himself to the "sense, constantly renewed, that Chad *was*— quite in fact insisted on being—as good as he thought. . . . It seemed somehow as if he couldn't *but* be as good from the moment he wasn't as bad." It "gratified his mental ear" to assume Chad is a Pagan, since "a Pagan was perhaps, at the pass they had come to, the thing most wanted at Woollett"—or rather by the Woollett ambassador who wants to relinquish the old ways. Believing in his theory, Strether is ready to accept the attachment as "virtuous," for however much he has abandoned the old ways, he has not abandoned its categories of perception.* A Pagan bound to a Countess conforms to Strether's romantic fancy of pleasure, but if the Countess is married and the Pagan is "our Chad," naturally, Strether assumes, pleasure will be sought with restraint.

What makes Strether's mistake so much more definitive than similar errors involving characters like Milly or Isabel is James's refusal to soften his hero's responsibility by hardening those who deceive him. For example, little Bilham, who gives Strether the lovely, muffling, "virtuous attachment," has honorable motives for doing so, as Strether ultimately admits. A man of character doesn't go about besmirching people's reputations; and, as James handles the scene, Bilham could scarcely have acted otherwise. Inviting the young painter to a café, Strether begins to question

---

* As Frederick C. Crews says, "The very earnestness with which he denounces Woollett can be traced to an insufficiency that Woollett instilled in him." *Tragedy of Manners* (New Haven, 1957), p. 39. But his denunciation does not cut him off entirely.

In *The Ambassadors* James stigmatizes in Strether a tendency toward polarizing experience that accounts, in large part, for failures among his own works.

him about Chad. As the conversation progresses, Bilham hints that an improvement in Chad's manners doesn't necessarily signify an improvement in every sense, but Strether will not pick up the hint. When Bilham says, "[Chad] wants to be free. He isn't used, you see . . . to being so good," Strether responds, "Then I may take it from you that he *is* good?" "*Do* take it from me," Bilham graciously replies to the man who has taken him out for coffee; and James underlines the fact that Bilham speaks to recompense rather than to enlighten Strether by timing the key utterance to Strether's payment of their bill. In short, while Strether pays the waiter, Bilham pays his host; and to put a fine point on it, James has Bilham remark that Strether overtips and has Strether acknowledge that giving too generously is a fault in his character.

But if any doubt remains that James emphasizes his hero's self-deception, we might consider the scene in which Strether becomes so enchanted with his Parisians that he reverses his mission and asks Chad to remain. Previously believing that the young man was in love with Jeanne, Strether has by this time abandoned that supposition and come round, or so he thinks, to the real truth. Nevertheless, he is still discomforted by Chad's involvement in the young girl's marriage. To his question about this detail, Miss Barrace responds with that "ah, ah, ah" which is her equivalent of Bilham's gracious euphemism or of Maria Gostrey's determination to escape from Paris rather than tell Strether the truth. Though the air is thick with their sense that he is getting in deep, Strether complicates his entanglement:

> "I've made it out for myself . . . I've really, within the last half hour, got hold of it. I understand it in short at last; which at first—when you originally spoke to me—I didn't. Nor when Chad originally spoke to me either."
>
> "Oh," said little Bilham, "I don't think that at that time you believed me."

"Yes—I did; and I believed Chad too. It would have been odious and unmannerly—as well as quite perverse—if I hadn't. What interest have you in deceiving me?"

"What interest have *I*?". . .

"Yes" [Strether says, congratulating himself on his skepticism]. "Chad *might* have. But you?"

[To which, borrowing a ploy from Miss Barrace, Bilham replies] "Ah, ah, ah!"

Through the rest of the scene, James reminds us that it is Strether who is talking himself into the "virtuous attachment," Strether who "proceeded as if not for little Bilham's benefit alone," Strether who "with his head back and his eyes on the ceiling, seemed to lose himself in the vision" of "a friendship of a beautiful sort [which is] what makes [Chad and Madame de Vionnet] so strong."

One wants to insist on this point because most critics of *The Ambassadors* pay entirely too much attention to Strether's nobility and too little to his foolishness. But to so misrepresent the novel's emphasis is to lose its delicious irony as well as the knowledge of how great a break it is from that sentimentalizing of innocence that is James's greatest fault.[78] Strether should not be admired for failing to realize at his age that two young lovers would take advantage of their opportunities; and if the conventional reading of *The Ambassadors* is accepted, then the irritation which the book produces in critics like Quentin Anderson and Robert Garis is quite valid.[79] Instead, James himself is aware that Strether is a fool, and one can never understand what redeems that folly until its extent has been measured.

We see it even in the novel's loveliest scenes, for Strether is not only foolish about Chad, who turns out to be base, but about Madame de Vionnet, whose excellence James takes such pains to create. In the great scene at Notre Dame, for example, we are meant to be thrilled by their little luncheon with its "intensely white table-linen . . . *omelette aux tomates* . . . [and] straw-coloured Chablis," but we are also meant to laugh at how easily Madame de Vionnet can crush his doubts concerning her morals by referring to their innocent outing as a "scandal." Moreover, we must remark the ingenuous way in which Strether turns the evidence of her anguished prayers into proof of her innocence: "Unassailably innocent was a relation that could make one of the parties to it so carry herself. If it wasn't innocent why did she haunt the churches?—into which, given the woman he could believe he made out, she would never have come to flaunt an insolence of guilt."

"Given the woman he could believe he made out." The point is that Strether cannot believe the real woman any more than he was able to believe the real man. He can no more believe that passion might reduce a splendid creature like Madame de Vionnet to begging than he could believe that in a man like Chad, after passion has fulfilled itself, no love might be left behind to sustain the appetite. But Chad had already told Strether this long before Notre Dame. "I've *never* got stuck—so very hard," the youth declared; "I always had my own way. . . . And I have it at present." To which Strether had innocently replied, "Then what are you here for? What has kept you . . . if you *have* been able to leave?" "Do you think one's kept only by women?" asks the young ladies' man of the tender gentleman whose regard for the sex is so nearly based on ignorance.

In the mass of criticism on James's masterpiece, too little attention is paid its plot. Seldom does one get a hint of what Chad or Madame de Vionnet is up to, yet this, and not the adultery itself, is what disillusions Strether. As in *What Maisie Knew*, the "villains" in *The Ambassadors* are involved in human exploitation; this activity, which Strether learns may be ubiquitous, is their real sin. Though Strether thinks he is using Chad to extend his own adventure in Paris (and reacts to this with poignantly excessive shame), Chad is really using him. Apparently, the young man had promised his mistress one more chance to keep the lover she had bored, so Chad uses Strether to pacify Madame de Vionnet, who thinks that by using Strether she will keep Chad. This is all indicated in Book Five, when Chad, summoning as much emotion as he possesses, acknowledges that his lover is "too good a friend, confound her . . . for me to leave . . . without my arranging somehow or other the damnable terms of my sacrifice." Again, Strether ignores what is sinister in this avowal, preferring instead to concentrate on what is amiable: "It *will* be a sacrifice then?" "It will be the greatest loss I ever suffered," Chad exhales; "I owe her so much." On Strether goes, like a faithful spaniel with the poor bone he has been tossed: "Chad owed Madame de Vionnet so much? What *did* that do then but clear up the whole mystery? . . . What was it that had suddenly so cleared up? It was just everybody's character; that is everybody's but—in a measure—his own. Strether felt *his* character receive for the instant a smutch from all the wrong things he had suspected or believed."

Such pathos is inseparable from Strether's innocence. Drowning in a sea of intrigue, Strether gets nothing to drink, for he has taste only for purer liquids than are found on earth. If he is noble, he is so first in the sense that Quixote is. But eventually James brings him to face facts, and here Strether becomes noble in a higher sense, passing through his innocence, admitting its folly, and then largely accepting the complexity of life.

Just as Strether is started on the road to error by an intrusive fact, so an intrusive fact begins the process of undeception. Throughout his strenuous rehabilitation of the affair, Strether has always stuck on one item: Chad's relation to Jeanne. In Book Nine, this relation provides the first blow to his beautiful construction, when he sees that Chad and Madame de Vionnet are arranging the girl's future. Now he perceives that the lovers act with great calculation. Learning that Marie has forced Chad to be civil to the Pococks, Strether senses stratagem ("She spoke now as if her art were all an innocence and then again as if her innocence were all an art"), and when he also learns that Marie is willing to "do" Paris with Jim, he is frightened by the force of purpose that could lie behind so grotesque a combination. The penultimate blow is delivered by Chad's cousin Mamie, a person whose real innocence and love, equally protective of the man who spurns her and a girl she scarcely knows, shatter Strether's confident transvaluation of Paris into virtue and Woollett into vice. From this, it is but a short journey to the novel's famous moment when reality suddenly swims into Strether's ken, reminding him of how distant he had been from the stream of life.

The boat scene in which Strether discovers the adultery has been too widely discussed to require much analysis, but a few facts should be emphasized. First, though Strether's discovery is an accident, he sets himself up for it. That is, we are meant to recall that Strether needn't have been there, needn't have taken his theory into the open air, and that the honesty that kept him from quitting Europe before he had comprehended things must be taken to mitigate his fabrications. Second, what disturbs Strether is not so much the fact that they are lovers as the way they deal with the revelation. Chad puts it off on Marie, who, lapsing into French and leaning on the table, shows the reality underneath her decorous manners. Finally, Strether responds to their deceit in a manner unusual for a Jamesian innocent: by feeling ashamed for his folly and saddened at the loss of pleasure with which the lovers unwittingly reproach him.

If the novel ended here, it would be James's supreme confrontation with the cost of innocence, showing even more clearly than *The Awkward Age* that fixation on innocence threatens and falsifies life. Making Strether comic for exemplifying James's own reluctance to face life's limits, the author rids himself of additional sentimentality. The world is irrevocably flawed, but innocent or moralistic characters offer no viable alternative. James now admits both harsh truths.

As I have said, *The Ambassadors* goes beyond such negation to celebrate life despite its moral impurity. In the twelfth book, this affirmation takes gradual shape. When other Jamesian protagonists have encountered vice, they have either renounced its source or demanded punishment. Initially, Strether feels the same instinct. Thus, when he learns of his idols' mendacity and infidelity, though he has also learned of Woollett's hypocrisy, he reverts to its tradition: "the notion that the state of the wrong-doer, or at least this person's happiness, presented some special difficulty." When he visits Madame de Vionnet for the last time, however, he discovers that her suffering doesn't please him. Reflecting that "their eminent 'lie' . . . was simply after all such an inevitable tribute to good taste as he couldn't have wished them not to render," Strether hopes that Madame de Vionnet "will make deception right." What she does instead is show Strether how she has been ground into the dust:

> it was like a chill in the air to him, it was almost appalling, that a creature so fine could be, by mysterious forces, a creature so exploited. For at the end of all things they *were* mysterious: she had but made Chad what he was—so why could she think she had made him infinite? She had made him better, she had made him best, she had made him anything one would; but it came to our friend with supreme queerness that he was none the less only Chad. Strether had the sense that *he*, a little, had made him too; his high appreciation had, as it were, consecrated her work. The work, however admirable, was nevertheless of the strict human order, and in short it was marvellous that the companion of mere earthly joys, of comforts, abberrations (however one classed them) within the common experience, should be so transcendently prized.

From his last vision of her, Strether takes away two important truths. One is that even cultured, fine people don't necessarily prize what is morally adorable. The other is that passion's prizing itself commands respect. Life's marvel, which Strether is the first Jamesian protagonist to sense, is this intensity of commitment that can make claims as great as those of morality. Maisie rejected Sir Claude because he was bound to a passion in which his soul did not enter, but Madame de Vionnet's passion is total. However much it may reduce her to lies and pleading, it is also the source of her grandeur and creativity. Seeing this, Strether realizes that such a force must be served. Though he regrets that passion has confounded her judgment, he does not, that is to say James does not, condemn her. Instead, he determines to restore her, insofar as he can, to the position she is so desperate to retain.

When we think of James's difficulties with sex, not to mention the Victorian attitude toward adultery, we can appreciate the significance of Strether's insistence that Chad not quit the woman who has so powerfully loved him. But alongside James's queasiness about sex there had always been his recognition that love is an ideal. Fleda Vetch may be wrongly admired for her virginal hysteria, but she does opt for love freely given and maintained. Kate Croy may be a villainess, but her crime is subjecting Eros to Mammon, not eroticism itself. Even though he wants to shield her from censure, James confesses that Isabel's fall was partly caused by her frigidity. In none of his other books, however (except, in part, *The Bostonians*), have we seen James accept the connection between the ideal of love and the fact of sexuality. Madame de Vionnet's desire is the very heart of her affection, and Strether, unlike others before him, does not ignore this morally disruptive fact.

Moreover, he condemns not the adulterous woman but the cold young fornicator who is ready to move on. Nothing in the book so reveals its ethical toughness as James's final judgment of Chad. After all he has enjoyed, after all the growth that love made possible, Chad wants to cast his benefactress away. Profit calls, and for the callow American (as James was to confirm when he revisited his native land [*The American Scene*]), monetary gain is more seductive than passion. But it is not only love that Chad desecrates. To a nearly fainting Strether, who must "coerce" his own attention, Chad outlines the brilliant future that awaits him in advertising: "It's an art like another, and infinite like all the arts." Surely, one day, when Chad is as rich as his mother, he will endow another *Woollett Review* in which innocents like Strether can fool themselves into thinking that culture survives.

Be that as it may, Strether now has a better understanding of culture and its involvement with passion. If the beauty and elegance of culture can't be had in any other way, James now seems to be saying, then let them be had through Chad's necessary faith in Madame de Vionnet. At last, Strether sees that although what is beautiful and sentient may not always be moral or disinterested, the better part of morals is to serve the beauty and sentience as best one can.

Still, though Strether can work for Madame de Vionnet, he cannot forgive her for having deceived him, just as Maisie cannot forgive Claude for having wanted her to lie. Strether no longer believes in absolute value, but he still cannot excuse deliberate deceit. James could construct a fable admitting the intrigues of life, but Strether cannot live in a world that embodies them.

The Ambassadors's last scene has been widely criticized as a failure of nerve because it is assumed that James wishes us to applaud when Strether rejects Maria Gostrey. Thus, Yvor Winters has fulminated against the hero's "sacrifice of morality to appearances," while H. R. Hays, who recognizes that the book is satiric, complains that James retreats from satire at the finale.[80]

Read carefully, however, the scene accomplishes just what its critics deny.

Maria offers Strether a permanent version of his romantic distance: a "retreat . . . back of the house, with a view of a scrap of old garden that has been saved from modern ravage." Her *objets* and her love can reconstruct the mythic world into which Chad and Madame de Vionnet had brought so disturbing a reality. But Strether will not seize this escape; by now he knows too much to lapse back into old wish fulfillments. "I'm not . . . in real harmony with what surrounds me," he admits to her. "You *are*. I take it too hard. You *don't*. It makes—that's what it comes to in the end—a fool of me."

Strether, who had momentarily transcended his New England conscience, cannot root it out. Thus, he begs to be excused from happiness, at which Maria rightfully rages: "It isn't so much your *being* 'right'—it's your horrible sharp eye for what makes you so." But, as Strether reminds her, she shares his taste for moral refinements: "Oh but you're just as bad yourself. You can't resist me when I point that out." Recognizing the truth of what he says, Maria can only confirm his logic. By his standards, he cannot join the lovers, who haven't paid for their duplicity, by not paying for his folly. Since what she loves him for is this quixotic morality, she must agree that he should renounce profit: "She sighed it at last all comically, all tragically, away, 'I can't indeed resist you.' 'Then there we are!' said Strether." And so the novel ends in an arrested movement, which, as James now admits, is the fate of cherished innocence.

Beyond Good and Evil

In James's last major novel, he goes beyond *The Ambassadors*'s tough candor, but he also looks backward to the sentimentality of *The Dove*. Split between all that is best and worst in his fiction, surrounded by a representative critical controversy, *The Golden Bowl* provides the perfect vantage point to summarize his art.

In *The Ambassadors* Strether accepts the mixture of good and evil, success and failure, that makes life so mysterious. Maggie Verver, in *The Golden Bowl*, goes further in this direction, learning to accept life's ambiguity and manipulate it for her own ends. Critics have emphasized her choice of success over renunciation as the novel's revolutionary feature; Maggie's revolution, however, includes not only her victory but her means. Whereas most Jamesian innocents, even at the cost of life, seek a glittering moral clarity, Maggie agrees not to know or judge, labors to keep things fuzzy, sacrifices clarity to erotic fulfillment.

Her story distills James's major themes. Innocent and Ameri-

can, though armed with native verve and the riches of a new
continent, she is enchanted by Europe's elegance and beauty,
which she seeks to possess in the person of an Italian prince. With
her adored father, Maggie had enjoyed a kind of paradisiacal
affection that knew neither the pleasures nor the pains of adult
love. Thus, when Adam buys Amerigo for Maggie, she cannot
understand how much he costs. By the end of the novel, both she
and Adam have learned:

> [Charlotte and Amerigo] seated, in conversation and at tea fell
> thus into the splendid effect and the general harmony: Mrs. Verver
> and the Prince fairly "placed" themselves, however unwittingly, as
> high expressions of the kind of human furniture required aestheti-
> cally by such a scene. The fusion of their presence with the dec-
> orative elements, their contribution to the triumph of selection,
> was complete and admirable; though to a lingering view, a view
> more penetrating than the occasion really demanded, they also
> might have figured as concrete attestations of a rare power of
> purchase.

The Ververs had originally bought Charlotte and the Prince as
if they were *objets*; but when Maggie and Adam learn that fine
human pieces come high, they reveal the necessary spiritual
capital to possess what they had only procured.

To purchase her husband, Maggie realizes that she must pay
with her father. She cannot earn her passion until she abandons
the presexual world in which she was a child playing games in
an atmosphere from which cash had banished suffering. Having
been freed from his bond to Maggie by her self-indulgent bond
with Adam, Amerigo resumes his affair with Charlotte, who had,
ironically, been bought to keep things orderly. Thus Maggie
learns that her ordered Eden was itself the cause of disorder;
and faced by this discovery, she understands that she cannot give
way to righteous indignation since her own cherished righteousness helped to bring her trouble about.

When proposing that Adam marry Charlotte so as not to be lonely, Maggie had responded carelessly to Adam's warning ("If we get her here to improve *us* don't we . . . then make use of her?" "We're old, old friends—we do her good too"); and she compounds her initial error by trying to maintain her service to Adam despite their respective marital obligations. Ironically, Amerigo and Charlotte can claim equally good intentions; as they assert, their affair facilitates the Ververs' intimacy. All this teaches Maggie the great lesson that James himself sometimes tried to ignore: doing good can produce effects similar to doing evil. Acknowledging this ironic equation, Maggie does not withdraw from benighted life; rather, she learns to use evil, thus relinquishing her status as innocent victim in order to take up her rightful place in the world. Making artful use of the dubieties and machinations characteristic of society, Maggie manages to regain her husband, unite her father and stepmother, and restore these relationships to their proper balance with as little pain as possible.

Because James so clearly dramatizes the Ververs' responsibility for their own suffering, he can't have written the novel that some critics make of *The Golden Bowl*. Tributes to Maggie's divinity, like those of Blackmur and Quentin Anderson, neglect her determinant shortcomings.[81] Moreover, by treating the action as if it were allegorical, they ignore its social orientation. However obsessed James may have been by the war between good and evil, he saw both as social forces. The book's significance is its transformation of social forms into means of resisting the very evil they embody, and this significance is lost if *The Golden Bowl* is read as a Swedenborgian allegory or Dantean parable.

On the other hand, the contrary view, expressed by Leavis and Ferner Nuhn (that the Ververs are wicked and the lovers inadvertently preferable), is also incorrect.[82] At no point does James deny the appeal of Charlotte and Amerigo, and he shows exactly what may be said against the Ververs: "Nothing stranger surely had ever happened to a conscientious, a well-meaning, a perfectly passive pair: no more extraordinary decree had ever been launched against such victims than this of forcing them against their will into a relation of mutual close contact that they had done everything to avoid." The prime fact about Amerigo is his desire to "be much more decent as a son-in-law than lots of fellows he could think of had shown themselves in that character." Bought for his physical charm, he is sincerely grateful to the man who had rescued him from elegant poverty and a sinister past, and he fully intends to give value for money. For this reason, he initially resists Charlotte, participates passively in their affair, and gives her up as soon as she threatens to prove troublesome. Trying to avoid the mess they all get into, Amerigo warns Maggie that she doesn't know him, just as Charlotte warns Adam. Neither intends to harm his benefactors. Charlotte even risks losing Adam when she offers to show him the telegram of advice that he had agreed she solicit from Amerigo.

James is too honest about their virtue and extenuating pressures to be accused, as Nuhn accuses him, of misplaced sympathy. He is also precise about the lovers' flaws—which amply support his contention that they deserve to be separated. Though the Ververs' bizarre arrangements are cruelly tempting, temptation doesn't justify malfeasance. Moreover, once the threat to marital regularity was clearly evident, Charlotte and Amerigo should at least have made some attempt to retain their respective spouses. Instead they take advantage of the Ververs' putative indifference.

Under the circumstances, their great show of protecting their *sposi* seems pure sophistry. Like the gilded but cracked bowl with which Charlotte had thought to commemorate Maggie's marriage, the concern showed by Charlotte and the Prince is specious, as James suggests by the way he describes it: "It put them, it kept them together . . . [made] a mystic golden bridge between them, strongly swaying and sometimes almost vertiginous, for that intimacy of which the sovereign law would be the vigilance of 'care,' would be never rashly to forget and never consciously to wound." Their support, then, is literally flimsy; for all their protestations, their moral position sways over a chasm of initial deceit. The first wrong was theirs: not telling the Ververs that they had once been intimate.

James underlines this sophistry in his narration of their affair. First, he shows their elegance prostituting itself when Lady Castledean invites them to Matcham only so that they may screen her affair with Mr. Blint. Then, after they have performed this service, he makes Charlotte and Amerigo seem not only corrupt but blasphemous. Stating as their purpose a visit to a cathedral, they embark for Gloucester, where they plan to go to bed.

Despite the sympathy that Charlotte's suffering provokes, despite James's admission that she has been used, her right to Amerigo is clearly inferior to Maggie's. Not only is Maggie his wife; she, unlike Charlotte, is willing to fight and sacrifice for him. The way she fights and what she sacrifices constitute not only the superiority of her claim but the toughness that is the book's most revolutionary feature. For once, James approves of a character who uses her sexual power.

Nowhere is the novel's sexual freedom and specificity better displayed than in the stages of Maggie's awakening. For example, she becomes certain of his affair only when Amerigo refuses to allow her to accompany him to the bath he takes on his return from Gloucester. Yet when he rejoins her, freshly turned out and fragrant, Maggie immediately understands how he wishes to use his sexuality to banish her fears. This calculation she checks, and throughout her subsequent maneuvering she insures her freedom by refusing to consent to his advances.

Maggie's unworldliness had smoothed Amerigo's path; accordingly, to make things rough for him, she begins to deck herself out and to join the set from Matcham. Cleverly, she tests his loyalty when one of their frequent vacations looms by pretending that she wants him to go off with Adam, in order to see if he could express a preference for remaining with his wife. These are all stages in Maggie's acceptance of what more typical Jamesian protagonists had feared:

> She had lived long enough to make out for herself that any deep-seated passion has its pangs as well as its joys, and that we are made by its aches and its anxieties most richly conscious of it. She had never doubted of the force of the feeling that bound her to her husband; but to become aware almost suddenly that it had begun to vibrate with a violence that had some of the effect of a strain would, rightly looked at, after all but show that she was, like thousands of women, every day, acting up to the full privilege of passion.

Privileges involve obligations. Maggie is superior to Charlotte because she will meet them by giving up her father and rewinning her spouse. Her greatness is the mercy which she brings to such acts. Disdaining to play the wronged wife, Maggie makes use of the very techniques that had wronged her, gaining her ends, however, while minimizing her adversary's pain. Telling Amerigo that she knows of his affair, she refuses to tell him what she will do about it, thus correctly relying upon his sense of honor to prevent him from seeking to check her course. Deciding not to tell Charlotte what she knows, she saves her rival from the pain of exposure while also depriving her of the cue to battle. Finally, making use of the nearly occult sympathy between them, she hints to her father that all would be improved if he and Mrs. Verver returned to America, thereby removing the threat to her happiness without having recourse to a public explosion.

Maggie is thus the craftiest, most worldly of James's innocents. But in putting on worldliness she does not blacken herself. Feel-

ing sympathy for her rival, she moderates the complacency produced by new-found skills. The famous imagery comparing Charlotte to a soul in pain all occurs in Maggie's imagination; thus it
exists primarily to exonerate Maggie from the charge of merciless
justice. That she is just, James proves by the shallowness of Charlotte's and the Prince's love; that she is merciful, James proves
by her attitude toward it. Maggie can imagine how Charlotte
must feel, but Charlotte says, "I can't put myself into Maggie's
skin—I can't, as I say. It's not my fit—I shouldn't be able, as I see
it, to breathe in it." Not only can Maggie breathe in Charlotte's
skin; she can try to save it.

By the end of her program, she has grown so in Amerigo's esteem that he wants to educate the mistress he has decided is not
clever about the wife they had thought a fool. "Isn't it my right
to correct her," he asks when Maggie protests. "Correct her?" his
wife wails. "Aren't you rather forgetting who she is?" It is Maggie's regard for Charlotte's stature—both the depth of her pain
and the dignity of her capitulation—that ultimately places Maggie above the woman she has, in one sense, wronged.

The Golden Bowl, then, brings the innocent through the fires
of her own guilt, where she may stand purged of self-righteousness and accept her place among those who feel passion, and sin,
and strive. Maggie takes her position in the world, becomes a
Princess, but we cannot accuse her of wresting it through the
brute power of propriety and wealth. She wins, instead, through
intelligence and compassion. That is why, at the end of the book,
when she has banished everything but herself from Amerigo's
field of vision, she can look at the light in his eyes with "pity and
dread"—pity for what she had done to put it there and dread at
her enormous obligation to fulfill its demands. In this moment,
James admits that love can be as stern a discipline as morality.

But this admission, which makes *The Golden Bowl* the most
humane of his novels, is compromised. In language and rhetoric

throughout the book there is evidence that James was far from comfortable with his theme; as in more seriously ambiguous works, where contradictory characterizations occur, James hedges his fine portrait with sentimentality. As a result, Maggie Verver shares in the ambiguity surrounding the governess, Newman, and Milly Theale. Those figures were intended to be wholly good but weren't, so that James's exposure might be deemed inadvertent. Maggie should be good and becomes so, but James wants her to be more than someone who outgrows a damagingly self-protective innocence: he wants her to be perfect. This is where *The Golden Bowl* reverts to his earlier flaws.

Soundly, James identifies Maggie's stature not with her virtue but with her ability to love. Thus, when she shows mercy to Charlotte, we may regard this as penitence for her exclusive and self-referring father-fixation. Unfortunately, James doesn't strictly connect her mercy with her guilt, because he allows her to disclaim wrongdoing. Toward the end of the novel, for example, he places in her mouth a lament for the loss of Adam that confuses the moral causality already dramatized: " 'Oh yes,' Maggie quite lucidly declared, '[we are] lost to each other really much more than Amerigo and Charlotte are; since for them it's just, it's right, it's deserved, while for us it's only sad and strange and not caused by our fault.' " As I have said, the soundness of the book depends on James's admission that the Ververs are partly at fault for events which lead to their separation; moreover, he suggests that the separation is crucial to Maggie's development. How then are we to reconcile this speech? Perhaps we should regard it as the expression of momentary grief, but neither Maggie nor Fanny Assingham, to whom it is made, ever points out the fallacy in its contention. Nor does James. Rather, he frequently vouches for Maggie's innocence, thus contradicting his own plot. Thus, he can refer to her as "our young woman, who had been, from far back, by the habit of her nature, as much on her guard against sacrificing others as if she felt the great trap of life mainly set for one's doing so," though we have already seen her sacrifice Charlotte to insure Adam's happiness and both Adam and Charlotte to insure her own.

What we have here is James's old tendency to make rhetorical love to surrogate characters: what I should call the "Milly Theale syndrome." "More and more magnificent now in her blameless egoism," James can exclaim, by way of introducing one of Maggie's most ruthless ploys. Perhaps the best example of this aspect of her characterization is the awful exchange she has with Fanny that so recalls Milly's pretentious refusal of Lord Mark's suit:

> "My dear child, you're amazing," [Fanny says, not for the first time].
> "Amazing?—"
> "You're terrible."
> "No; I'm not terrible, and you don't think me so. I do strike you as surprising, no doubt—but surprisingly mild. Because—don't you see?—I *am* mild. I can bear anything."
> "Oh, 'bear'!"
> "For love."
> "Of your father?"
> "For love."
> "Of your husband?"
> "For love."

Remarking "something slightly sickening in this wide-open declaration of being in love with love without discrimination between kinds,"[83] F. O. Matthiessen should have gone on to note that it also contradicts Maggie's presumed awakening to the distinction between passion and filial devotion. One also wants to deplore in this speech a conceit that almost justifies Nuhn's reference to the "crafty-innocent, smugly virtuous, coolly victorious little Princess."[84]

James clearly didn't see it this way. Even though Maggie doesn't turn her face to the wall, away from her own failings, he brings to her the same worship that cloys in the characterization of Milly Theale. So we get the same effluvium of Christianity, the same rumblings about magnificence, the same recourse to miraculous conversions. Surely the book's ugliest detail is Maggie's reformation of the venal Jewish shopkeeper (who had been sketched with an anti-Semitic nastiness elsewhere evident in James).[85] Though the man is willing to sell Charlotte and the Prince damaged merchandise at inflated prices, one look at Maggie suffices to restore his probity. Thinking back on the accomplishment, Maggie modestly attributes it to her "kindness, gentleness, grace, her charming presence and easy humanity and familiarity."

Even more disturbing than these testimonials to Maggie's magnanimity are touches in the portrait of her father. Though James is aware of Adam's avidity and causes the millionaire to discuss his selfishness, often we find James applying the whitewash with broad strokes. The chapter that introduces Adam solicits "our attention—tender indeed almost to compassion" in a way that recalls James's introduction of Milly Theale. Though we are subsequently given evidence that Adam is an egotist, in chapter seven we are told that his "depravity" is "imitate[d]," something "which for amusement . . . he practised 'keeping up,' " and that a "quarter of an hour of egoism was about as much as he . . . usually got." Several critics have celebrated James's satire of Adam's philanthropy, which plans to rifle Europe for the benefit of American City, but James seems to approve of the project. Indeed, he states that Adam's connoisseurship is not destructive:

It was all at bottom in him, the aesthetic principle, planted where it could burn with a cold still flame; where it fed almost wholly

on the material directly involved, on the idea (followed by appro-
priation) of plastic beauty, of the thing visibly perfect in its kind;
where, in short, despite the general tendency of the "devouring
element" to spread, the rest of his spiritual furniture, modest scat-
tered and tended with unconscious care, escaped the consumption
that in so many cases proceeds from the undue keeping-up of
profane altar-fires.*

We have only to compare this with James's treatment of Mrs.
Newsome's motive for endowing the *Woollett Review* to see
that James is scarcely hard-headed in his conception of Mr.
Verver.

Instead, Adam is both a fantasy figure of odd punctilio and a
man of deep unwitting egoism, just as Maggie is, simultaneously,
an innocent user and virtuous refuser of other people's unhappiness. James was ambivalent toward both protagonists; but whereas Maggie is mostly clear, Adam is mostly obfuscated. How, for
example, are we to understand his feelings for Charlotte? If he
married her solely for Maggie's peace of mind (for which reason
he also takes her back to America), why should James think we
ought to admire him? But perhaps he really loves Charlotte. In
that case, something might be said in his behalf.

The passage describing his decision to propose is long, but
some of it must be quoted to establish the ambiguity surrounding
Adam's motives:

> The sharp point to which all his light converged was that the
> whole call of his future to him as a father would be in his so man-
> aging that Maggie would less and less appear to herself to have for-

* Shortly before this passage, James writes: "Nothing perhaps might affect
us as queerer, had we time to look into it, than this application of the same
measure of value to such different pieces of property as old Persian carpets, say, and
new human acquisitions; all the more indeed that the amiable man was not without
an inkling on his own side that he was, as a taster of life, economically constructed."
Considering the obtrusiveness of this shortcoming, one wonders why James bothers
to point it out. But how are we to take the "had we time to look into it"? Viewed
as an ironic come-on, it has the fault of pointing up James's subsequent omissions.

saken him. And it not only wouldn't be decently humane, decently possible, not to make this relief easy to her—the idea shone upon him, more than that, as exciting, inspiring, uplifting. . . . He had seen that Charlotte could contribute—what he hadn't seen was what she could contribute *to*. When it had all supremely cleared up and he had simply settled this service to his daughter well before him as the proper direction of his young friend's leisure, the cool darkness had again closed round him, but his moral lucidity was constituted. . . . Oh if Charlotte didn't accept him the remedy of course would fail; but, as everything had fallen together, it was at least there to be tried. And success would be great—that was his last throb—if the measure of relief effected for Maggie should at all prove to have been given by his own actual sense of felicity. He really didn't know when in his life he had thought of anything happier. To think of it merely for himself would have been, even as he had just lately felt, even doing all justice to that condition—yes, impossible. But there was a grand difference in thinking of it for his child.

This last sentence seems ironic. If so taken, it can only mean that Adam wanted Charlotte because he desired her, and that marrying her for Maggie's sake is partly a pretext allowing him to go ahead despite the difference between his and Charlotte's ages and the indelicacy of proposing marriage to his daughter's best friend. Support for this belief is provided by Adam's graphic impatience while Charlotte hesitates before accepting him. But once this possibility is introduced, the whole novel takes on a different color.

If Adam really loved Charlotte, why did he do so little after their marriage to prove it to her. Virginal Maggie might be forgiven a certain naiveté; Adam seems suspiciously sterile. This, in turn, adds interesting emphasis to Charlotte's contention that she wanted children but that Adam couldn't give her any. Perhaps he is guilty of her adultery not only because of his affection for Maggie but through a refusal to love. Did Maggie cause this refusal? Left to himself, Adam might have loved Charlotte more; he is, after all, not too old for passion.* The reading I previously outlined makes Charlotte's account of her marriage a high-handed ruse which Maggie, to her great credit, pretends to believe. But if we consider the evidence I am now collecting, Charlotte may be telling the truth.

In their final confrontation (one of the most powerful scenes in a novel full of them), Charlotte accuses Maggie not of breaking her affair but of attempting to break her marriage. To be sure, we are meant to read the former charge into the latter since Maggie's machinations make it impossible for Charlotte to speak of Amerigo without tipping her hand. But perhaps Charlotte had fallen in love with Adam between the day of her marriage and her resumption of the affair. Perhaps she resumed the affair only because Adam had become indifferent, and perhaps he became indifferent only because Maggie began actively to compete for his affection. As in similar cases, most of the evidence supports the standard reading, but *The Golden Bowl* does permit grave doubts about its characters' motives and thus about its ostensible theme.

In this novel James is further from moral melodrama than in any of his other books, for he shows that all parties to the predicament share in guilt and that all may claim extenuating circumstances. But though he goes far toward a mature vision, he is drawn to the old habit of pitting black against white. However, the more he tries to separate his characters into opposing moral camps, the more dubious become the grounds of separation. Had he relaxed about the Ververs' virtue, his plot would have made

* The obscurity concerning Adam's age is one of the book's most puzzling features. Even before Maggie suggests Charlotte, her father proclaims his reluctance to remarry (his first match was apparently a flop), and he denies Maggie's contention that he is still young enough to taste life's joys. So far as I can make out, he is forty-seven; however he speaks of himself as much older. This psychological senescence is another disturbing feature in Adam about which James seems imperfectly aware.

his point with tolerable conviction. But the more he vouches for them, the more he invites our skepticism.

Why does he vouch for them so fervently? Here again we come to the underside of James's advocacy of life and individual freedom. Though he can applaud Maggie's decision to live up to passion and commend both her means and her mercy, part of James prefers the sexless relationship she had had with Adam: a lost paradise gilded by wealth. Despite Oscar Cargill, who counters Matthiessen's attack on Adam Verver with an *ad hominem* attack on Matthiessen's politics,[86] this character is not convincing as a millionaire. It would be tendentious to deny that millionaires can be nice, but James's conception of a saintly rifler of the Golden Isles is equally partisan, reaching beyond the shrewdly observed Newsomes to Christopher Newman, who, at least, had been saved for us by his charm. In addition, when we are asked to share James's delight in the Ververs' relationship, we needn't invoke Freud to explain our inability. Despite Marx, all millionaires aren't robber barons, just as, despite Freud, all closely knit families aren't incestuous. But the point of the novel is that Maggie must outgrow her fixation on papa—incestuous or not—because maturation means accepting sex. Yet as late as chapter thirty-seven we find James recording a tête-à-tête between the Ververs with a sympathy that contradicts his theme:

> it was wonderfully like their having got together into some boat and paddled off from the shore where husbands and wives, luxuriant complications, made the air too tropical. . . . Why, into the bargain, for that matter—this came to Maggie—couldn't they always live, so far as they lived together, in a boat? She felt in her face with the question the breath of a possibility that soothed her; they needed only *know* each other henceforth in the unmarried relation. That other sweet evening in the same place he had been as unmarried as possible—which had kept down, so to speak, the quantity of change in their state. Well then that other sweet eve-

ning was what the present sweet evening would resemble; with the quite calculable effect of an exquisite inward refreshment. They *had* after all, whatever happened, always and ever each other; each other—that was the hidden treasure and the saving truth—to do exactly what they would with: a provision full of possibilities.

Of course, this passage reflects Maggie's feeling, but James approves of it in a personal interpolation ("Who could tell as yet what, thanks to it, they wouldn't have done before the end") that identifies this mood with the Ververs' ultimate accomplishments. But this mood is sick. As the potential pun in "know" suggests, Maggie is escaping from sex with her father, having an asexual fling in a little boat far away from the tropics. Without digging very deeply, one can read in such details a fear of sex, yet by this time in the novel Maggie is supposed to be motivated primarily by her desire to recapture Amerigo. This is a good example of how James's rhetoric can contradict his plot.

One must describe *The Golden Bowl*, then, as a novel whose wisdom is qualified by nostalgia for immaturity. Maggie grows up, but James's enthusiasm is less than complete. Though he isn't admiring a character who is hostile to growth (as he may be in "The Turn of the Screw") or one who will not grow (as in *The Princess Casamassima* and *The Wings of the Dove*), he cannot easily accept the process he seems to be espousing. Testimonials to the Ververs' virtue (and the ambiguities that these produce) indicate all that is most backward-looking in their author. Within the moral skeptic capable of subtly apportioning praise and blame there is a moral idealist who would rather keep them ineluctably separate so as to cleave to one. The skeptic wrote *The Golden Bowl*, but the idealist also lives in its pages.

As I have already indicated, most critics choose to recognize only half the novel's effect, making it either a melodrama about the angelic Ververs and the "thing hideously behind" or a canny attack on the Ververs' moral pretensions together with a covert celebration of Charlotte and the Prince. The former group takes James at his word (see *The Notebooks*) and accords with much of his practice.[87] The latter group seeks to save James from his own defects.[88] When, as occasionally happens, some critic sees that *The Golden Bowl* is ambiguous, he congratulates James for its complexity, however uncontrolled.[89]

But *The Golden Bowl* reminds us that ambiguity and complexity are not arrived at by the same routes. If Maggie is both good and bad, then she is complex; if her badness is both demonstrated and denied, then she is ambiguous. *The Golden Bowl* is superior to *The Wings of the Dove* because James does acknowledge and make Maggie's flaws functional, whereas he ignores Milly's; but, as I have tried to show, he does not freely connect Maggie's flaws with the more dominant virtues which they presumably help to produce.

Fine though it is, this novel is imperfectly coherent. Written with dazzling elegance and metaphoric brilliance, it is darkened by obscurities. As much may be said against the entire Jamesian canon. I do not know if my qualitative distinctions will turn out to have been the correct ones; I do know that qualitative distinctions must be made. After James's first books, there are remarkably few lapses in his technical mastery. In symmetry of plotting, complexity of situation, suavity of expression, he has few peers in English fiction. But we should not follow his lead in using his technical victories to divert our attention from his conceptual flaws. Edmund Wilson is correct when he contends that James's *Notebooks* are oddly extroverted, as if James was escaping internal doubts by emphasizing the job at hand.[90] Though the Jacobites revived James as a saint of art, we must remember that artistic devotion and mastery cannot guarantee sanctity, cogency, or any achievement except skill.

James is great not only because of his skill but because of his centrality. Despite exclusions and timidities, he attempted to answer the most important problem placed before the moral intelligence: How can we construct reasonable values in a world that confounds certainty? Moreover, he demonstrates the problem at the same time that he attempts to express it, for any James story that has attracted attention has also divided its critics about the moral value of its characters.

It is finally this problem that gives James his enduring interest even for readers who do not share his parochial artistic concerns. Reading through his work, one begins to see that he was representative of modern man. Disbelieving in supernatural sanctions but intensely moral, James tried to construct his own ethics. Like most of us, he found it easiest to offer injunctions: one should respect privacy, should love and not use other people. But he was also too intelligent to deny that egotism may take high as well as low forms, so that his investigative zeal was often lessened by the paucity of positive evidence.

Warring against the dispassionate observer was the moral celebrant. Occasionally, needing something to celebrate, he finds it at the cost of plausibility. Personal preferences for chastity or culture, themselves either morally neutral or dubious, further weaken his advocacy. Then his intelligence whispers his doubts and his constructions begin to totter. Judiciousness collapses into tendentiousness and special pleading, while the world comes more and more to seem not a field for his researches but the enemy of his dreams. Still, the world is actual; it will not go away: how can one make peace with it?

One must know what to value. Could any other knowledge be half so precious? Henry James is supremely interesting not, as decades of criticism have argued, because he shows what is right, but because he shows how difficult it is to show it.

BIBLIOGRAPHICAL NOTES

1. The history of James's contemporary reputation is told in Leon Edel's biography. Another useful source is Richard N. Foley, *Criticism in American Periodicals of the Works of Henry James from 1866 to 1916* (Washington, 1944).
2. They are: Joseph Warren Beach, *The Method of Henry James* (New Haven, 1918); Van Wyck Brooks, *The Pilgrimage of Henry James* (New York, 1925); Ford Madox Ford, *Henry James: A Critical Study* (New York, 1916); Rebecca West, *Henry James* (London, 1916).
3. F. W. Dupee's book is *Henry James* (New York, 1951) and Maxwell Geismar's is *Henry James and the Jacobites* (Boston, 1963).
4. Edmund Wilson, "The Ambiguity of Henry James," reprinted in *A Casebook on Henry James' "The Turn of the Screw,"* ed. Gerald Willen (New York, 1959). All my citations are to this edition of Wilson's essay.
5. These novels seem negligible—as juvenilia (*Watch and Ward*) or as pot-boilers (*The Outcry, The Other House*)—but I also omit two that are not negligible: *Roderick Hudson* and *The Tragic Muse*. These novels, together with a host of stories (the majority of which were collected by F. O. Matthiessen under the title *Stories of Writers and Artists*), form a coherent group that seemed to me to call for more explicitly biographical criticism than I have attempted for James's other fiction. Since, for all their undeniable merits, these works also seem unlikely to attract the general reader, I have decided to treat them on another occasion.
6. Samples of this controversy and a good bibliography of further debate

can be found in Willen's *A Casebook on Henry James' "The Turn of the Screw."* Reading through this volume will prove that there is ample evidence for both famous interpretations.

7. See John Silver, "A Note on the Freudian Reading of 'The Turn of the Screw,'" in Willen, *A Casebook.*

8. *The Selected Letters of Henry James*, ed. Leon Edel (New York, 1960), p. 146.

9. *The Novels and Tales of Henry James* (New York, 1908), XII, xiv.

10. Ibid., p. xix.

11. Of three representative critics who have found the story radically ambiguous, one, Marius Bewley, derides it for this reason. See *The Complex Fate* (New York, 1954). Leo B. Levy ("*The Turn of the Screw* as Retaliation," *College English*, XVII [February, 1956], 286–288) asserts that the tale is incomprehensible because James wanted to take vengeance on those who found *Guy Domville* obscure; he'd show them what obscurity was! Louis D. Rubin, Jr. ("One More Turn of the Screw," *Modern Fiction Studies*, IX [Winter, 1963–64], 314–328) finds the story successful because it can't be understood: "the whole point about the puzzle is its ultimate insolubility. . . . The Master indeed!" (p. 328).

12. Wilson, "The Ambiguity of Henry James," p. 123.

13. West, *Henry James*, p. 108.

14. See relevant entries in *The Notebooks of Henry James*, ed. F. O. Matthiessen and Kenneth B. Murdock (New York, 1961), and the letter quoted in the cited edition of *The Sacred Fount*, p. 9.

15. Tony Tanner makes a rather different use of "The Patagonia" analogy in "Henry James's Subjective Adventurer: *The Sacred Fount*," *Essays and Studies* (London, 1963). His is one of three representative essays which argue that the book's narrator is a hero. Each makes an unqualified claim, ignoring contrary evidence in the text. To Tanner, the narrator is an artist-figure comparable to Sir Philip Sydney, Conrad, etc. To James Reany, he is a "God, a Providence, and also a sort of Prospero." See "The Condition of Light: Henry James's *The Sacred Fount*," *University of Toronto Quarterly*, XXXI (January, 1962), 136–151. For Robert A. Perlongo, he is a "tragic figure in the Greek tradition." See "*The Sacred Fount*: Labyrinth or Parable?" *Kenyon Review*, XXII (Autumn, 1960), 635–647. Several critics have deemed the narrator a fool or worse. The most extensive argument against him (with copious references to other critics) is to be found in Jean Frantz Blackall, *Jamesian Ambiguity and The Sacred Fount* (Ithaca, 1965). Though not so famous, the controversy surrounding this work exactly parallels the notorious battle about "The Turn of the Screw."

16. *The Novels and Tales of Henry James*, XXI, xix.

17. Wayne Booth, in *The Rhetoric of Fiction* (Chicago, 1961), finds the story ambiguous precisely because it contains no clear statement of James's sense of the past. Oddly enough, Booth finds no ambiguity in "The Turn of the Screw."

18. *The Novels and Tales of Henry James*, II, ix.

19. Ibid., p. xxii.

20. See John A. Clair, "*The American:* A Reinterpretation," *PMLA*, LXXIV (December, 1959), 613–618.

21. J. A. Ward, *The Imagination of Disaster: Evil in the Fiction of Henry James* (Lincoln, 1961). See also a recent article that cites further evidence of James's inadvertent derogation of Newman: Edward R. Zietlow, "A Flaw in *The American*," *CLA Journal*, IX (March, 1966), 246–254.

22. Richard Poirier, *The Comic Sense of Henry James* (New York, 1967), p. 87.

23. Clair, "*The American*," p. 613.

24. Yvor Winters, *In Defense of Reason* (Denver, n.d.), p. 205.

25. *The Novels and Tales of Henry James*, V, xxii.

26. *Notebooks*, p. 68.

27. George Woodcock, "Henry James and the Conspirators," *Sewanee Review*, LX (Spring, 1952), 220.

28. Dupee, *Henry James*, p. 157.

29. Brooks, *The Pilgrimage of Henry James*, p. 83.

30. Bewley, *The Complex Fate*, p. 47.

31. Quentin Anderson, *The American Henry James* (New Brunswick, 1957), p. 237.

32. The reader should compare my discussion to the essay by Leo Bersani, which it resembles: "The Narrator as Center in *The Wings of the Dove*," *Modern Fiction Studies*, VI (Summer, 1960), 131–144.

33. *Notebooks*, p. 137.

34. Ibid.

35. *The Novels and Tales of Henry James*, X, vii.

36. Ibid., p. xv.

37. Ibid., p. xvi.

38. Winters, *In Defense of Reason*, p. 318.

39. Patrick Quinn, "Morals and Motives in *The Spoils of Poynton*," *Sewanee Review*, LXII (Autumn, 1954), 563, 564.

40. *Notebooks*, p. 214.

41. The parallel here to Clair's essay on *The American* and all those debunkings of the governess or the Newmarch narrator is Robert C. McLean, "The Subjective Adventure of Fleda Vetch," *American Literature*, XXXVI (March, 1964), 12–30. The best testimonial for Fleda, which my argument resembles, is James W. Gargano, "*The Spoils of Poynton:*

Action and Responsibility," *Sewanee Review,* LXIX (Fall, 1961), 650–660.

42. Himself tending to downgrade Ransom, Oscar Cargill gives a useful summary of critical objections to the southerner in *The Novels of Henry James* (New York, 1961). Critics who assert James's derision of Ransom give a less accurate view than those, like Philip Rahv and Lionel Trilling, who overestimate James's admiration. Rahv's and Trilling's comparisons of Ransom to Eliot, the southern agrarians, and other representative moderns are to be found respectively in Rahv's introduction to his 1945 edition of the novel and in *The Opposing Self* (New York, 1955).

43. As usual, one sees evidence of James's ambiguity in the criticism. Most critics line up too firmly for or against Isabel, despite the fact that her virtues and failings are more intelligibly intermixed than the virtues and failings of the governess, Fleda Vetch, Milly Theale, etc.

   From the first reviews through discussions by recent critics like Leavis and Dupee, Isabel's luminosity has impressed itself upon her commentators. But after the excellent essays by Dorothy Van Ghent (*The English Novel: Form and Function* [New York, 1953], pp. 211–228, 428–439) and Richard Chase (*The American Novel and Its Tradition* [New York, 1957], pp. 117–137), a shift became perceptible. Once committed to the notion that James believed and adequately conveyed Isabel's greatness, critics began to acknowledge her determinant shortcomings. Lately, this emphasis has become excessive. So we have R. W. Stallman asserting that Isabel is *"a pretentious and shallow creature duped by her own presumptuous ideas"* (*The Houses That James Built* [Lansing, 1961], p. 23) and W. B. Stein contending that James intended Isabel as an illustration of Henry Adams's notion that American women are frigid: "*The Portrait of a Lady:* Vis Inertiae," *Western Humanities Review,* XIII (Spring, 1959), 177–190.

44. Philip Roth, *Letting Go* (New York, 1963), p. 10.

45. A few critics have noted the tension behind James's novel, but they have not explained it plausibly. The weakest point in Chase's admirable essay is his confrontation with the book's mixture of tragedy and melodrama. His concluding hypothesis ("Is James . . . subtly vindictive toward Isabel?") is singularly fruitless, and Chase retreats behind a frail evasion ("Isabel is so completely created a character that she lives her life independently of the approval or disapproval the author may feel toward her"). *The American Novel and Its Tradition,* pp. 128–129.

   J. M. Newton argues that "James's deep and strenuously active will not to know how very unattractive and unintelligent his heroine really is" comes from excessive identification; but this argument is no more plausible than that of Richard Chase. See "Isabel Archer's Disease and Henry James's," *The Cambridge Quarterly*, II (Winter, 1966–67), 3–22. As I argue, James knows all that he must, though he tries to soften the blows thus rained on his dearest loyalties. The matter is nicely put by C. B. Cox, though he treats the book too briefly to follow up his insight: "In spite of James's sympathy for Isabel's love of independence, his intelligence urges him both to criticize her by means of irony and to provide a tragic conclusion. His understanding of the dangers of liberal idealism pulls against his admiration for Isabel's aspirations, and the resulting tension has set all his critics at variance over the total effect of the novel." *The Free Spirit* (London, 1963), p. 45.

I have found only one critic who balances what James did against what he did not do: A. B. Moody, "James's Portrait of an Ideal," *Melbourne Critical Review*, IV (1961), 77–92. This first-rate essay deserves to be widely reprinted.

46. See F. R. Leavis, *The Great Tradition* (London, 1948).

47. James, "Gustave Flaubert," *The Future of the Novel*, ed. Leon Edel (New York, 1956), pp. 138–139.

48. James, "*Daniel Deronda*: A Conversation," in Leavis, *The Great Tradition*, p. 264.

49. Two exceptions are Moody, whose discussion parallels mine (see note 45), and William H. Gass, "The High Brutality of Good Intentions," *Accent*, XVIII (Winter, 1958), 62–71.

50. Arnold Kettle, *An Introduction to the English Novel* (London, 1953), p. 31.

51. See Jacques Barzun, "James the Melodramatist," *Kenyon Review*, V (Autumn, 1943), 508–521.

52. Dupee, *Henry James*, p. 104.

53. Poirier, *The Comic Sense of Henry James*, p. 136.

54. F. R. Leavis, "The Novel as Dramatic Poem III: *The Europeans*," *Scrutiny*, XV (Summer, 1948), 209.

55. In the little written about *Washington Square* a simple melodramatic reading predominates. For examples, see S. Gorley Putt, *Henry James: A Reader's Guide* (Ithaca, 1966), and Leo B. Levy, *Versions of Melodrama* (Berkeley, 1957).

56. Ward, *The Imagination of Disaster*, p. 34.

57. R. P. Blackmur, "In the Country of the Blue," *The Question of Henry James*, ed. F. W. Dupee (New York, 1945), p. 193.

58. This is true of all early criticism. Representative examples are Morton Dauwen Zabel's introduction to the Anchor reprint and Albert C. Friend's "A Forgotten Story by Henry James," *South Atlantic Quarterly*, LIII (January, 1954), 100–108. The tradition of uncritical ad-

miration for the telegraphist is most recently represented by Muriel G. Shine, *The Fictional Children of Henry James* (Chapel Hill, 1969). Even Tony Tanner, who recognizes that the style is ironic, treats the story by analogy with *The Sacred Fount*, as a serious comment on art. See *The Reign of Wonder* (Cambridge, 1965), pp. 310–319.

59. E. Duncan Aswell, in the first convincing reading of the tale, accurately collects instances of her erroneous conclusions. See "James's *In the Cage*: The Telegraphist as Artist," *Texas Studies in Language and Literature*, VIII (Fall, 1966), 375–384.

60. This reading crops up now mostly in articles that stress the story's relationship to *La Princesse de Clèves*. See Benjamin C. Rountree, "James's *Madame de Mauves* and Madame de Lafayette's *Princesse de Clèves*," *Studies in Short Fiction*, I (Summer, 1964), 264–271. Another advocate of the Baroness is Charles F. Hoffman, *The Short Novels of Henry James* (New York, 1957), pp. 9–16. Most recent critics take my approach.

61. See Rebecca Patterson, "Two Portraits of a Lady," *Midwest Quarterly*, I (July, 1960), 343–361.

62. Marius Bewley, *The Eccentric Design* (New York, 1959), pp. 224–232.

63. See George Stevens, "The Return of Henry James," *Saturday Review of Literature*, XXVIII (March 3, 1943), 7–8, 30, 32–33, and Christof Wegelin, *The Image of Europe in Henry James* (Dallas, 1958), pp. 43–46.

64. This is stressed in the most satisfactory study of the tale that I have found: J. A. Ward, "Structural Irony in 'Madame de Mauves,'" *Studies in Short Fiction*, II (Winter, 1965), 170–182.

65. See Dupee, *Henry James*, pp. 196–202.

66. Representative examples of modern opposition to the book may be found in Joseph Warren Beach's study (see note 2 above) and in D.W. Jefferson, *Henry James and the Modern Reader* (New York, 1964).

67. Dorothea Krook, *Ordeal of Consciousness* (Cambridge, 1967), p. 151.

68. Henry James, *The Question of Our Speech* (Boston, 1905), p. 10.

69. Ezra Pound, "Henry James," *Literary Essays of Ezra Pound* (London, 1960), p. 325.

70. Krook, *Ordeal of Consciousness*, pp. 159–162.

71. Pound, "Henry James," p. 325.

72. Mildred Hartsock, "The Exposed Mind: A View of *The Awkward Age*," *Critical Quarterly*, IX (Spring, 1967), 56.

73. See, for examples, James W. Gargano, "*Daisy Miller*: An Abortive Quest for Innocence," *South Atlantic Quarterly*, LIX (Winter, 1960), 114–120, or the second volume of Edel's biography.

74. Criticism of this masterwork has been singularly unsatisfying. My reading most resembles that of Terence Martin, "James's 'The Pupil': The

Art of Seeing Through," *Modern Fiction Studies*, V (Winter, 1958–59), 335–345.

75. When Marius Bewley asserted that Mrs. Wix resembled the other governess, his mentor, F. R. Leavis, responded with anger to this suggestion. (See Bewley, *The Complex Fate*.) But by now Mrs. Wix's flaws are widely acknowledged. Studying characters of her type, Sister M. Corona Sharp gives a good account of Mrs. Wix in *The "Confidante" in Henry James* (Notre Dame, 1963). Along with *The Portrait of a Lady*, *What Maisie Knew* is the best analyzed of James's major novels. Notable studies are: Joseph A. Hynes, "The Middle Way of Miss Farange," *ELH*, XXXII (December, 1965), 528–553; James W. Gargano, "*What Maisie Knew*: The Evolution of a Moral Sense," *Nineteenth-Century Fiction*, XVI (June, 1961), 33–46; Edward Wasiolek, "Maisie: Pure or Corrupt?" *College English*, XXII (December, 1960), 161–172.

76. Two critics believe that Maisie actually makes a sexual offer here. See John C. McCloskey, "*What Maisie Knew*: A Study of Childhood and Adolescence," *American Literature*, XXXVI (January, 1965), 485–513, and Harris W. Wilson, "What *Did* Maisie Know?" *College English*, XXII (December, 1960), 167–172.

77. Despite its popularity with critics, *The Ambassadors* is, I think, almost as badly understood as *The Awkward Age*. Most of its famous critics give too much attention to Strether's discovery that he hasn't lived and have thus misrepresented the significance of his speech in Gloriani's Garden. (Though it must be admitted that James himself encouraged this error through his prefatory remarks.) Representative examples of this widespread emphasis are to be found in F. O. Matthiessen, *Henry James: The Major Phase* (New York, 1944), and in Leon Edel's introduction to the Riverside edition. Oscar Cargill (*The Novels of Henry James*) shows why the "live" speech can't be the book's theme.

Though there have been some fine essays on this novel, notably a superb, though specialized, study by Ian Watt ("The First Paragraph of *The Ambassadors*," *Essays in Criticism*, X [July, 1960], 250–274), I do not think that the book's satiric spirit has been caught.

78. Cf. "People really ought to try to live up to such an imagination of them as Strether's—that finally is what the book asks us to believe, not anything so tiresome as that Strether has failed to be in touch with reality." Richard Poirier, *A World Elsewhere* (New York, 1966), p. 136. But why should people aspire to a vision recognized as either "grandly cynical or grandly vague" even by its possessor?

However, in restoring what I believe to be the proper emphasis, I should like not to go too far in the other direction. Still, Strether's nobility is not, as many critics contend, his romantic vision of the lovers' chastity but rather his fundamental vision of general welfare. Because he believes that all fine people restrain themselves for the common good, he is shocked to find this expectation betrayed by people he was sure were virtuous. For this reason James is careful to start Strether on the road to truth by having him learn that Chad and Madame de Vionnet can sacrifice Jeanne's happiness for their own convenience. (Frederick Crews is unique in placing due emphasis on this fact.) Both as value and sin, the adultery is symptom rather than principal, as Strether demonstrates when he ultimately comes to countenance the affair in order to enhance something under which it may be subsumed.

79. To Mr. Anderson, Strether is the "supreme instance of selfishness" because he insists on being wholly good. Fortunately, James anticipated whatever is correct in Anderson's stricture. See "Henry James, His Symbolism and His Critics," *Scrutiny*, XV (December, 1947), 12–19. In "The Two Lambert Strethers," *Modern Fiction Studies*, VII (Winter, 1961–62), 305–316, Robert Garis comes to the wrong conclusion (that Strether learns nothing from his experience) but, along the way, he shows that the novel would be that faulty if it meant what most critics have contended.

80. Yvor Winters, *Maule's Curse* (Norfolk, 1938), p. 207, and H. R. Hays, "Henry James, the Satirist," *Hound and Horn*, VII (April–May, 1934), 521–522.

81. See Anderson's *The American Henry James*, in which Maggie is regarded as the embodiment of a religious dispensation, and R. P. Blackmur's "The Loose and Baggy Monsters of Henry James," *Accent*, XI (Summer, 1951), 129–146, in which she is compared to Dante's Beatrice.

82. See Leavis, *The Great Tradition*, and Ferner Nuhn, *The Wind Blew from the East* (New York, 1942).

83. Matthiessen, *Henry James: The Major Phase*, p. 97.

84. Nuhn, *The Wind Blew from the East*, p. 137.

85. For a full discussion of this issue see Leo B. Levy, "Henry James and the Jews: A Critical Study," *Commentary*, XXVI (September, 1958), 243–249.

86. See Cargill, *The Novels of Henry James*, p. 410.

87. In addition to Anderson and Blackmur, this view is expressed by Dorothea Krook and by Caroline Gordon ("Mr. Verver, Our National Hero," *Sewanee Review*, LXII [Winter, 1955], 29–47), among others.

88. This group includes Leavis, Nuhn, and, most forcefully, Joseph J. Firebaugh, "The Ververs," *Essays in Criticism*, IV (October, 1954), 400–410. See also Jean Kimball, "Henry James's Last Portrait of a Lady: Charlotte Stant," *American Literature*, XXVIII (January, 1957), 449–468.

89. See, for example, Walter F. Wright, "Maggie Verver: Neither Saint nor Witch," *Nineteenth-Century Fiction*, XII (June, 1957), 59–71. Miss

Krook's last-minute attention to ambiguity in her unconscionably extended analysis of the book can serve as the very model of Jacobite evasion. See *Ordeal of Consciousness*, pp. 310–324. A. R. Gard, "Critics of *The Golden Bowl*," *Melbourne Critical Review*, VI (1963), 102–109, gives by far the most honest available estimation of the book's ambiguity, but although he confesses bafflement concerning its "moral cogency," he is willing to affirm its "bizarre kind of success."

90. "Though he talks to himself a good deal . . . about his relation to his work, his 'muse,' he never notes down personal emotions in relation to anything else as possible subjects for fiction. One comes to the conclusion that Henry James, in a special and unusual way, was what is nowadays called an 'extrovert'—that is, he did not brood on himself and analyze his own reactions . . . but always dramatized his experience immediately in terms of imaginary people." Edmund Wilson, "The Ambiguity of Henry James," p. 147.

A NOTE ON THE AUTHOR

Charles Thomas Samuels, associate professor of English at Williams College, holds degrees from Syracuse University (1957), Ohio State University (1958), and the University of California at Berkeley (1961). He has previously published a pamphlet on John Updike for the University of Minnesota Pamphlets on American Writers (1969), *A Casebook on Film* (1970), and articles in a wide variety of magazines. He writes a quarterly film column for *The American Scholar* and reviews books regularly for *The New Republic*. He has been a Fulbright lecturer, has received fellowships from the American Council of Learned Societies and the American Philosophical Society, and is currently a senior fellow of the National Humanities Endowment.

University of Illinois Press